The Unvarnished Truth about The Prison Family Journey ©

Carolyn Esparza, LPC
Phillip Don Yow, Sr.

Published By:

PRISONER'S
FAMILY & FRIENDS
UNITED

The Unvarnished Truth about The Prison Family Journey ©

For information please contact:

Prisoner's Family & Friends United
2200 N. Yarbrough, B 245
El Paso, Texas 79925
www.pffunited.org
915-861-7733
e-mail: info@pffunited.org

ISBN: 1490392386
ISBN-13: 978-1490392387

Library of Congress Control Number: 2013909793
Carolyn Esparza LPC, El Paso, TX

This book is dedicated to all prison family voyagers,
past, present and future.

TABLE OF CONTENTS

TO THE READER

Long-standing erroneous and undeserved myths have resulted in the perpetual marginalization of the prison family. Shunned by society with almost as much disdain as the prisoner, the prison family typically retreats from the mainstream community. As a result of this self-imposed isolation, our society has lost millions of remarkable, intelligent, talented members who, instead of benefitting our communities actually diminish our quality of life by their self-imposed absence.

Millions of people are affected by incarceration. It is our belief that by understanding the truth about this large segment of our society; by reaching out to them instead of disenfranchising them; by embracing them instead of shunning them we will significantly enhance and strengthen the quality of life in our communities.

With over fifty years combined professional and personal experience with the criminal justice and prison systems, we knew fully that the prison family is among the most-forgotten of all populations. In an effort to reach out and support the prison family, we initiated an on-line resource for those affected by the incarceration of a loved one. That website, Prisoner's Family & Friends United or www.pffunited.org provides resources and services addressing critical concerns and needs of prison families. In the process of creating that website, this book evolved.

Initially the book was conceived as an aide for prison families, especially with hopes of preventing new initiates from stumbling and falling. However, it quickly became evident that this book serves a greater purpose. Not only will it benefit those directly affected by the incarceration of a loved one, but it will equally benefit those who serve prisoners and their families through secular and faith-based organizations, such as those in the fields of criminal justice; social service, mental and medical health, academia and ministry. Professionals and lay-workers will benefit greatly by understanding the unvarnished truth about the operation of our criminal justice and prison systems and how those systems indelibly impact prisoners and their loved ones.

We remain committed to continuing to compile valuable information from our ongoing experiences and the experiences of other prison families. There is much more to come. New information will be incorporated on our members' only website: www.pffunited.org and certainly will be incorporated in any subsequent editions of this book. Notices of the addition of new information will be posted on the Prisoner's Family & Friends United Facebook page—"like" the page to remain updated.

It is our sincere hope that this book will encourage and strengthen prisoners and their families. It is also our hope that this book will provide those serving prisoners and their families with a broad and honest picture of those they serve, enabling them to provide more effective services than ever before.

With regard to legal information contained herein, although we do have qualified and licensed legal consultants, Prisoner's Family & Friends United and the authors of this book, while exceptionally knowledgeable on the topics are not licensed legal authorities and do not hold themselves out as attorneys. All information herein is provided as "food for thought," based on many years—well over a half a century combined—of personal and/or professional experience both inside and outside the criminal justice system.

ACKNOWLEDGEMENTS

It is with sincere gratitude that we thank the hundreds of prisoners and their families who have touched our lives and our hearts and provided us with the inspiration and insight for writing this book. It is our hope that sharing what you have taught us will provide a legacy of encouragement, healing and ultimate success for many prison families, as well as those who serve them in the fields of corrections, social service, academia and ministry.

Thank you to Kimberly Dearman for your belief in this project and your loving and tangible support that encouraged us to complete this project in the most meaningful manner possible.

Thank you to Grace Bauer, Co-Director of Justice for Families. Your enthusiastic support of this project is greatly appreciated. Your unwavering determination and unstoppable advocacy on behalf of all families touched by incarceration is a powerful legacy and exceptional inspiration to fight for what we know is right.

Thank you to Carol Miller and Barbara Castellone, mother and daughter who have walked the prison family walk and successfully reunited. We appreciate the knowledge you have shared with us. We are grateful for the feedback you have provided.

Last, but definitely not least, thank you to our children—Carolyn's: Kayla, Jeffrey, Melissa and Joshua and Phillip's: Phillip Jr., Malik and Tamara. Each one of you uniquely inspires each of us to follow our hearts and to do the right thing, even though we may not always see eye to eye. We love each one of you uniquely and dearly.

INTRODUCTION

Most prison families will not find this book (let alone find the stamina to read it) until *after* experiencing a great deal of pain. The hope is that whenever you read this book you will receive insight and encouragement for the remainder of your prison family journey. And when the prison family experience engulfs others, we hope you will quickly share the insight to be found here with the new voyagers to help them avoid pitfalls and even tragedy. We hope this information will provide encouragement to boldly face the confounding situations we all experience on our prison family journeys.

The United States is an "Incarcerated Nation." With 5% of the world's population this country has almost 25% of the world's *prisoners*. The reasons for this mass incarceration in our nation are many. However, the *primary* reason is *money*. Prison has become a lucrative industry in the United States generously padding the pockets of a few at the horrid expense of multitudes—many of whom some refer to as "sheeple." That is the unvarnished truth.

Like sheep to the slaughter, "We the People" have blindly allowed "them" (those "we" put in power) to run slipshod over us; even surreptitiously passing laws we knew nothing about until "they" enforced those laws and our lives became tragically affected by mass incarceration, especially of the poor and the racial minorities—although we **all** are horribly affected. There is hardly a person alive in this country who does not know someone who is or was incarcerated.

We have casually come to accept incarceration as a rite of passage, at least for "some people," instead of the aberration it once was. The fact is that we gave them an inch by not watching what they were doing, and they took the proverbial mile until it now stretches into 2.5 MILLION "miles" of humanity warehoused in their prisons—2.5 MILLION prisoners with

2.5 MILLION children and countless loved ones and friends devastated by their absence. Now they are privatizing their prisons to assure the continued growth of their lucrative industry. We gave them the power; now it is time we wake up and take the power back.

This book is written for two primary reasons: First, we must all now learn to live with what we have sown, at least until we can turn the tide. So it is our fervent hope that the unvarnished truth you will find on these pages will provide prison families, as well as those serving prisoners and their families with insight to empower the family for the journey and lessen the excruciating pain resulting from the incarceration of a loved one.

Second, we are hopeful that in learning the unvarnished truth about the reality of the painful prison family journey you will become as outraged as we have become. We want you to become so outraged that you will be compelled to join the fight to stop the persistently creeping tentacles of mass incarceration by joining in one-voice to be heard over the clanging cash registers of the entrepreneurs of mass incarceration, before more of our loved ones are snared and dropped into the cesspool called "prison." ONLY by joining forces; ONLY by becoming one powerful voice will we ever be able to undo the mess we have allowed to be created. We need YOU and your voice to strengthen the outcry.

There are golden nuggets to be found on these pages. It is our prayer that you will pocket and use many of those nuggets to lighten the load and ease the pain of the prison family journey. Then join in forming one voice. Together we *will* make a difference.

CHAPTER I

"LEGALLY SPEAKING"

THE INITIATION

The initiation to become a Prison Family Member is swift. It only takes a five minute phone call to announce that your loved one is in jail.

Your heart lurches; your stomach falls to the ground; your knees buckle; your mind races and the voice on the other end of the phone sounds as though it is funneling through an echo chamber a thousand miles long.

From this moment forward, life will never be the same. But, although most new initiates into the prison family will not believe it as they stand speechless staring at the suddenly silent phone clenched in their hand, many long-time prison family members will tell you, "These *can become* some of the best years of your life."

What lies ahead is a challenging and often painful and frustrating journey no one ever asked for and certainly no one intended or desired to travel. It is a journey that will lead to incomparable confusion and extreme frustration. There will be infuriating encounters with injustice and irrational madness. At the very same time this journey can lead to the most remarkable, comforting and understanding friends anyone could ever hope to find. At the end of this journey many prison family members look back down that very dark road they have traveled and find they have become stronger more confident people than they ever imagined was possible.

When hanging up from that first startling phone call, there is a tendency to scramble frantically to find help. What most people actually find are pitfalls on those first wobbly steps of the prison family journey. However, for those who persevere and keep on walking, we know as fact that it is possible to find the help needed to live comfortably and even *thrive* as a member of the prison family.

With that one phone call, the initiation is complete. The prison family journey now begins. Whether the new member has traveled this road before or not, they have no idea of what now lies ahead.

"Unknowns" are the most anxiety-producing experiences in life for all of us, and the legal process is abundant with its "unknowns." Therefore, each step of the court process that the new prison family member will immediately be immersed in will increase their anxiety. At the same time however, despite drowning in a sea of emotions it is crucial to find a way to remain as composed and calm as possible. Maintaining a clear head is critical to making good decisions about things the family may know little or nothing about as they begin this journey.

Court hearings are among the most anxiety producing experiences on the prison family journey. They are filled with numerous unknowns from the moment of first learning of a loved one's arrest throughout seemingly endless trips to court—many of which are totally unproductive. The best way to reduce the tension is to reduce the number of unknowns that lie ahead. The only way to reduce the unknowns is to become knowledgeable about what to expect on the dark road ahead. Hopefully the information provided here will substantially reduce the unknowns by revealing a good deal about what to expect both EMOTIONALLY and LEGALLY.

INNOCENCE

Not everyone in prison is guilty. Despite the sarcastic comments we often hear that "everyone in prison says they're innocent," the truth is—many **are** innocent! These are some very cold unvarnished facts about "innocence:"

The University of Michigan Law School and the Center for Wrongful Convictions at Northwestern University Law School recently issued reports that between 1989 and mid-2012 there were 873 prisoners exonerated of the crimes for which they had been convicted.

I just heard a court official say that of the many thousands of cases heard by courts in this country "873 is a very small percentage of mistakes" made by the courts. Mathematically, he may be right. However the human cost is anything but small.

An even colder fact is that these 873 exonerees tell us that many innocent people have been **executed;** put to death before they could prove their innocence, because the justice system is often not just.

Further, the 873 prisoners were exonerated because there was DNA evidence to *scientifically* prove their innocence. That leaves us to wonder how many **thousands** of prisoners are wrongly convicted and falsely incarcerated who do not have DNA evidence involved in their cases and therefore cannot prove their innocence *scientifically*.

The National Innocence Project reports that as many as five percent of prisoners are falsely incarcerated. While other reports indicate the figure to be much higher—as high as twenty-five percent—the National Innocence Project points out that **if only one percent** of today's prisoners were innocent of crimes for which they have been convicted, that **one percent** would represent **20,000 innocent human beings sitting in our nation's prisons today**. In fact, a new study on wrongful convictions indicates that between 5,000 and 10,000 wrongful convictions occur in the United States EVERY YEAR!

Even worse, most of those who were exonerated spent **fifteen to twenty years** or more of their lives in prison trying desperately to prove their innocence; **many of them on death row**. And always the prosecutors fought bitterly to uphold their record of convictions, not caring one iota and even objecting vehemently to the testing of DNA evidence available in the case that would prove or disprove for once and for all the innocence or guilt of the now convicted felon.

And, it gets worse. In many exoneration cases the truth was finally uncovered by *citizens*; not by the justice system. In fact, in many cases the winning "attorney" was not an attorney at all, but was the convicted innocent prisoner them self; a writ writer.

The sad, sad unvarnished truth is that today there is an overabundance of attorneys, making competition among them very fierce. There is also an overabundance of lawsuits, because we have become an aggressively litigious society suing at the drop of a hat and all for only one purpose—not for justice, but for money.

Logic tells us that the more cases an attorney can represent, the more money they will make. At the same time the less cases the court has to hear in full, the faster they can clear the docket and the less money it will cost the government to prosecute cases.

Sadly, it is all about money and not about justice. So, if convicted of a crime you may want to consider engaging a writ writer to help you fight your case—certainly to fight any *appeal* that becomes necessary due to the injustices inherent in today's legal system.

Here is some food for thought: No matter who represents the defendant in court, **defendants have RIGHTS**. Legal rights are not handed to any of us on a silver platter. Access to our legal rights requires gaining knowledge, accepting responsibility and darn hard work! If you become a defendant or an appellee in a court case, these are some of your rights whether you have a paid or court-appointed attorney:

- You have a RIGHT to ask questions, so ask lots of them.
- You have a RIGHT to receive logical, honest answers to your questions, so demand the truth.

- You have a RIGHT to get 2nd opinions; demand 2nd opinions.
- You have a RIGHT to compare services.
- You have a RIGHT to compare rates.
- Within reason, you have a RIGHT to take your time. The court postpones; the prosecution postpones—the defense can also postpone while CAREFULLY weighing options.
- You have a RIGHT to fire your attorney, if you honestly do not believe they are adequately representing you.
- Although the courts don't like it and it is not necessarily the wisest thing to do, you have a RIGHT to have the person of your choice represent you in court, even if that person is YOURSELF, even with the assistance of a writ writer to prepare your court documents.

What is a "writ writer," you ask?

Well that's getting way ahead of ourselves. We don't meet writ writers until we're in prison and fighting to overturn our conviction. That is an entirely different stage of the prison family journey. Right now, you're going to need an attorney!

SHOPPING FOR AN ATTORNEY

Years ago a client who had gotten himself into some legal trouble asked me to suggest an attorney. In addition to being new in the community I'd never had the need for an attorney, so I knew no one to suggest, but told him I'd check around. A few days later, at lunch with a friend who worked at a homeless shelter, I mentioned the client's need for an attorney. She suggested I call her boss, the Director of the homeless shelter.

I had heard that the executive director of the city's largest homeless shelter was once a practicing attorney. He left what I'd heard was a thriving practice when he felt called to take the helm of the shelter.

In very short order he had turned the shabby struggling facility into a meaningful program for the homeless. He was very well respected for his faithfulness and his unwavering persistence in following his calling. My friend said that while he no longer practiced law he had maintained some good contacts in the legal community and she was sure he would be glad to talk with me.

Although it was many years ago, my memory of that call is crystal clear. Perhaps I already knew what he would say, but to hear it from an attorney was rather startling at the time.

After introducing myself I said, "David, I understand you left the legal profession many years ago, but still have some good contacts in the local legal community."

He responded in a most friendly manner. "Yes, I sure do, and I even attend some bar functions from time to time to keep up with my old cronies!"

"Well, I have a counseling client who has gotten himself into a bit of legal trouble. I'm just wondering if you could suggest an honest attorney who will really fight hard for this guy?"

Amidst clearly audible chuckles David responded, "That's an oxymoron if I ever heard one!"

"What's that?" I questioned, suddenly thinking to myself that David would think I didn't know the definition of the word "oxymoron."

"I never heard the word 'honest' mentioned in the same sentence with the word 'attorney' before!" David burst into full scale laughter at the thought.

Stunned by his utter honesty, I feigned a chuckle and said, "Well, I was just hoping!"

"I'm really stumped," David responded, still chuckling. "If you really want 'honest,' I'm not sure I can come up with anyone. But, if you'll settle for 'good natured and qualified' I've got a few names I can give you."

I settled for "good natured and qualified."

It's not that we believe only crooks become lawyers; it is rather that lengthy experience tells us many well-intentioned lawyers seem to take on the characteristics of crooks once immersed in the profession. Sadly, that's just the unvarnished truth.

Over the years I've actually known dozens of young law students who were very wide-eyed and eager to pass the bar so they could begin saving clients from the perils of the legal system. They genuinely seemed to think they could avoid the corruption. A handful has. The remainder has succumbed to the numerous unscrupulous practices that have been allowed to grow and fester and ultimately putrefy the legal system. Today, as an attorney you either play the courthouse games or you're essentially run out of town. While young attorneys may fight the corruption for awhile, many ultimately resort to playing the game to eke out a living, and that is exactly why attorneys have gotten a well deserved bad name over the years.

Here is another very alarming unvarnished truth about our court system and attorneys that everyone ever facing a legal dilemma should know.

Not long ago I attended a meeting of a social reform organization at which a criminal court judge was invited to speak on the workings of the court and their responsibilities as judge. I suppose everyone attending felt much as I did upon learning a judge would be speaking. So, recognizing that building relationships with those at all levels of law enforcement is critical to effecting social change, I prepared for an hour or so of politically correct nodding and smiling at the usual boring rhetoric of politicians.

We were all in for a surprise—a very pleasant and refreshing surprise.

The judge began by divulging a bit of their own background, which included having several family members who had been incarcerated. As such they seemed to understand the criminal justice system to be "imperfect." The judge went on to add that one of the gravest problems with the criminal justice system, including the court system is that there is no accountability. There is absolutely no oversight of the courts, which is why judges can, if they so choose, make up their own rules and treat defendants (and others) with insensitive rudeness and even hostility.

Wow! No one at the meeting ever expected to hear such words coming from the mouth of a judge!

In fact, this judge urged the members of the social reform organization to spend time sitting in on court hearings in "every court," because the courtrooms are "public." Unless an individual will be a witness in a specific case, any member of the public has open access to observe any court hearing. We were told that if the court personnel attempted to bar us from entering the courtroom, they were actually violating our constitutional rights! This judge noted that sometimes, due to fire department regulations on room capacity, when too many people wanted to observe a court hearing they asked their staff to locate a sufficiently large room to accommodate the crowd and had even moved hearings to buildings outside the courthouse!

I observed some fellow-members' jaws drop in amazement at this judge's candor! However, the fullness of their candor was yet to come.

In responding to a question about attorney competency, the judge stated, "There is an extremely low bar set for attorney competency. In fact, the Supreme Court has previously ruled that an attorney who literally slept during a court hearing on a criminal case was fully competent in representing their client."

I observed members' jaws drop wide open with that revelation!

The judge went on to say that in fact attorneys routinely misrepresent their clients, using what the attorney would call "strategy that just didn't work," but the "strategy" was clearly designed to assure the client would be convicted and punished harshly. Never-the-less, the attorney would be considered to have competently represented their client.

"In fact," the judge went on to say, "When cases are being appealed on the grounds that an attorney was incompetent, the higher courts will say that it is the **defendant's responsibility to assure their attorney**

is adequately representing them. The higher courts will say that the Defendant hired the attorney, and if they didn't feel they were being adequately represented, they should have FIRED THEM!"

In unison, the members of the social justice group audibly gasped!

Despite the corruption prison families will encounter, compounded by their profound emotional turmoil, they must know the rules of the courtroom and actually police their own attorney! It is apparently THEIR RESPONSIBILITY to assure they are being adequately represented!

Regardless of the corruption, defendants still need to find the best attorney possible for their circumstances. The first thing they will likely do is exactly what I did; ask friends.

Caution! While some attorneys may have done a great job for some of their clients they may not be the proper attorney for your particular circumstances. Unless you have a lot of experience with the criminal justice system, it is difficult to know whether an attorney will be beneficial to you or not. But, there are some questions to ask that may help you make a better decision than simply playing Russian roulette with your loved one's legal life.

Of course it's OK to check out attorneys that friends suggest. It's just important not to allow emotions to rush you into grabbing the one who seems most friendly or the one with the best gift of gab. This is a most serious decision, so let's be practical about it and ask some hard hitting questions to see who these attorneys really are. Set appointments for consultation with at least three attorneys. The initial consultation for them to hear your case is (or should be) free of charge and usually lasts only thirty minutes. The purpose of this meeting is to learn what each lawyer thinks of the case and to have them clearly explain what they will do and how much it will cost. They should also be willing to answer any reasonable questions.

Because emotions are high, to make the most of this meeting it is best to have a *written* list of questions for these attorneys. There will be a very limited time. So, it is important to stick closely to that list and avoid chatting!

The following questions cover different areas of possible concern when shopping for an attorney. Defendants and their loved ones should not be afraid to ask these questions and even add more questions specific to their case. When paying for a service; you have every right to know what you are getting for your money. You'd be asking questions of a roofer repairing the roof on your house, so why wouldn't you ask questions of an attorney who has your life or the life or your loved one in his or her hands?

1. **EXPERTISE: What types of cases do you handle most frequently?**
    a. Is my case in your area of legal expertise?
    b. Is my case in the area of law you studied for in law school?
    c. What licenses or training do you have to qualify you to handle this type of case?

2. **PROCEDURE: How much experience have you had with cases like mine?**
    a. If they have not handled many similar cases you will probably want a different lawyer. Ask if they will suggest an attorney with more experience in that area.
    b. What procedure do you prefer to use in handling such a case?
        i. Jury trial?
        ii. Judge only?
        iii. Plea bargain? (**Note:** If they prefer is this option, we strongly advise you to say "thank you" & leave. More on that topic, later.)
    c. Why do you believe that particular legal procedure will work best for my case?

    d. What investigators, witnesses or experts do you think are needed?

    e. What do you think the outcome will be? (**Note:** If they give you an absolute definitive outcome, say "thank you" & leave. More on that topic, later.)

3. **ROLES: Will you, or will a paralegal or intern handle our case?**

    a. If a paralegal or intern is handling my case, how are they qualified to do so?

    b. If a paralegal or intern handles my case, what responsibilities will they undertake?

    c. If a paralegal or intern handles my case, how are they supervised?

    d. If this case goes to trial, what will the paralegal's role be in court?

    e. If paralegals or interns are handling my case, exactly what will your role be?

    f. What responsibilities will be expected of me?

    g. If things don't go well, who will handle the request for a new trial or an appeal?

4. **CONTACT: How will we communicate with you about the case, and how often?**

    a. I understand you are busy, but what are your thoughts about frequent updates?

    b. What is the best way and what are the best times to contact you?

    c. What times do you usually return calls?

    d. Will you respond personally to e-mail contact? May I have your e-mail address?

5. **FEES: What are your fees and what other expenses should we expect to pay?**
   a. Will the fee you have given us cover everything, including a trial if needed?
   b. If "no," what is your fee for a trial?
   c. What is your fee if the case is plea bargained?
   d. What additional legal expenses do we need to plan for?
   e. What are the fees we will be required to pay the court?
   f. Will there be additional fees for expert witnesses or investigators?
   g. Do we sign a contract with you to confirm your services and the fees you've stated?
   h. Can we establish a payment schedule, or will you want the total fee paid up front?

GOING TO COURT

When preparing to go to court, it may help to become familiar with the following chart produced by the American Bar Association. It is most arguably complex, but it is a good resource for understanding the general process of a criminal court case.

~ **EMOTIONALLY:** Confusing! Intimidating! Overwhelming!

~ **LEGALLY:** Complicated! So, let's simplify the process by addressing each of the most critical stages for most criminal court cases.

There will be many delays! It is safe to say that the likelihood the judge or one of the attorneys will request a postponement of a court hearing is *one hundred percent.* To reduce anxiety, prepare for numerous delays. Becoming angry about the many delays serves no purpose in speeding the process and only increases anxiety. The wheels of justice definitely grind slowly. Postponement times should be used productively to prepare for court by becoming very knowledgeable about what to expect, both EMOTIONALLY and LEGALLY.

The Sequence of Events in the Criminal Justice System

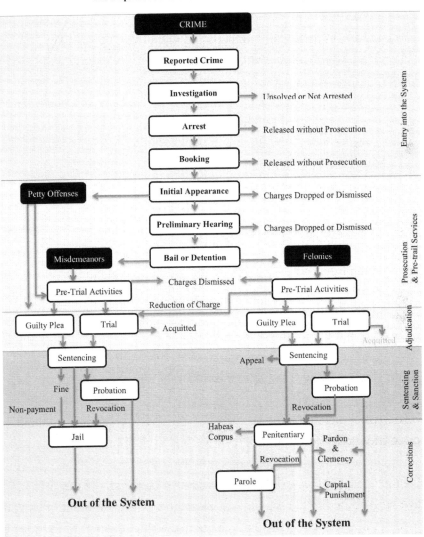

~ **EMOTIONALLY:** Knowing that the feelings elicited by this emotional roller coaster ride are "normal" can help reduce anxiety. In explaining what to expect on the journey through the legal process we will provide insight on typical emotions associated with each step.

~ **LEGALLY:** To eliminate some "unknowns," it is important to learn as much as possible about the court process. The defendant and their support team should research their attorney's responsibilities to assure they are receiving the most effective representation. While it is impossible to predict every anxiety-producing incident that may or may not occur during the legal process, this legal section will provide a good deal of information to lessen apprehensions and reduce stress.

THE JOURNEY BEGINS

When a person is arrested they are booked into the local jail. If policy is followed (and it is our experience that it usually is) the prisoner is allowed that infamous "ONE phone call" to notify their family or a friend that they have been arrested. The call is very brief (usually no more than 5 minutes) and as long as a loved one is incarcerated, the family should prepare for all too brief, *monitored* communication whether by phone, written correspondence or visitation.

You probably want to know what family and friends can do during the initial arrest stage?

The unvarnished truth is, there is absolutely nothing they can (or should) do, but wait. In some, but not all local jails the arrested individual may have access to a phone system that will allow them to make collect calls IF their family or a friend has a land-line. If the prisoner is not able to reach anyone by phone, there is little that can be done except to wait until they can write or can receive a visit during scheduled jail visitation hours.

~ **EMOTIONALLY:** When first receiving the call informing you that your loved one is arrested and booked into the local jail, a host of conflicting emotions will be experienced, often simultaneously. Initially you will be numbed by shock during which you will deny the experience altogether. Denial quickly turns into fearful confusion and unproductive panic. It is likely you will simultaneously feel angry and embarrassed by the circumstances. When hanging up the phone you may be flooded with feelings of self-doubt and possibly even guilt, in some way taking responsibility for your loved one's poor choices leading to their incarceration. Staring at that silent phone you will likely be overcome by feelings of helplessness.

~ **LEGALLY:** During the next 24 hours (often rather quickly depending on the number of arrests and bookings occurring at the jail at that time) someone from the jail will speak with the prisoner and explain that they will be taken before a lower court judge or magistrate in a courtroom usually inside the jail. At that time the judge or magistrate will tell the prisoner what the charges are and what their rights are and they will determine the prisoner's eligibility (if indigent) for a court-appointed attorney (a public defender). At this hearing a bond may be set. (Bonds are a distinct subject and will be discussed separately.)

If the prisoner is unable to call home, the jail MAY be able to tell a family member the approximate time this initial hearing will take place. It does not hurt to call the jail and ask. Calling may temporarily relieve some anxiety. However if the jail cannot or will not provide a time, all you can do is wait until the prisoner can call or until a jail visit can be arranged.

As difficult as it may be to hold back, **the family should not retain an attorney** until clearly knowing what the charges are! You begin paying for legal services the minute you hire an attorney. There is not much an attorney can do at this stage except WAIT WITH YOU and you will pay them for holding your hand.

Here are some examples of why that is true: If this is the loved one's very first arrest and the alleged offense is not a major crime (i.e. murder; rape; child abuse, etc.), in all likelihood the prisoner will be bonded out on their own recognizance. (That means, there will be no monetary bond to pay.) In that case, an attorney is not required at the initial hearing and an attorney will have been paid for an unneeded service.

If this is a very serious charge (i.e. murder; rape; child abuse, etc.) or if it is one of many times the loved one has been arrested and/or convicted of an offense, no bond may be offered. This means they will remain in jail to await further court hearings to set a bond regardless of any amount of pleading by an attorney. In this case retaining an attorney for the initial hearing will serve no purpose and the attorney will be paid for an unneeded service.

Incarceration is very expensive. The unvarnished truth is that when you hire an attorney, every single, solitary moment they spend on your case, including phone calls and letter writing, as well as court appearances will be charged to you. Therefore, it is important from the outset to prioritize where your money will be best spent, especially if funds are limited. The initial hearing is one place to save some money, because no permanent, life-altering decisions are made at this stage.

BAIL BONDS

~ **EMOTIONALLY:** While waiting for a bond to be determined, loved ones may randomly experience high levels of anxiety in anticipation of the prisoner being released and returning home, as if bonding would erase the incident altogether! This leads to being easily distracted and unable to focus on issues necessary for making critical decisions. It is not unusual for anxiety to be mixed with all of the initial feelings of denial, confusion, embarrassment, guilt, anger and fear. This paralyzing mixture of emotions often leads to standing by helplessly unproductive watching as total strangers make critical decisions for your life and the life of your loved one.

~ **LEGALLY:** At the initial hearing or arraignment the judge or magistrate will determine if a bond will be set and if so, the amount of the bond will be determined. In very serious cases, or when the arrested party has had numerous prior arrests and/or convictions or if there is some reason to consider the prisoner a flight risk, the court may order that no bond will be allowed.

If no bond is set at the initial hearing, a date for a separate bond hearing may be scheduled. The defendant will be returned to the jail until that date (or until a date is later set), at which time a higher court will determine if a bond will be set and if so, the amount of the bond.

If no bond is set or the amount set is far too high for the defendant or their loved ones to pay, the defendant will remain in jail until the case goes to trial. However, if decided beneficial to the defendant, additional hearings may be requested to set a bond or to lower a bond at a later date. Just know that every time an attorney represents you in court it costs more money. The legal costs mount quickly. Financial priorities should be established very early in the process.

If a bond is set at an amount that is believed to be *unjustly* high, the defendant can request a bond reduction hearing. If this is the case, an attorney may be helpful.

The court may set certain conditions before allowing the defendant to make bond. For example they may order the defendant to turn over their passport so they cannot leave the country; they may ask for the defendant's driver's license so they cannot drive a vehicle; they may order that the defendant have no contact with their alleged victim or many other stipulations. When bonded out of jail, it is very important that these requirements be followed to the letter. If a violation of the court's orders is learned of by the court or district attorney, the defendant will quickly be re-arrested and returned to jail and all money paid for the bond will be forfeited.

When a bond is set, the monetary amount set for the bond is not the cash amount required to be paid to the bail bondsman. In most cases you are expected to pay cash for ten percent of the total bond. However, you will be expected to *prove* you can pay the ENTIRE bond if your loved one absconds and does not appear for a court hearing.

Sometimes, especially for small bonds, the proof of ability to pay is only that you have a steady job. For larger bonds, you will be required to sign over collateral. "Collateral" is sufficient personal property that the bondsman believes will cover the entire bond amount if the defendant is nowhere to be found when there is a scheduled court hearing.

Putting up property for collateral is **a very serious decision** and one that can literally financially ruin a family. While collateral may be jewelry or perhaps a vehicle, many people use stocks or bonds or even their family home as collateral. That is where things can get very sticky.

No matter how friendly and helpful a bondsman may be, they are **not your friend**. They are in business to make a living.

And, do not ever think, "Oh my loved one would never run. They would never put me in such a predicament as to lose our family home!"

Never say "Never." YOU HAVE NO IDEA WHAT FEAR CAN DO TO A PERSON!

If a loved one does something totally unexpected and does not show up for court, the bondsman **will** take ownership of your property, including your home, without hesitation. It has happened many times before. We are all too aware of families having used their life savings or their home as collateral on a felony bond and having lost it all when the defendant got scared and did not appear for a court hearing. Those families learned that bounty hunters are definitely real.

When a bondsman must hire a bounty hunter to track down a missing defendant, they also must pay that bounty hunter. If the bounty hunter cannot find the defendant, the bondsman is required to pay the court the *entire* amount of the bond—even if it is a million dollars! If that happens the bondsman will definitely not be shy about taking possession of your home (or any other property you have signed over as collateral) to cover their expenses.

Mathematically, let's clarify how bonding works. If, for example, the court sets the bond at $25,000.00, you must pay the bondsman ten percent, or $2,500.00 in cash AND you must sign a document and even hand over property such as jewelry or stock certificates or the deed to your home, committing to the bondsman whatever you have of value that will cover the remaining $22,500.00 if something goes wrong.

After paying the fee for the bond and arranging for any required collateral, the bondsman will give the jail the necessary paperwork to have the defendant released.

The unvarnished truth is that bonding a loved one out of jail is not always in their (or your) best interest.

The owner of the air conditioning company that recently installed a new unit at our house asked me what kind of work I do. When I told him I work with prison families, he eagerly told me about his nephew (also his Godson) who he had bonded out of jail "many times for DUI's."

He said his nephew had just been arrested again and he did not know if he would pay another bond for him because, "He doesn't seem to learn his lesson. I bond him out and the next day he's drinking and driving like a maniac again."

When I asked him how many times he had bonded his nephew out of jail, he thought for a few moments before saying, "I really don't know. Maybe five or six times!"

Then he looked at me almost pleadingly and asked rhetorically, "That's too many times, isn't it?"

The harsh truth is that while only one minute in jail may be all it takes to alter some people's troubled thinking and troubled behavior permanently, in most cases, especially where drugs or alcohol are involved, short stays in jail or prison rarely provide sufficient time for the person to accept responsibility for their own behavior.

Their loved ones think they are doing them a favor by paying for their bond time and again. However, when the arrested party walks out of the jail, nothing has changed their way of thinking or their lifestyle. In fact, on top of their originally troubled thinking they are now angry and blaming the policeman who arrested them for interrupting their life. The entire incident becomes nothing more than an inconvenience to them and their troubled thoughts and behaviors remain unchanged. The truth is that bonding them out "again" is actually **enabling** their troubled behavior to continue.

Before making a decision to pay the bond, it may be helpful to have a checklist of the pros and cons for bonding a loved one out of jail. If there are more pros than cons—bonding may be the best thing to do. However, if there are more cons than pros, remember this: **In life there really are worse things than jail and while you may not believe it right now, in some cases jail may actually be a blessing in disguise.** Many prisoners and former prisoners and certainly their family members will attest to this.

The following "Bonding Decision Checklist" created by Prisoner's Family & Friends United may help in making a decision to pay for a bail bond. It is important to be totally honest when using the Checklist or it will not be helpful.

BONDING DECISION CHECKLIST			
X	**PRO'S FOR BONDING**	**X**	**CON'S FOR NOT BONDING**
	They are DEFINITELY NOT guilty of this offense		They are DEFINITELY (or very likely) guilty of this offense
	Making bond will not severely deplete your finances		Making bond will require a loan and/or will severely deplete your finances
	A chemical substance was NOT involved; your loved one is NOT addicted to a chemical substance		A chemical substance WAS involved; your loved one IS addicted to a chemical substance
	This is the first time, as an adult or a juvenile that your loved one has ever been arrested		Your loved one has been arrested before. If your loved one has been arrested/convicted multiple times this is a bigger con. Give it 2 X's.
	You can honestly say you have never known your loved one to exhibit the alleged behavior leading to their arrest.		You must honestly admit your loved one has exhibited the alleged behavior before. If the behavior is known to have been exhibited multiple times before it is a bigger con. Give it 2 X's.
	Your loved one typically faces their problems head on.		Your loved one has a history of running from their problems.
	Your loved one has a steady job and a stable work history.		Your loved one is unemployed at this time. If your loved one has an unsteady work history, this is a bigger con. Give it 2 X's.
	You do NOT in any way feel responsible for your loved one's behavior and arrest in this incident.		You feel some responsibility for your loved one's behavior and arrest in this incident.
	Your loved one typically makes very good life choices and decisions.		Your loved one has a history of making poor life choices and decisions.
	Your loved one is a teenager.		Your loved one is age 21 or older.
	TOTAL PRO'S FOR BONDING		**TOTAL CON'S FOR NOT BONDING**

Of course this is not an exact science. However, consider what the responses to these questions tell you about your loved one in considering the risk involved in bonding them out of jail.

By the way, if you do pay for the bond and put up any collateral, once the court process ends and the defendant is found not guilty and released or found guilty and transferred to prison, be sure to return to the bondsman and ask for all property or documents used as collateral to be returned to you. The collateral is not part of the payment for the bond. It was only left with the bondsman as "insurance" in the event the defendant disappeared. If all went according to plan, you have a right to have your property returned.

PRE-TRIAL HEARINGS

~ **EMOTIONALLY:** Each and every pre-trial hearing (and there will likely be several) increases the stress level. During this time it is typical to feel agitated and discouraged while at the same time feeling hopeful that the final outcome will be positive. These conflicting emotions are compounded by feelings of impatience with the slowness of the legal process and anger at your loved one for bringing these shameful and embarrassing circumstances on your family. Underneath it all is fear that the final outcome may remove your loved one from the family for a very long period of time. Such fear leads to profound sadness and depression as you are overcome by feelings of hopelessness and helplessness.

~ **LEGALLY:** In most criminal court cases there is a series of hearings before an actual trial begins. These hearings (including the arraignment described above) typically clarify legal issues, including the charges and the range of applicable sentences. A date is set for a trial (although that date may be delayed many times). At these preliminary hearings the defendant's attorney will likely move that the case be dismissed! That is appropriate standard procedure to essentially "cover all bases." It is very unlikely the case will be dismissed at this stage, so no one should get their hopes up.

Throughout this legal section there are insertions from the American Bar Association (ABA) website. These insertions are literally "cut and pasted" from the ABA website exactly as they appeared on that site. We need to point out that while there are many similarities between the federal and state legal processes, there are also some differences. The legal information provided here from the ABA is most relevant to state courts.

This is what the American Bar Association says about pre-trial hearings in felony cases.

FELONIES

The process [for felony cases] is quite similar [to that for misdemeanors], except that [for felonies] there is the additional step of the preliminary hearing as an additional safeguard warranted by the more serious nature of the charges.

Step 1 [This describes the arraignment.] The first step is an initial appearance or an arraignment before a judge of a lower court or magistrate, at which:
The charge is read to the defendant, and penalties explained.

The defendant is advised of his/her right to a preliminary hearing and the purpose of that procedure, as well as his/her right to trial and right to trial by jury in trial court.

The right to counsel (legal representation) is explained, and the judge or magistrate appoints a lawyer if the defendant requests one and is found to be indigent (too poor to afford a private lawyer).

The defendant does **not** enter a plea. The matter is set for preliminary hearing (a hearing to establish if a crime has been committed and if there is probable cause to believe that the defendant committed the offense(s) alleged in the complaint). The judge or magistrate sets the amount of bail.

Step 2 - The second step is the preliminary hearing, at which:

The government must demonstrate to a judge or magistrate that there is sufficient evidence, or probable cause, to believe the suspect committed the crime with which he or she is charged. Defendants usually must be present at this hearing [& if the Defendant is still in jail, the jail will transport them to & from the courthouse], although **[defendants] do not commonly offer evidence in their defense.** This procedure has a similar function to grand jury proceedings, in that it is a safeguard against unfettered government action. (Clarification and emphasis added.)

We wish to clarify the meaning of "unfettered government action." This step was established in the criminal legal process to prevent the government from "railroading" defendants. "Railroading" means the defendant is either coerced to admit guilt and accept a plea bargain or other unscrupulous tactics have taken place behind-the-scenes to assure the defendant is found guilty.

Unfortunately, the unvarnished truth is that this "safeguard" is **not** an absolute assurance. All too often defendants **are "railroaded," especially to take a plea bargain.** Understanding the facts about "Plea Bargains" is very important and will be discussed separately.

> If the court finds there is no probable cause, the matter is dismissed (this would be the equivalent of a grand jury declining to press charges). If this happens, defendants are released.
>
> If the court finds there is probable cause, the matter is transferred to trial court. Many courts use the term bound over, as [in] "the defendant is bound over to the district or circuit court for trial."

A specific court will be assigned to hear the case and a date will be set on the docket for a hearing in that court. Although the hearing court is unlikely to change, the trial date may be postponed several times.

Perhaps the most comforting thing to know about the preliminary hearing is that other than the highly unlikely possibility that the defendant may be released for lack of evidence, no decisions regarding the final outcome of the case are made at this stage.

A VERY SERIOUS WORD ABOUT PLEA BARGAINS

~ **EMOTIONALLY:** Making a decision about accepting the offer of a plea bargain is extremely stressful as you must wrestle with numerous "what if's" and unknowns that all plea bargains present. The plea bargain stage may activate a tangled web of conflicting and confusing emotions filled with hopefulness for the offer of a light sentence and simultaneous feelings of trepidation, uncertainty and fear that the harshest of punishments will ultimately be enforced. Feeling intimidated by the legal authorities to accept their plea bargain offer will lead to extraordinary anxiety and ultimate exhaustion. Overwhelmed by weighing critical life-altering options, most people are left feeling angry and helpless.

~ **LEGALLY:** Once a trial court is assigned and the hearing date is scheduled, the defense attorney and the government's attorney (more commonly referred to as the "DA" or "District Attorney") will hold some behind-the-scenes negotiations that most often result in offering the defendant a plea bargain.

Before even describing the "plea bargain" let us point out that we have learned from lengthy experience that unless the government offers to **completely** dismiss the case or unless the government offers probation in a case where guilt is **completely** acknowledged by the defendant, it is wise to **SAY "NO" TO PLEA BARGAINS!**

To understand why we highly recommend saying "NO" to the offer of a plea bargain, here are some facts about "plea bargains":

- Defendants are routinely pushed very hard, even intimidated to accept plea bargains, because plea bargains help the court clear the docket (the court's caseload) swiftly and economically.

- Defendants are pushed hard and even intimidated to accept plea bargains, because prosecutors are evaluated by the number of convictions they obtain. **A plea bargain is a conviction** in the prosecutor's favor and the fastest and cheapest way to get a conviction.

- Plea bargains give the **illusion** of offering the defendant a "good deal" when compared to **MAXIMUM** possible sentencing time.

- Accepting a plea bargain may sound safer than going to trial and in your fearful and fragile emotional state the plea bargain will be tempting.

- It IS possible that the defendant MAY get more time than a plea bargain offer, if they insist on a trial.

- The defendant and the prosecutor may agree on the plea bargain, but **the judge does not have to accept it**. (The judge will tell the defendant that if they do not accept an agreed upon plea bargain, the defendant will have the right to proceed with a trial.)

- Judges have actually been known to engage in the process of intimidating defendants to accept plea bargains by threatening longer sentences, if the defendant insists on taking the case to trial.

- With very few exceptions, accepting a plea bargain agreement is final, if accepted by the judge.

- By accepting a plea bargain the defendant forfeits his or her right to appeal. There is no turning back. The defendant will begin serving the time agreed upon—period, if accepted by the judge.

- Although a plea bargain may be more economical for the defendant as well as the prosecution and the court, plea bargains are **not** intended to do the defendant a favor.

- **Accepting a plea bargain is an admission of guilt.** The defendant must admit guilt when accepting a plea bargain; the defendant will then be convicted of the offense and the conviction will remain on the defendant's record, permanently.

The unvarnished truth is that if every criminal case filed with the courts went to a full trial the court dockets would be so back-logged it would be impossible for the courts to ever hear all of the cases. The purpose of the plea bargain is NOT to be nice to the defendant. The purpose of the plea bargain is to clear the court docket as quickly and cheaply as possible. The whole purpose of a plea bargain is to help the court and the prosecutor, **not** the defendant.

Despite feeling threatened to take the plea bargain, defendants should always remember that HASTE MAKES WASTE!!! They should not feel forced to make a hasty decision by the overbearing prosecutors and the intimidating nature of the court. Despite being in a vulnerable position, there is no good reason to rush to make any decision related to a criminal court case. The defendant should take the time needed to carefully weigh the options. When in doubt, they should always, always, always get a second opinion & even a third opinion. Most attorneys will provide one free consultation to hear the circumstances of the case. The most ethical attorneys will provide a suggested course of action based on the facts of the case.

Remember this: While many young attorneys have a genuine passion to serve their clients judiciously, after years in the courtroom many attorneys become jaded and begin engaging in practices that are not fully ethical, but are accepted in our courts. Attorneys have acknowledged this fact to us. One most recently said it this way: *"Court is nothing more than a human chess game."* No defendant should allow them self to become a pawn in the game of human chess.

Remember this: No ethical attorney can promise any outcome of any court case. If an attorney promises they will get your case dismissed or get you probation or if they promise any other outcome before the case is heard in court, they are being *untrue*. (That is the nice way of saying **they are lying**.) They will gladly take your money and when things don't go exactly as they promised, they will say they're sorry and walk away, while you will face the consequences.

Remember this: Most of us were taught to trust in a court system that was established to "determine the absolute truth" when neighbors disputed a legal fact or when those arrested for crimes denied their guilt. Most of us operate under the belief that justice will prevail when matters are taken to court. The very sad unvarnished truth is—**justice does not always occur in our justice system.** At times like these we must unlearn

28

what we always believed to be true and then relearn the realities of what "justice" has become in our country.

And, always remember this: There is no accountability in the criminal justice system. Therefore judges are free to make up their own rules as the case unfolds.

While speaking with the mother of a teenager who had been accused of inappropriate sexual contact with a young girl, the boy's mother informed me that the first attorney they hired had "gotten him transferred out of the juvenile system," into the adult criminal justice system. The original attorney was described as "specializing in juvenile cases," so the family had now hired a new attorney.

To be very honest, I was shocked when she told me this and had to wonder what would have possibly prompted this action. After all, if found guilty a fifteen year old tried as a juvenile has a better chance of having the case erased from his record, than if found guilty of a sex offense as an adult. Now, if found guilty as an adult, her son would be labeled as a sex offender and possibly be required to register as a sex offender for the rest of his life!

The mother stated adamantly, "He is innocent!"

"All the more reason to have him tried as a juvenile," I responded.

"Well, the attorney and judge and everyone wanted to ship him off to the juvenile authorities immediately if he remained in the juvenile court. We wouldn't have had a chance to prove he is innocent!"

I was stunned. "They can't just 'ship him off' without a hearing whether he is a juvenile or an adult," I responded incredulously.

"They told us that if he stayed in the juvenile system, they would 'ship him off' without a trial, right there and then," the mother responded.

I thought I'd already heard it all after more than thirty years wrestling with the criminal justice system, but I absolutely could not believe what I was hearing. Surely this mother was mistaken and in her anxiety and fear she had totally misunderstood what the legal authorities had told her. So, of course I questioned her further.

After several minutes of explanation, it became clear that indeed she had heard exactly what she had told me, and when she informed me what the judge from the adult court had told her son just the day before, it only took me a few seconds to understand why she had been given this totally false information.

The day before our conversation her son had gone with his attorney to meet with the district attorney about the possibility of a plea bargain. The boy's father and grandfather had accompanied him.

The whole arrangement in itself was very unusual. Typically the defendant has no active front-line role in negotiating plea bargains. To make matters even more baffling, the mother stated that during the negotiations her son had continued to insist on his innocence, so the district attorney along with the boy's own attorney suggested they talk with the assigned judge in the case—another extremely unusual move— defendants don't talk to judges **before** their case is in Court!!!

The entire scenario became even more peculiar and concerning when she told me, "The judge told him that if he refused to take the plea bargain and took the case to a jury trial and was found guilty, the minimum sentence the jury could give him was five years in prison, but if he let the judge hear the case and is found guilty the minimum sentence could be probation."

My mouth literally fell open. "I'm not an attorney," I gasped in disbelief attempting to guard my words, "But I believe that is not true."

The mother again repeated what the judge had told her son and I responded in what I hoped was a manner that she would fully understand, "There are prescribed ranges of sentences for every offense. Even if your son is found guilty he would be sentenced from the same range of prescribed sentences whether a judge or jury hears the case. A judge cannot suddenly make up new sentences for those that are written in statutes and law. There's an entire legal process for changing the rules!"

"Well, I don't know," said the mother. "All I know is that's what the judge said, so now we want to go with the plea bargain."

I then said firmly, "A plea bargain is an admission of guilt. If your son accepts that plea bargain and pleads guilty he will be convicted of a sex offense. Do you understand that he will be labeled as a sex offender for the rest of his life?"

"I know," said the mother, "But we don't want to risk the possibility that he will go to prison when the judge has practically promised he will give our son probation."

"No he hasn't!" I nearly shouted at her. "He hasn't promised you anything," He gave you a picture of what COULD happen in HIS Court. **He lied to you.** He didn't promise anything."

Extremely distressed by what I was hearing, I had to remind myself that I am not an attorney and so I told the mother that I would double-check with one of our legal consultants, although I felt that I was pretty accurate with the information I'd already given her.

Hanging up from this incredible phone conversation, I phoned an attorney we feel quite confident provides us with accurate information. She was far more adamant about the situation than I had been. She said sharply, "If that is what they were told, that is an out and out lie."

She then repeated what I had already told the mother about prescribed sentences. Then she added, "Those people need to fire their attorney. If their attorney didn't correct the judge right there and then; or if he didn't at least tell the family the judge had lied to them, that attorney is definitely not going to fight for her son. He is trying to force the boy to take a plea bargain."

She went on to add that attorneys and judges will take advantage of the vulnerability of the defendant and their family just to coerce them into taking plea bargains. She explained what I already knew about trying to quickly clear the court docket by pushing all defendants to take plea bargains, adding, "Attorneys and judges like that never have the defendant's best interest in mind; they are only interested in making a quick buck, getting a conviction and moving on to the next case so they can make more money," and then the attorney added, "And you can quote me on that."

———

If, after carefully weighing all of the options, the choice is to accept a plea bargain assure you are not paying the same attorney fee as you would for a full trial. The truth is that a plea bargain agreement only requires a standard form (essentially installed on every defense attorney's computer). The attorney carries a stack of those forms in his or her briefcase! The minute a defendant succumbs to the plea bargain, the attorney zips out that form and scribbles in a few blanks or a paralegal or secretary (not the attorney) plugs in names and numbers in a pre-existing form and submits it to the court. It requires very little time or effort for attorneys to file a plea bargain or to represent a defendant in plea bargained matter. After all, the whole purpose of the plea bargain is to save time for the court and to get a conviction for the prosecutor!

This is what the American Bar Association says about plea bargains.

> Defendants can avoid the time and cost of defending themselves at trial, the risk of harsher punishment, and the publicity a trial could involve.

Don't be fooled by the first statement on the subject of plea bargains out of the mouths of the ABA. The plea bargain is not for the benefit of the defendant. It is first and foremost for the benefit of the judicial system. The ABA explanation is written for lay people and not for judges and lawyers. They'd like us to think the plea bargain benefits defendants. They're going to fess up to the truth in just a minute.

The prosecution saves the time and expense of a lengthy trial.

Both sides are spared the uncertainty of going to trial.

The court system is saved from the burden of conducting a trial on every crime charged. (Emphasis added.)

Either side may begin negotiations over a proposed plea bargain, though obviously both sides have to agree before one comes to pass. Plea bargaining usually involves the defendant's pleading guilty to a lesser charge, or to only one of several charges. It also may involve a guilty plea as charged, with the prosecution recommending leniency in sentencing. The judge, however, is not bound to follow the prosecution's recommendation. Many plea bargains are subject to the approval of the court, but some may not be (e.g., prosecutors may be able to drop charges without court approval in exchange for a "guilty" plea to a lesser offense).

Plea bargaining is essentially a private process, but this is changing now that victim rights groups are becoming recognized. Under many victim rights statutes, victims have the right to have input into the plea bargaining process. Usually the details of a plea bargain aren't known publicly until announced in court.

The victim has the right to be present and/or represented at every stage of the court process and may even meet with the district attorney to discuss the provisions of a plea bargain, often providing their own input. It is common for the district attorney to honor the wishes of the victim or their family in determining the terms of a plea bargain offer.

Other alternatives are also possible in the criminal justice system. Many states encourage diversion programs that remove less serious criminal matters from the full, formal procedures of the justice system. Typically, the defendant will be allowed to consent to probation without having to go through a trial. If he or she successfully completes the probation – e.g., undergoes rehabilitation or makes restitution for the crime – the matter will be expunged (removed) from the records.

Note: Expunging is a legal process; it does not happen automatically just because you have successfully completed restitution; probation, etc. You must file for it with the Court.

ABOUT SEEKING "CLOSURE"

Going to trial is an extremely stressful period filled with many unknowns and frightening thoughts of the worst potential outcome. Fear and anxiety are mixed with guarded hopefulness for total freedom, or at least probation. The whole experience is so incredibly surreal that it is very likely the defendant and their support team will experience denial throughout the entire trial. This couldn't possibly be happening! Surely this is the proverbial nightmare from which they will awaken very soon. In large part they will remain in denial because they are seeking "closure." Everyone wants the suffering to end and life to return to "normal." However, nothing ever seems to have an ending and the process remains dangling and incomplete.

You've probably heard about victims of heinous crimes seeking "closure." They are actually seeking an end to their pain and suffering. For example, families of murder victims often believe "closure" will come once the murderer is found guilty and sentenced. But when the trial is over and the convicted perpetrator is hauled away in handcuffs and shackles, regardless of the length of sentence given the victims will typically say, "They deserved a *harsher* sentence." In other words, the conviction and sentencing did **not** bring them "closure."

Even in death penalty cases after the victim's family witnesses their loved one's murderer executed many years after the crime, they will invariably state, "I thought watching him die would bring closure, but it hasn't. The only way I would ever have closure is to have my loved one back with me." They cannot seem to find the closure they are so desperately seeking.

Among the most painful unvarnished truths about the prison family journey is the fact that **closure never comes**. In fact, consciously seeking "closure" to resolve the pain you are experiencing probably only serves to intensify your pain. That is because you are seeking something that does not exist.

Perhaps it would help not to seek closure at all, but instead to accept the milestones along the journey as achievements; as successes. Looking at the entire journey that lies ahead can easily become overwhelming. If you could possibly look at the prison family journey much as we look at planning a long car trip perhaps that will help.

When planning a long car trip we will map out the rest stops; the places to fill up with gas; the places to take a break for a meal, perhaps even where we may take a moment for some sight seeing along the way. Maybe looking at reaching the next rest area or the next place you'll fill up again makes the trip seem less tedious. Each time you fill up with gas you realize you are that much closer to your destination. Each rest stop ahead gives you something to look forward to and those brief moments for sight seeing can be very refreshing. Could looking at the prison family journey in smaller stages like that make the journey feel less tedious; less painful; more tolerable?

At this point, you've made it through the arrest and arraignment. You've stopped for several pre-trial hearings and now you are about to reach a major milestone—the trial. Emotions are exceptionally high. It is common to feel almost suffocated by anxiety during the trial stage. Despite the anxiety however, it is extremely crucial to keep a clear head. You must pay attention to what the attorneys are doing. You must be alert to the judge's rulings and the jury's reactions. You must take note of whether your own attorney is protecting your right to appeal, if you are found guilty. Take a deep breath.

THE TRIAL

~ **EMOTIONALLY:** The beginning of the long awaited trial will bring with it a host of mixed emotions. While there may be a sense of relief that you have finally reached this fearfully anticipated milestone and a sense of guarded hopefulness that freedom may be near, there will also be a sense of trepidation that the defendant will be found guilty and harshly punished. Explaining the circumstances to friends, family and colleagues is generally fraught with embarrassment and shame, which often leads loved ones to withdraw from interaction with others to avoid discussing any aspect of the case. Once the trial begins there are feelings of frustration and confusion over seemingly unnecessary delays and senseless legal jargon all of which may lead to anger and a sense of helplessness at the inability to stop the process once it begins as though you are on a run away roller coaster teetering on the brink of disaster.

~ **LEGALLY:** No one cares more about the outcome of a criminal trial than the defendant and their loved ones. Therefore, for the best outcome, everyone on the defendant's support team must become very knowledgeable about what is and what is not supposed to be happening. It is now their responsibility to assure the defense attorney is diligently representing the defendant.

Often the defendant will have little contact with their defense attorney before trial. Further, most attorneys will refuse to speak to the defendant's loved ones, even if they are paying the legal fees. This is a matter of "legal ethics." The attorney only represents the defendant and not the defendant's family or friends regardless of how well-intentioned they are. The attorney is ethically only supposed to speak with the defendant.

Isn't it interesting that attorneys can become so highly ethical at times it serves their own purpose? If they don't have to talk to the defendant's loved ones, so much the better. It certainly saves them time and a lot of grief, because those family members and friends are sure to ask some hard questions and demand logical answers! Well, let's take care of that! You will find the forms you will need to be able to talk to the defendant's lawyer without fear of breaching any ethics in the "Forms Section" right in the back of this book!

To enable the attorney to talk with members of the defendant's support team a Release of Information or a Power of Attorney must be signed by the defendant and notarized (at the jail, if they are still being held) and then delivered to the attorney. The form should specifically name those individuals the defendant wishes their attorney to talk with about their case. Once the signed and notarized form is provided to the attorney, you may be able to communicate with them. However do not be surprised if no one on the defendant's support team talks with the attorney before going to court—not even the defendant them self!

One of the biggest complaints we hear at the trial stage is that the attorney has NEVER talked to the defendant before going to trial. Even though most attorneys are bright, intelligent people who think quickly on their feet and are articulate spokespersons, it is a sad fact that the first time some attorneys meet their client is when they go to trial. We've actually seen attorneys who were unable to identify their client when the court called their case, because they never met their client in person. This especially happens when the primary attorney you believe you hired sends younger attorneys or even interns or aides to the pre-trial hearings on their behalf. Of course we believe this should never happen, however the unvarnished truth is it *does* happen all too often.

Of course, it is also our opinion that all attorneys should be like Perry Mason, devoting hours to strategizing with their client; diligently researching the case; hiring the best investigators imaginable and of course always pulling a magical rabbit from a hat during cross examination of the prosecution's star witness and thereby winning all cases!

Well folks that is Perry Mason's incredible TV magic! That is not real life. So here's what you can expect in real life.

Expect many more postponements. These are some typical excuses for court hearing and trial postponements: Your attorney isn't ready to go to trial; the prosecution isn't ready to go to trial; the assigned judge is tied up in another hearing; a critical witness (on either side) is unavailable until next month; a key player is sick; it's an obscure holiday and court is not in session; there's a farewell party for a retiring judge; your attorney or the prosecutor or even the judge planned a family vacation months ago! You name the excuse for postponement, we've heard it! The best thing you can do about postponements is to expect them and use the delays to further prepare for trial.

Expect your attorney and the prosecutor and even the judge to be friends or at least to be friendly with each other. Defendants are often disturbed by the friendly chatter and jovial laughter they observe between their attorney and the members of the prosecution team and even with the judge. This is especially true when a court-appointed attorney is representing the defendant.

It is important to recognize that outside of the courtroom these courtroom adversaries may very well be friends. They may have attended law school together; they may attend the same church; they probably go to local bar association luncheons together and they may even play golf together. The fact is that they have learned to play their roles in the courtroom without letting their friendship outside of the courtroom interfere—at least not too much.

Remember, this is a human chess game! The defense attorney and prosecutor have learned to be adversaries in the courtroom, even if they are personal friends. It is important to each of them to win cases or at least satisfy their client, or they won't remain in practice very long. Even public defenders are expected to win a case now and then!

Similarly, it behooves the judge to portray the appearance of a stoic and impartial referee in the courtroom, or too many of their verdicts will be overturned and they won't maintain their judgeship very long! So, while you can certainly inquire of your attorney about any discomfort you have with the apparent friendliness between the parties; do not be frightened by it. To be honest, that is the least of your worries!

Expect that your attorney will not be solely dedicated to your case. The fact is that attorneys must make a living just like the rest of us, so they take on many cases representing many clients at the same time. In fact, don't be surprised if your attorney suddenly dashes from your courtroom to run to another courtroom to take care of business in another case.

Additionally attorneys have their own lives; their own families and the same daily ups and downs; joys and tragedies we all experience. So, they are not devoted solely to you and your case. For that reason in the midst of your emotional turmoil you must become very knowledgeable about the legal process and very alert to points your attorney may miss, especially if they are otherwise distracted. Defendants and their loved ones must absolutely advocate for themselves and essentially become the watchdogs of the very attorney who is supposed to be representing them. The defendant may even need to assure their own witnesses are prepared to effectively testify. It may not seem right; it may not seem fair, but it is reality.

Expect to live with numerous unknowns for months on end; in some cases years on end. There may be talk of "swift and speedy trials," but the reality is that the wheels of justice grind ever so slowly. Your attorney may try to appease you by saying there are benefits in the delays. They may say that the longer you wait to go to trial the more witnesses will forget. They may say that the longer the defendant is out on the street causing no problems, the better the chance the court will realize they are really a good person and will go easy on them. Maybe those things are actually strategically beneficial in some cases, but certainly not in all. So, regardless of whether delays are strategic or not, all you can do is WAIT! There is nothing more stressful than living with unknowns, but that is a reality in this situation. For that reason, everyone must find ways to cope effectively with stress.

Expect to feel intimidated by the cold austerity of the courtroom and the numerous unknowns ahead. The court is intended to be an intimidating forum. Regardless of your fears, to protect your best interests you must become your own assertive advocate. You must not be afraid to speak out on your own behalf, especially if you feel you are not being adequately represented. To effectively become your own advocate you must arm yourself with solid information about what should and should not be happening during the trial. You must speak up if your attorney overlooks an important point. If you do not speak up for yourself, these matters will go unaddressed and if things don't go your way **you** must live with the consequences, not your attorney.

Expect that the trial will eventually begin and there will again be some serious decisions to make. It is then that you will realize how important it has been to have prepared for the trial while waiting for it to begin.

Even before the trial begins the defendant is faced with daunting decisions, such as choosing whether to request a jury trial or not. In fact, it is the defendant's option to choose whether to have a jury or only the judge hear their case. This is an overwhelming decision.

~ **EMOTIONALLY:** The uncertainty involved in determining whether to choose a jury or not is confusing and filled with overwhelming doubts that elicit feelings of anxiety, fear and frustration.

~ **LEGALLY:** Deciding whether to have a jury to hear your case or whether you only want to present your case to the judge is a very tough call because a lot depends on the particular judge who will hear the case and where their interests, prejudices and sympathies lie. A lot also depends on the type of offense the defendant has been charged with.

Essentially, this decision is like rolling dice; either choice is a gamble! Some "experts" will tell you that it's harder to convince one solitary judge of innocence than it is to convince at least one of twelve jurors. With a jury you have twelve chances of winning at least one person over to your side. With a judge, you are putting all of your eggs in one basket. However, other experts will tell you that a judge has heard unpleasant things many times before and won't be as shocked or appalled by the sordid and graphic details of your case as twelve inexperienced jurors might be.

The truth is that in some cases the ability to persuade a judge or a jury boils down to what side of the bed they woke up on that morning! You simply have to make your best guess; hopefully an *educated guess* based on the specific circumstances of the case and what is known about the judge. What is their track record? How have they ruled in similar cases? What is most important is that you are as fully convinced as possible that you've made the right choice, because you will have to live with the consequences of your decision.

If the defendant chooses to go with the judge, the trial date will be set and the trial will begin. If the defendant chooses to go with a jury, a date will be set at which time the prosecutor and defense attorney will begin questioning potential jurors from the jury pool to select those most beneficial to "their side."

Here is what the American Bar Association has to say about jury selection in criminal cases.

JURY TRIALS

Juries…are selected from the jury pool. The size of jury varies from state to state and depends to some extent on the type of case at trial. … in serious criminal cases twelve jurors are generally required.

Alternate jurors are selected in some cases to take the place of jurors who may become ill during the trial. Alternate jurors hear the evidence just as the other jurors do, but they don't participate in the deliberations unless they replace an original juror.

In many jurisdictions, jury selection begins with the court clerk's calling twelve people on the jury list and asking them to take a place in the jury box. The judge usually makes a brief statement explaining what kind of case is to be tried and inquiring whether there is any reason the potential jurors cannot serve. The judge or the lawyers then ask them questions as to whether they have any knowledge of the case or have had specific experiences that might cause them to be biased or unfair. This questioning of the potential jurors is known as voir dire (to speak the truth).

If either lawyer believes there is information that suggests a juror is prejudiced about the case, he or she can ask the judge to dismiss that juror for cause. For example, a juror can be dismissed for cause if he or she is a close relative of one of the parties or one of the lawyers. Each lawyer may request the dismissal of an unlimited number of jurors for cause. Each request will be considered by the judge and may or may not be allowed.

In addition to challenges for cause, each lawyer has a specific number of peremptory challenges. These challenges permit a lawyer to excuse a potential juror without stating a cause. In effect, they allow a lawyer to dismiss a juror because of a belief that the juror will not serve the best interests of the client. Peremptory challenges are limited to a certain number determined by the kind of lawsuit... They can't be used to discriminate on the basis of race or sex.

Once impaneled, the jurors' role is to listen to the evidence conscientiously and not draw premature conclusions. They are instructed by the judge not to discuss the case with outsiders or each other (until deliberations). They generally do not have the right to ask questions of witnesses, but some judges permit jurors to submit written questions for the judge and lawyers to consider. (The lawyers have a right to object to these questions, just as they do to questions posed by lawyers during the trial.) If appropriate, the questions may be asked.

The following information is primarily that provided by the American Bar Association for each factor affecting the trial process.

THE TRIAL PROCESS

Opening Statements

The purpose of opening statements by each side is to tell jurors something about the case they will be hearing. The opening statements must be confined to facts that will be proved by the evidence, and cannot be argumentative.

The trial begins with the opening statement of the party with the burden of proof. This is the party that brought the case to court–the government in a criminal prosecution….. The defense lawyer follows with his or her opening statement. In some states, the defense may reserve its opening statement until the end of the…government's case [if it is believed strategically beneficial to the defendant]. Either lawyer may choose not to present an opening statement.

In a criminal trial, the burden of proof rests with the government, which must prove beyond a reasonable doubt that the defendant is guilty. The defendant does not need to prove his or her innocence–the burden is on the government.

It should be noted that *proof* is based on "reasonable doubt" and NOT "beyond all doubt." That is why many cases are won on circumstantial evidence, rather than actual concrete evidence.

EVIDENCE

The heart of the case is presentation of evidence. There are two types of evidence --
direct and circumstantial.

Direct evidence usually is that which speaks for itself: eyewitness accounts, a confession, or a weapon.

Circumstantial evidence usually is that which suggests a fact by implication or inference: the appearance of the scene of a crime, testimony that suggests a connection or link with a crime, physical evidence that suggests criminal activity.

Both kinds of evidence are a part of most trials, with circumstantial evidence probably being used more often than direct. Either kind of evidence can be offered in oral testimony of witnesses or physical exhibits, including fingerprints, test results, and documents. Neither kind of evidence is more valuable than the other.

Strict rules govern the kinds of evidence that may be admitted into a trial, and the presentation of evidence is governed by formal rules.

DIRECT EXAMINATION [OF THE WITNESSES]:

Witnesses may testify to matters of fact, and in some instances provide opinions. They also may be called to identify documents, pictures or other items introduced into evidence.

Generally witnesses cannot state opinions or give conclusions unless they are experts or are especially qualified to do so. Witnesses qualified in a particular field as expert witnesses may give their opinion based on the facts in evidence and may give the reason for that opinion.

Lawyers generally may not ask leading questions of their own witnesses. Leading questions are questions that suggest the answers desired, in effect prompting the witness. An example is, "Isn't it true that you saw John waiting across the street before his wife came home?"

Defense witnesses should be well prepared to testify. The prosecution will have spent a good deal of time preparing their witnesses. It just stands to reason that defense witnesses should be equally well prepared. This means that the defense attorney or at least their aides should have taken *ample* time prior to the trial to present their witnesses with the types of questions they might expect in the courtroom. The defense attorney or at least their aides should have even spent face-to-face time practicing how those questions should be answered.

If children are to be used as witnesses, a member of the defense attorney's team should take them into an empty courtroom and even have them sit in the witness stand. They should engage the child(ren) in face-to-face practice, preparing them for what to expect and to be as comfortable as possible when they actually testify in court.

A defense attorney should be very aware of the responses all of their witnesses are likely to give in the courtroom. No attorney should ever ask a witness a question without knowing what the answer will be, *especially when it is their own witness*!

DIRECT EXAMINATION

Lawyers for the plaintiff or the government begin the presentation of evidence by calling witnesses. The questions they ask of the witnesses are direct examination. Direct examination may elicit both direct and circumstantial evidence. Witnesses may testify to matters of fact, and in some instances provide opinions. They also may be called to identify documents, pictures or other items introduced into evidence.

Generally witnesses cannot state opinions or give conclusions unless they are experts or are especially qualified to do so. Witnesses qualified in a particular field as expert witnesses may give their opinion based on the facts in evidence and may give the reason for that opinion.

Lawyers generally may not ask leading questions of their own witnesses. Leading questions are questions that suggest the answers desired, in effect prompting the witness. An example is, "Isn't it true that you saw John waiting across the street before his wife came home?"

Objections may be made by the opposing counsel for many reasons under the rules of evidence, such as [when the opposing attorney has used] leading questions [or] questions that call for an opinion or conclusion by a witness, or questions that require an answer based on hearsay.

Most courts require a specific legal reason be given for an objection. Usually, the judge will immediately either sustain or overrule the objection. If the objection is sustained, the lawyer must re-phrase the question in a proper form or ask another question. If the objection is overruled and the witness answers the question, the lawyer who raised the objection may appeal the judge's ruling after the trial is over.

As a handbook for federal jurors points out, a ruling by the judge does not indicate that the judge is taking sides. He or she is merely saying, in effect, that the law does, or does not permit that question to be asked. Even if the judge decides every objection against a certain party, he or she is not taking sides or indicating to jurors how they should decide the case.

If the defendant believes the judge is indicating partiality to the prosecution, they are strongly urged to discuss this with their attorney. If the attorney does not satisfactorily explain the judge's appearance of partiality, the defendant may insist that their attorney make an audible statement to reflect the defendant's belief that the judge is showing preference to the prosecution. This type of statement, as well as the defense attorney's objections made throughout the trial, whether sustained by the judge or not, protects the defendant's right to appeal in the event of a guilty verdict. If the defense attorney does not make objections throughout the trial, the defendant may be left with little recourse for an appeal, if found guilty.

CROSS EXAMINATION:

When the lawyer for the…government has finished questioning a witness, the lawyer for the defendant may then cross-examine the witness. Cross-examination is generally limited to questioning only on matters that were raised during direct examination. Leading questions may be asked during cross-examination, since the purpose of cross-examination is to test the credibility of statements made during direct examination… [and] the witness is usually being questioned by the lawyer who did not originally call him or her…[and] is likely…to resist any suggestion that is not true. When a lawyer calls an adverse or hostile witness (…such that his testimony is likely to be prejudicial) on direct examination, the lawyer can ask leading questions as on cross-examination.

On cross-examination, the attorney might try to question the witness's ability to identify or recollect or try to impeach the witness or the evidence. Impeach in this sense means to question or reduce the credibility of the witness or evidence. The attorney might do this by trying to show prejudice or bias in the witness, such as his or her relationship or friendship with one of the parties, or his or her interest in the outcome of the case. Witnesses may be asked if they have been convicted of a felony or a crime involving moral turpitude (dishonesty), since this is relevant to their credibility.

Opposing counsel may object to certain questions asked on cross-examination if the questions violate the state's laws on evidence or if they relate to matters not discussed during direct examination.

On cross-examination, the attorney might try to question the witness's ability to identify or recollect or try to impeach the witness or the evidence. Impeach in this sense means to question or reduce the credibility of the witness or evidence.

The attorney might do this by trying to show prejudice or bias in the witness, such as his or her relationship or friendship with one of the parties, or his or her interest in the outcome of the case. Witnesses may be asked if they have been convicted of a felony or a crime involving moral turpitude (dishonesty), since this is relevant to their credibility.

Opposing counsel may object to certain questions asked on cross-examination if the questions violate the state's laws on evidence or if they relate to matters not discussed during direct examination.

MOTION FOR DIRECTED VERDICT/DISMISSAL

At the conclusion of the…government's evidence, the…[prosecutor] will announce that the… government rests. Then, when the jury leaves the courtroom, the defendant's lawyer… can ask for a motion to dismiss the charges, arguing that the government has failed to prove its case.

In effect…the lawyer asks the judge to direct a verdict for the defendant. The judge will either grant or deny the motion. If it is granted, the case is over and the defendant wins. If the motion is denied, as it usually is, the defense is given the opportunity to present its evidence.

PRESENTATION OF EVIDENCE BY THE DEFENSE

The defense lawyer [whether paid or appointed by the Court] may choose not to present evidence, in the belief that the…[the prosecution] did not prove its case. Usually, however, the defense will offer evidence.

In a criminal case, the witnesses presented by the defense may or may not include the defendant. Because the Fifth Amendment to the U.S. Constitution protects against self-incrimination, the prosecution cannot require the defendant to take the stand and explain what happened, nor can it comment or speculate on the reasons the defendant has chosen not to testify. The jury will be instructed not to take into account the fact that the defendant did not testify.

The defense presents evidence in the same manner as the…state, and the…government in return has the right to cross-examine the defense's witnesses. Re-direct and re-cross examination also are permitted.

This type of action on the part of the defense attorney is very important, because it sets the groundwork for an appeal if the defendant is found guilty. During the trial a defense attorney should be heavily focused on three things: 1) attempting to prove the defendant's innocence and/or 2) attempting to lessen the degree of a defendant's guilt to minimize the severity of punishment and *always* 3) attempting to protect the defendant's right to appeal if found guilty.

The decision for the defendant to testify or not testify is a very sensitive issue. While most would agree that juries want to hear directly from the defendant, the more important fact to be considered is whether (guilty or not guilty) the defendant will make a good witness.

Not all defendants make good witnesses; therefore it is not always in the defendant's best interest that they testify. For example, if the defendant is especially hostile toward his/her accusers, they may easily anger and their emotions may cloud the jury's perception. If the defendant has difficulty articulating and is unable to effectively organize their thoughts and express them self clearly, it may confuse the jury, rather than clarify information for them.

There are many good reasons a defendant may choose not to testify. The judge will instruct the jury not to take a defendant's failure to testify into consideration when deliberating guilt or innocence.

On the other hand, if it is believed the defendant's testimony is crucial to a favorable outcome of the trial, it is also crucial that the defense attorney and/or their representatives spend a good amount of time preparing the defendant to testify effectively long *before* the trial begins. A large part of that preparation should be devoted to anticipating questions the prosecutor might ask and helping the defendant (and all of their witnesses for that matter) manage their emotions appropriately.

REBUTTAL

At the conclusion of the defendant's case, the…government can present rebuttal witnesses or evidence to refute evidence presented by the defendant. This may include only evidence not presented in the case initially, or a new witness who contradicts the defendant's witnesses.

FINAL MOTIONS

After all the evidence has been presented and the jury has left the courtroom, either side may move for a directed verdict. If the motion is granted the trial is over; if not, the presentation of evidence is complete and the case is ready to be submitted to the jury.

Again, this is another opportunity for the attorney to protect the defendant's rights to appeal. However, the defendant should not get their hopes up that the judge will dismiss the case based on this motion. Rarely in a jury trial would a judge make such a decision unless, based on the evidence the prosecution clearly had no basis for bringing the case to the court in the first place and it is very rare that a case would be brought to trial with insufficient evidence.

CLOSING ARGUMENTS

The lawyers' closing arguments or summations discuss the evidence and properly drawn inferences. The lawyers cannot talk about issues outside the case or about evidence that was not presented.

The judge usually indicates to the lawyers before closing arguments begin which instructions he or she intends to give the jury. In their closing arguments the lawyers can comment on the jury instructions and relate them to the evidence.

The lawyer for the…government usually goes first. The lawyer sums up and comments on the evidence in the most favorable light for his or her side, showing how it proved what he or she had to prove to prevail in the case.

After that side has made its case, the defense then presents its closing arguments. The defense lawyer usually answers statements made in the…government's argument, points out defects in their case and sums up the facts favorable to his/her client.

Because the…government has the burden of proof, the lawyer for that side is then entitled to make a concluding argument, sometimes called a rebuttal. This is a chance to respond to the defendant's points and make one final appeal to the jury.

Occasionally the defense may choose not to make a closing statement. If so, the… government loses the right to make a second argument.

When the attorneys rest their cases the judge will announce any variations by which the defendant may be found guilty or not guilty for the particular offense with which they have been charged. The range of punishment is determined **prior to beginning the trial** based primarily on the type of offense with which the defendant is charged. In some cases, a defendant may have more than one charge against them, such as "robbery and assault." The defendant may or may not be found guilty on both charges. In some cases a defendant may be found not guilty of the most serious charges against them, but can still be found guilty of lesser charges, or vice versa.

There is a significant difference in assessing an offense to be "aggravated" as opposed to a non-aggravated offense. Of course "aggravated" charges are more serious and result in more severe sentencing than non-aggravated charges. The difference often relates to whether a weapon was used in the offense or not.

There may be different degrees of guilt to be considered in some cases. For example, in murder cases a person may be charged with "murder in the first degree," but the judge or jury may also be given the option of finding the defendant guilty of the much lesser charge of "manslaughter." Often the difference in degrees is related to "intent," i.e. whether the person charged truly intended to kill the victim or not.

So, assessing guilt is not a simple cut and dried process. It is the defense attorney's responsibility to do all they can at the **outset** of the case to assure that lesser charges are included in the guilt or innocence phase of the trial, because if found guilty the degree of guilt will largely determine the severity of punishment. This is not always possible, as some offenses have the degree of severity ascribed by law, such as "capital" offenses.

A capital offense typically is one that falls under one of three categories. It may be a murder that occurred during the perpetration of another crime; it may be the commission of more than one murder at the same time—even that of a pregnant woman, as the fetus is considered a "second person," or it may be the murder or possibly the attempted murder of a peace officer or even another public servant. Capital offenses are usually punishable by life sentences (with or without the possibility of parole) or death, where the death penalty exists.

Despite the prescribed sentences for various offenses, often the finding of guilt or innocence and the application of sentencing is not meted out in a fair and equitable manner. This is when we question the reality of "justice" as it is delivered by our judicial system.

EQUITY OR LACK THEREOF

On the topic of "equity," we will start with the bottom line: From our perspective there is sometimes *luck*, but there is rarely equity to be found in the criminal justice system.

Generally speaking, minorities are more frequently arrested and minorities are more frequently arrested *without* cause than whites. More minorities are also found to be innocent of charges and convictions than whites. The unvarnished truth is that whether we like talking about it or not it is a statistically proven fact that race plays a major role in dispensing justice (or the lack thereof) in our country. Therefore, we will broach the subject, because of its relevance.

The stress of the trial is intensified by the fairly common knowledge that there is a lack of equity in our criminal justice system. It is of significant interest that the American Bar Association's description of "jury selection" indicates that no potential juror may be dismissed due to anything related to "**race** or gender." That looks very nice when written into law, but unfortunately reality tells us a very different story through factual statistics.

Simply using U.S. Census statistics it is clear to virtually everyone involved with criminal justice that this country has only 5% of the entire world's population, but proudly boasts almost 25% of the entire **world's**

prison population. The vast majority of those prisoners are minorities, especially Black males.

The United States Census also tells us that only 12.5% of our total population is Black, yet at last count statistics from the Federal Bureau of Prisons report that 72.7% (almost three-quarters) of our *prison* population is Black. The disparity found in those figures is nothing less than staggering.

It is not our intent to create racial strife in our depiction of the inequities within our judicial system. Actually, we believe the judicial system creates that strife on its own. But, the facts are the facts. In no way can that disparity be fully explained away by such mindless sweeping generalities as "Blacks commit more crimes than other races." Perhaps a picture will speak a thousand words on that subject.

The charts and graphs on the following pages (all a matter of public record and easily found on the internet) may best explain the significant disparities with which justice is administered in our country.

Generally speaking:

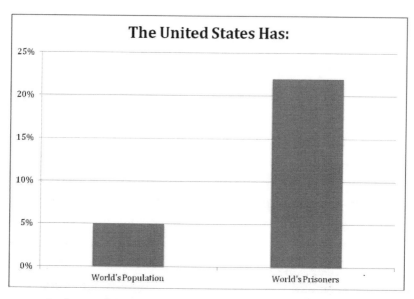

Comparatively speaking:

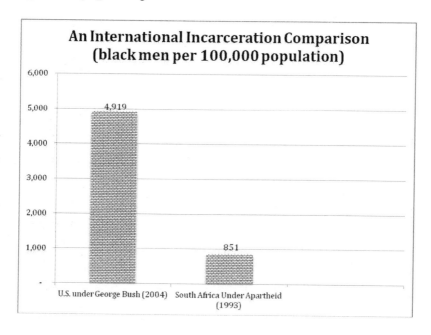

Who is in our prisons in the United States?

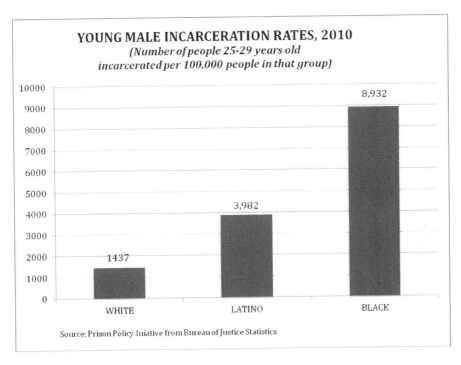

YOUNG MALE INCARCERATION RATES, 2010
*(Number of people 25-29 years old
incarcerated per 100,000 people in that group)*

Source: Prison Policy Iniative from Bureau of Justice Statistics

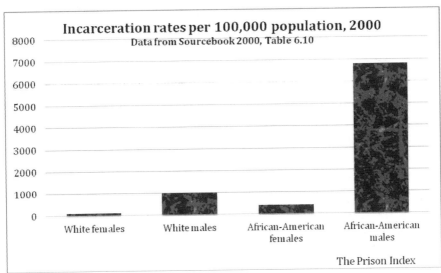

Incarceration rates per 100,000 population, 2000
Data from Sourcebook 2000, Table 6.10

The Prison Index

And, it is not only our nation's adults who are affected by this disparity.

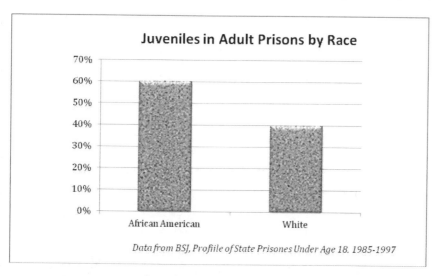

Expectations are the disparity will continue and even grow.

How does this disparity affect families?

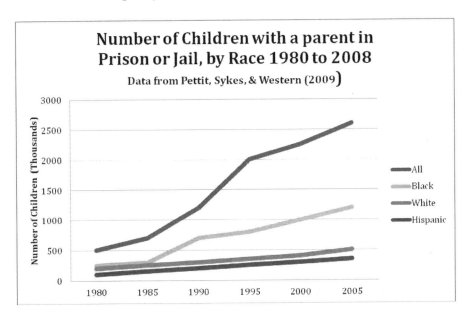

From an ABC News Report 12/27/12

So we won't seem biased, here is what *appears* to be some "balance." Unfortunately it is only an "appearance" of balance, because in reality whites commit more violent crimes than Blacks. Therefore, it stands to reason that more whites receive the death penalty than Blacks.

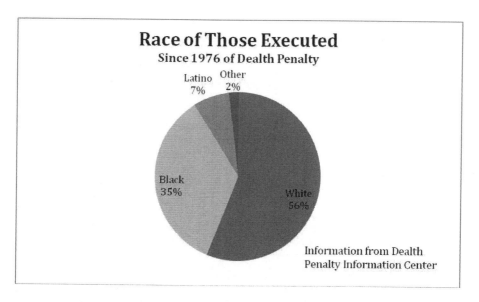

However, using only current statistics, even the *appearance* of "balance" seems to be disappearing!

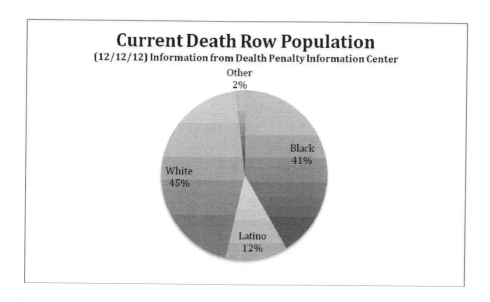

And what might this chart say about "disparity?"

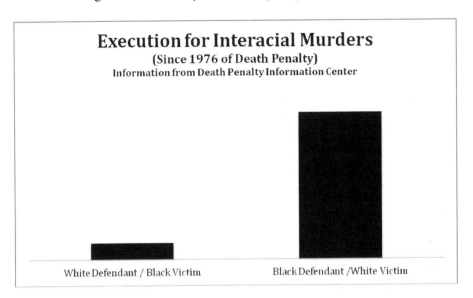

Something we found to be of interest:

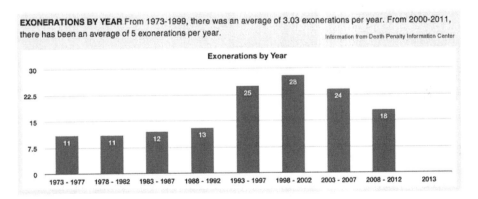

That was especially interesting, because of this:

Exonerations by Race

RACE	EXONERATIONS
Black	71
White	57
Latino	12
Other	2

Information from Dealth Penalty Information Center

Of course we all know that statistics can be skewed to prove a point. However we defy anyone to find statistics that refute the **blatant racial prejudice found throughout the criminal justice system from arrest through the trial through treatment in prison and reception upon re-entry.** The facts are the facts.

We cannot whitewash these facts by saying one race commits virtually all of the crimes in this country! That just is not true—especially as relates to violent crimes. In fact, more whites are in prison for murder; rape and other aggravated crimes than Blacks. The vast majority of Blacks are in prison for drug related offenses—possession; possession with intent to sell, etc.

Racial prejudice abounds throughout the criminal justice system. We mention it not to excuse any violation of the law or because we feel sorry for "those poor people." We mention it because of its relevance to the outcome of your case, regardless of what race you are.

We also mention the racial disparity because we believe it is wrong. We call it a "justice system" because it is supposed to be "just" in serving ALL peoples, not "just" to only one race of people or another.

Martin Luther King had an astute vision when he said he had a "dream of a society that would one day judge people by their character and not by the color of their skin." Tragically, not only did he not live to see his dream realized, but over a half a century later his dream is nowhere near fruition and this is especially true in our criminal justice system.

Our justice system was established to administer "justice" to all people, regardless of their heritage. We cannot simply give lip service to this inequity if we ever expect to right the wrong being done. It behooves each of us to speak out boldly when we see inequities of any kind, because, if for no other reason, "there, but for the grace of God, go I." Equity may be on my side *this time*, but what about next time? If I don't speak up for "you," who will be there to speak up for me?

When it comes to the law in this country we seem to be very good with the written word—especially the written word for public consumption. However, putting the written word on "equity" into practice in our criminal justice system is an entirely different story.

Whatever your race, we can almost guarantee that it **will** play a factor in the outcome of your case. We will leave it to you to determine from the facts **how** race plays a role in your case.

THE CONVICTION

At the end of a trial everyone typically tries to second guess what the judge or jury will determine about the defendant's guilt. This "second guessing" of course only creates additional stress for everyone. There may be some predictors of what the outcome might be, however whenever human beings are involved in making decisions, there are too many extenuating factors involved to scientifically determine the outcome *before* any actual decision is made.

~ **EMOTIONALLY:** While it is pointless to tell anyone to "relax" and patiently await the verdict, it may be helpful to know that it is perfectly "normal" for the defendant and their support team to be numbed by apprehension, anxiety and fear at this point. Some have even referred to this period as an "out of body experience." You may be physically present, but emotionally and mentally absent, just going through the motions necessary to live from moment to moment.

~ **LEGALLY:** Here is what the American Bar Association has to say about the judge's charge to the jury in determining guilt or innocence in criminal court cases.

INSTRUCTIONS TO THE JURY

The judge instructs the jury about the relevant laws that should guide its deliberations. ….. The judge reads the instructions to the jury. This is commonly referred to as the judge's charge to the jury.

The judge will advise the jury that it is the sole judge of the facts and of the credibility…of witnesses. He or she will note that the jurors are to base their conclusions on the evidence as presented in the trial, and that the opening and closing arguments of the lawyers are not evidence. Sometimes judges will explain what basic facts are in dispute, and what facts do not matter to the case.

The judge will point out that his or her instructions contain the interpretation of the relevant laws that govern the case, and that jurors are required to adhere to these laws in making their decision, regardless

---

of what the jurors believe the law is or ought to be. In short, the jurors determine the facts and reach a verdict, within the guidelines of the law as determined by the judge.

MISTRIALS

Mistrials are trials that are not successfully completed. They're terminated and declared void before the jury returns a verdict or the judge renders his or her decision in a nonjury trial.

Mistrials can occur for many reasons:
- death of a juror or attorney
- an impropriety in the drawing of the jury discovered during the trial
- a fundamental error prejudicial (unfair) to the defendant that cannot be cured by appropriate instructions to the jury (such as the inclusion of highly improper remarks in the prosecutor's summation)
- juror misconduct (e.g., having contacts with one of the parties, considering evidence not presented in the trial, conducting an independent investigation of the matter)
- the jury's inability to reach a verdict because it is hopelessly deadlocked.

Either side may make a motion for a mistrial. The judge will either grant the motion and declare a mistrial, or he or she will not grant the motion and the trial will go on.

JURY DELIBERATIONS

After receiving the instructions and hearing the final arguments, the jury retires to the jury room to begin deliberating. In most states the first order of business is to elect one of the jurors as the foreperson or presiding juror. This person's role is to preside over discussions and votes of the jurors, and often to deliver the verdict. The bailiff's job is to ensure that no one communicates with the jury during deliberations.

In some states, the jury may take the exhibits introduced into the record and the judge's instructions to the jury room. Sometimes the jury will have a question about the evidence or the judge's instructions. If this happens, the jury will give a note to the bailiff to take to the judge. The judge may respond to the note, or may call the jury back into the courtroom for further instructions or to have portions of the transcript read to them. Of course, any communication between the judge and jury should be in the presence of lawyers for each side or with their knowledge.

Usually the court provides the jury with written forms of all possible verdicts, so that when a decision is reached, the jury has only to choose the proper verdict form. In most instances, the verdict in a criminal case must be unanimous. ..... All federal cases require a unanimous decision.

If the jury cannot come to a decision by the end of the day, the jurors may be sequestered, or housed in a hotel and secluded from all contact with other people, newspapers and news reports. In most cases, though, the jury will be allowed to go home at night. The judge will instruct jurors not to read or view reports of the case in the news. Nor should they consider or discuss the case while outside of the jury room.

If the jurors cannot agree on a verdict, a hung jury results, leading to a mistrial. The case is not decided, and it may be tried again at a later date before a new jury. Or the …government may decide not to pursue the case further and there will be no subsequent trial.

VERDICT

After reaching a decision, the jury notifies the bailiff, who notifies the judge. All of the participants reconvene in the courtroom and the decision is announced… by either the foreperson or the court clerk.

Possible verdicts in criminal cases are "guilty" or "not guilty." The lawyer for either party may ask that the jury be polled, although the request usually comes from the losing party. This means each juror will be asked if he or she agrees with the decision, as announced. This is to make sure that the verdict announced is the actual verdict of the jury. After the decision is read and accepted by the court, the jury is dismissed, and the trial is over.

If the defendant is found "not guilty," of course everyone will be relieved and the court process ends. However, if the defendant is found to be guilty, after briefly sinking into the depths of shock and despair you must regain composure to remain acutely aware of the very important process that the defense attorney should be engaged in following a guilty verdict.

Almost immediately following the reading of a guilty verdict the defense attorney should be avidly protecting the defendant's right to appeal that verdict. There are at least two motions the attorney can make based on errors they should have been watching for and protecting throughout the trial. If the attorney does not vigorously make one or both of these motions immediately after a guilty verdict is read, the defendant and/or members of their support team should not be afraid to speak out in court to ask why they have not made these motions, and even *demand* (respectfully, of course) that they do so.

This is what the American Bar Association says about motions your attorney should be making on your behalf after the guilty verdict is read.

MOTIONS AFTER VERDICT

Motions permitted after a verdict is announced differ from state to state.

A **motion in arrest of judgment** questions the sufficiency of the indictment or information in a criminal case and asks that the judgment not be enforced. (Emphasis added.)

A **motion for a new trial** asks for a new trial to be granted, based on errors committed by the judge during the trial. In some states, the losing party must make a motion for a new trial before filing an appeal. (Emphasis added.)

If neither of these motions is awarded by the court, your attorney should notify the court that the guilty verdict will be appealed.

THE GUILTY VERDICT

~ **EMOTIONALLY:** Obviously anxiety continues to build to higher and higher degrees throughout the trial with constant thoughts of the conclusion of the trial when guilt or innocence will be determined. While awaiting the verdict there will be simultaneous, but conflicting feelings of hopefulness and hopelessness. Questions about the defense attorney's performance will raise fears and doubts and even anger.

Upon hearing a guilty verdict numbness from shock and disbelief leaves you feeling much as you did upon first hearing your loved one was arrested. Feelings of guilt crowd out a sense of relief at finally having at least half of the answer you have been seeking since day-one of the journey. Sadness, depression and despair wash over you like rising floodwaters in a sea of helplessness with thoughts of your loved one quite possibly heading for prison. While it is a relief to finally know the outcome, with a guilty verdict the waiting and anxiety and dread begin again and continue through sentencing when you will finally have the second half of the answer you have been seeking.

~ **LEGALLY:** Once found guilty, there will next be a sentencing hearing. There are variations from state to state on whether sentencing will be determined only by the judge or whether a jury is also an option in determining the sentence. In those states where either a judge or jury is a possibility for sentencing, the defendant will again be faced with another daunting decision. Now they must decide whether to have the judge or the jury determine sentencing. The decision is no less difficult than it was to decide whether a judge alone or a jury would determine guilt or innocence.

In either case, judge or jury there will be a hearing. It is at this hearing that the defendant has the opportunity to present extenuating circumstances that may have led to the offense of which they have now been found guilty.

SENTENCING

~ **EMOTIONALLY:** While awaiting sentencing tension continues to rise. By the time the day of reckoning finally arrives it is not unusual to feel numbed and paralyzed by fear.

~ **LEGALLY:** Prior to sentencing the judge will order (or at least "should" order) a pre-sentencing investigation. The stated purpose of the pre-sentencing investigation is to provide the judge or jury additional information regarding any extenuating circumstances that should be taken into consideration in assessing punishment.

Unfortunately, not only is this legally sanctioned assessment often not performed at all, but even when it is performed, it may not be thought to have much merit, especially for concrete thinkers. If the judge or members of the jury see things in "black or white" and have very little interest in gray matters, other than going through the formality of scanning the written report or listening to someone read it, they will likely disregard the results of the pre-sentencing investigation anyhow. The failure to perform a pre-sentencing investigation or the complete disregard of this evaluation may serve the defendant well in an appeal. However, it will probably mean the sentence assessed will be harsh.

The pre-sentence investigator is appointed by the court to meet with the newly convicted defendant to assess their risk for further criminal behavior and flight risk. The investigator may also look at some factors that indicate the defendant's potential to be "rehabilitated."

Some things a pre-sentencing investigator may look at are work history; family situation; community involvement; substance abuse/addiction and hopefully any medical and mental health issues that may have prompted the behavior that led to the incident for which there is now a conviction. In some cases the investigator actually recommends a prison sentence or alternatives to prison, such as a drug program or mental health treatment.

The pre-sentence investigation is not a scientific evaluation, but one similar to the Bonding Risk Assessment PFFUnited has created. It is essentially a list of possible risk factors. However, it is based on accepted knowledge of "typical" risk factors known to those who work with offenders. Those who are familiar with mental health principles know that you cannot generalize when it comes to understanding the complex make up of an individual. Psycho-social assessments, such as the pre-sentence investigation "should" be individualized. However, the pre-sentencing assessment is typically based on broad generalities.

It would be important that the now convicted defendant know that the investigator has little interest in what they have learned from this experience or their desperate promises to behave and to never use drugs or alcohol again or their fervent promises to go to anger management classes eternally *if the court is lenient with punishment.* It is also important for the defendant to know that once convicted (whether actually guilty or not) the unvarnished truth is that legal entities expect admissions of guilt and genuine expressions of remorse, the absence of which will significantly heighten the assessed risk level.

In the end the investigator will simply tally up the rather arbitrary score and report it to the court. The higher the score of course, the higher the anticipated risk factors the judge or jury will consider when assessing punishment.

The investigation may take several weeks or longer to complete after which the report is provided to the court, as well as to the prosecutor and defense attorney and a date is set for a sentencing hearing.

Regardless of the sentence, the prisoner and their family will experience additional trauma upon hearing the sentence. Whether the sentence is three months or three years or thirty-three years or more, the imposition of a sentence is the clearest indicator that *all hope is lost.* From the exact moment of sentencing there will be total loss of control over future contact with the prisoner.

This is what the American Bar Association says about Sentencing.

SENTENCING

If the defendant is convicted in a criminal case, the judge will set a date for sentencing. Before that time, a pre-sentence investigation will take place to help the judge [or jury in those States where a jury may] determine the appropriate sentence from the range of possible sentences set out in the statutes. The pre-sentence investigation may consider the defendant's prior criminal record, family situation, health, work record, and any other relevant factor.

We would also expect that the defendant's emotional state and/or mental health (both current and at the time of the offense) would be assessed for purposes of sentencing, however all too often it may not be considered relevant.

> In most states and in the federal courts, only the judge determines the sentence to be imposed. (The main exception is that in most states juries impose sentence in cases where the death penalty is a possibility.) The federal courts and some states have sentencing guidelines to guide judges in determining appropriate sentences and to encourage uniformity in sentencing.

In Texas (which vies with California for "Greatest Prison Population" and Florida for the title of "Death Penalty Capital of the World") the defendant may elect to have a jury assess punishment for other offenses, as well. The sentencing factors should be clarified with the defense attorney even **before the trial starts**, so everyone is knowledgeable about what to expect if the defendant is found guilty.

Let's be totally honest. Despite these "guidelines to encourage uniformity" in punishment, our experience tells us that there is no uniformity in sentencing at all. Fair and equitable sentencing is definitely not a reality. For example one person may receive a sentence of seven years for a murder, while across the hall in the courthouse another may receive sixty years for a robbery in which no one was physically injured. Or, one person may receive a sentence of seven years for a murder and another found guilty of murder with very similar circumstances may receive a life sentence which begs the question: "Is one life more valuable than another?" Obviously, the answer is "yes," when it comes to equity in our judicial system. Unfortunately there is no scientific formula for predicting or understanding such inequities.

Once the conviction and sentencing has become a reality, expect to be faced with numerous similar puzzling, illogical incidents throughout incarceration. From now on much will happen within the criminal justice and prison systems that will make little sense. Avoid trying to make sense out of senseless situations, because it will only frustrate and anger you further and render you a less effective team partner than the prisoner now needs you to be.

APPEALS

If the defendant is satisfied with the verdict and the sentencing, you will continue the prison family journey with no further involvement with the court system. However, if it is believed that an injustice has been done, you will now begin an extraordinarily lengthy appeals process while endeavoring to tolerate the role of a prison family member. (Note: In Capital cases, appeals are automatic. In other cases, the court must be notified by the defense attorney of your intent to appeal.)

Appeals are complicated and will take *years* to work their way through the judicial system. There are those who have been proven totally innocent and exonerated of crimes after sitting fifteen or even thirty years in prison—sometimes even on death row, struggling to have their appeals heard. If you are appealing a conviction, prepare for a long road ahead. Take some comfort in the fact that the appeals process does offer hope that a wrong can be corrected, although it will require jumping through many frustrating legal hoops and enduring many challenging years to accomplish.

This is what the American Bar Association provides about "appeals.

APPEALS

A popular misconception is that cases are always appealed. Not often does a losing party have an automatic right of appeal. There usually must be a legal basis for the appeal—an alleged material error in the trial—not just the fact that the losing party didn't like the verdict.

.....In a criminal case, only the defendant has a right to an appeal in most states. (Some states give the prosecution a limited right to appeal to determine certain points of law. These appeals usually occur before the actual trial begins. Appeals by the prosecution after a verdict are not normally allowed because of the prohibition in the U. S. Constitution against double jeopardy, or being tried twice for the same crime.)

Criminal defendants convicted in state courts have a further safeguard. After using all of their rights of appeal on the state level, they may file a writ of habeas corpus in the federal courts in an attempt to show that their federal constitutional rights were violated. The right of a federal review imposes the check of the federal courts on abuses that may occur in the state courts.

At the time of this writing, PFFUnited has initiated and is coordinating a national campaign to "Repeal AEDPA." AEDPA, the Antiterrorism and Effective Death Penalty Act may significantly come into play if the prisoner must file a 22.54 federal writ of habeas corpus attacking their conviction. So it will behoove everyone to know this information and prepare for the possibility of having to do battle with this ruling.

In 1996 Congress surreptitiously passed a bill, signed into law by then President Clinton unrealistically limiting the time for filing a 22.54

federal writ of habeas corpus in fighting a conviction to only one year. The law was passed with the purported intention of speeding up the executions of those on death row and preventing "frivolous" federal writs by prisoners. Unfortunately, the AEDPA not only prevents thousands of legitimate federal writs from being filed, but it is believed to be unconstitutional. We will explain more fully in a separate section.

An appeal is not a retrial or a new trial of the case. The appeals courts do not usually consider new witnesses or new evidence. Appeals… are usually based on arguments that there were errors in the trial's procedure or errors in the judge's interpretation of the law.

APPEAL PROCEDURE

.….The appeal is instituted with the filing of a notice of appeal. This filing marks the beginning of the time period within which the appellant must file a brief, a written argument containing that side's view of the facts and the legal arguments upon which they rely in seeking a reversal of the trial court. The appellee then has a specified time to file an answering brief. The appellant may then file a second brief answering the appellee's brief.

Sometimes, appeals courts make their decision only on the basis of the written briefs. Sometimes, they hear oral arguments before deciding a case. Often the court will ask that the case be set for oral argument, or one of the parties will request oral argument. At oral argument, each side's attorney is given a relatively brief opportunity to argue the case to the court, and to answer questions posed by the judges. In the U.S. Supreme Court, for example, an hour is set for oral argument of most cases, **which gives each side's lawyers about half an hour to make their oral argument and answer questions. In the federal courts of appeals**, the attorneys are often allotted **less** time than that – **10- or 15-minute arguments are common.** (Emphasis added.)

Once reaching the U.S. Supreme Court, for all practical purposes and with few exceptions it will be the final opportunity a convicted felon has to plead his or her case to attack their conviction. There is something very unsettling about the fact that crucial, often life or death decisions are allotted only ten to thirty minutes attention by the highest court in the land. Even more disturbing is the fact that the appellee is not even present at these hearings, as they are sitting in a prison cell, often on death row totally dependent upon an appellate attorney to convince the judges of the Supreme Court that their case deserves a second look.

The appellate court determines whether errors occurred in applying the law at the lower court level. It generally will reverse a trial court only for an error of law. Not every error of law, however, is cause for a reversal. Some are harmless errors that did not prejudice the rights of the parties to a fair trial. For example, in a criminal case a higher court may conclude that the trial judge gave a legally improper instruction to the jury, but the mistake… had no bearing on the jury's finding…and [they will] let a guilty verdict stand. However, an error of law, such as admitting improper evidence, may be determined to be harmful and therefore reversible error.

After a case is orally argued or otherwise presented for judgment, the appeals court judges will meet in conference to discuss the case. Appellate courts often issue written decisions, particularly when the decision deals with a new interpretation of the law, establishes a new precedent, etc. At the conference, one judge will be designated to write an opinion. The opinion may go through several drafts before a majority of the court agrees with it. Judges disagreeing with the majority opinion may issue a dissenting opinion. Judges agreeing with the result of a majority decision but disagreeing with the majority's reasoning may file a concurring opinion. Occasionally the appeals court will simply issue an unsigned opinion. These are called per curiam (by the court).

> If the appeals court affirms the lower court's judgment, the case ends, **unless the losing party appeals to a higher court**. The lower court decision also stands if the appeals court simply dismisses the appeal (usually for reasons of jurisdiction). (Emphasis added.)
>
> If the judgment is reversed, the appellate court will usually send the case back to a lower court (remand it) and order the trial court to take further action. It may order that a new trial be held, the trial court's judgment be modified or corrected, the trial court reconsider the facts, take additional evidence, or consider the case in light of a recent decision by the appellate court.

Regardless of whether an appeal will be pursued or not, the trial is over; the verdict was "guilty," and nothing will stop the journey now. You are on the road to prison.

THE "AEDPA" & THE "TIME BAR"

The Antiterrorism & Effective Death Penalty Act (AEDPA) was surreptitiously passed by Congress and in 1996 then President Bill Clinton signed the Act into law. If you are ever involved with the criminal justice appeals process, it is critical to know how this act will come into play.

We say the bill was "surreptitiously" passed into law, because it was quickly and quietly ushered through both houses of congress with little if any fanfare for the stated purpose of assuring those responsible for the tragic 1995 Oklahoma City Bombing would be quickly executed. Even had there been fanfare, it is highly unlikely the general public would have understood the intent, let alone the broader future impact of this law as it relates to a "writ of habeas corpus."

How many in the general public are even familiar with that Latin term? With such a horribly heinous crime, how many of the general public would have cared in 1995 whether Timothy McVeigh had sufficient time to file his writ of habeas corpus? After all, guilty or not, the media vilified him **before** he was even **arrested**. So who cared if he had time to file his 22.54 writ of habeas corpus or not? As it turned out, virtually no one became aware of the full impact of this act until years later when **innocent** people were convicted and unable to file their 22.54 federal writ of habeas corpus **because it was not filed within the newly imposed one year deadline**.

In addition to the law being specifically intended to speed the executions of those on death row, it was intended to curtail the filing of "frivolous" 22.54 federal writs of habeas corpus.

Well the truth is, there are numerous "frivolous" 22.54's filed daily; there always has been and there always will be. It is simply the nature of the beast and no amount of laws will stop it. The unfortunate truth is that many prisoners with "life without parole sentences" or sentences so lengthy that they are assured to die in prison have nothing better to do with their time than clog the federal court dockets with unnecessary and unsubstantiated claims that by law must be reviewed by the courts before being determined as "frivolous." What do they have to lose? What would anyone do differently in their situation? Unfortunately, their frivolity has adversely affected many with fully valid cases for filing 22.54 federal writs of habeas corpus.

Obviously reviewing frivolous cases is a substantial waste of time for the courts. We understand that. These are essentially the bad apples that have spoiled the entire barrel, aren't they? Or are they? With 873 people exonerated of their convictions by DNA evidence over the past twenty years, who is to say there aren't more innocents filing 22.54 federal writs of habeas corpus that the courts would rather not be bothered with? Therefore every 22.54 writ should be taken seriously and treated with fairness and equity.

Unfortunately, what "should be" and what "is" are two entirely different matters. It is therefore with a sense of urgency that we present what the AEDPA has done to prevent numerous legitimate 22.54 federal writs of habeas corpus from being reviewed, let alone ever heard by the federal courts.

Let's start at the beginning. This is the portion of the AEDPA that affects filing those writs of habeas corpus so critical in overturning wrongful convictions. This is copied and pasted here directly from the U.S. government website:

[104th Congress Public Law 132]
[From the U.S. Government Printing Office]
<DOC>
[DOCID: f:publ132.104]

[[Page 1213]]

ANTITERRORISM AND EFFECTIVE DEATH PENALTY
ACT OF 1996

[[Page 110 STAT. 1214]]

Public Law 104-132
104th Congress

An Act

To deter terrorism, provide justice for victims, provide for an effective death penalty, and for other purposes. <<NOTE: Apr. 24, 1996 - [S. 735]>>

Be it enacted by the Senate and House of Representatives of the United States of America in Congress assembled, <<NOTE: Antiterrorism and Effective Death Penalty Act of 1996.>>

Here we would like to point out the mention in this act that: Yes! The stated intent of the AEDPA is to deter terrorism and provide justice for victims, which we fully support. But, was that the **real** intent?

What was Congress actually referring to with their catchall phrase **"other purposes?"** What "other purposes" did they have in mind?

Would they have included the words *"other purposes"* if they had not had other intentions in mind? Why would the Congress of the United States of America write a bill—any bill that included the vague phraseology, **"and for other purposes"** if they did not intend this bill to apply to anything other than "deterring terrorism" and "providing justice for victims" (also phrases vague unto themselves)?

We believe this type of surreptitious and deceptive action is intended to dupe the public and obviously goes on secretly behind closed doors in congress **all of the time**. Well, let's not delay further; let's continue with an examination of this surreptitious Act.

SECTION 1. <<NOTE: 18 USC 1 note.>> SHORT TITLE.

This Act may be cited as the ``Antiterrorism and Effective Death Penalty Act of 1996".

SEC. 2. TABLE OF CONTENTS.

The table of contents of this Act is as follows:
Sec. 1. Short title.
Sec. 2. Table of contents.

TITLE I--HABEAS CORPUS REFORM

Sec. 101. Filing deadlines.

Sec. 102. Appeal.

Sec. 103. Amendment of Federal Rules of Appellate Procedure.

Sec. 104. Section 2254 amendments.

Sec. 105. Section 2255 amendments.

Sec. 106. Limits on second or successive applications.

Sec. 107. Death penalty litigation procedures.

Sec. 108. Technical amendment.

(Emphasis added.)

How can there be any doubt that the Antiterrorism & Effective Death Penalty Act was intended to block 22.54 federal writs of habeas corpus when **the very first thing mentioned** *before even considering victims of crimes,* **is the prisoner's right to file a federal writ of habeas corpus?** Isn't the first thing said usually the most important? The highest priority?

And, just look at this! Title I; Section 101—the very first topic under the very first heading is what? That's right! It is **"Filing deadlines"** for filing that federal writ of habeas corpus. Could it be that the **first intention** in passing this bill was actually to so stringently limit the time frame for filing these writs that it would become a virtual impossibility for prisoners with legitimate wrongful convictions to file 22.54 federal writs of habeas corpus? Let's proceed.

In its entirety, the AEDPA is 118 pages in length when copied and pasted into an 8 ½ x 11 Word document with one inch margins and size ten font. For obvious practical reasons, here we are only including the portion of the AEDPA critical to filing the federal writ of habeas corpus.

TITLE I--HABEAS CORPUS REFORM <<NOTE: Courts.>>

SEC. 101. FILING DEADLINES.

Section 2244 of title 28, United States Code, is amended by **adding** at the end the following **new** subsection:

``(d)(1) **A 1-year period of limitation shall apply to an application for a writ of habeas corpus by a person in custody** pursuant to the judgment of a State court. The limitation period shall run from the latest of--

``(A) the date on which the judgment became final by the conclusion of direct review or the expiration of the time for seeking such review;

``(B) the date on which the impediment to filing an application created by State action in violation of the Constitution or laws of the United States is removed, if the applicant was prevented from filing by such State action;

``(C) the date on which the constitutional right asserted was initially recognized by the Supreme Court, if the right has been newly recognized by the Supreme Court and made retroactively applicable to cases on collateral review; or

``(D) the date on which the factual predicate of the claim or claims presented could have been discovered through the exercise of due diligence.

``(2) The time during which **a properly filed application** for State post-conviction or other collateral review with respect to the pertinent judgment or claim is pending shall not be counted toward any period of limitation under this subsection."

(Emphasis added.)

Well, if you understand this and have a burning desire to learn more about the AEDPA you can read it in its entirety at: http://www.gpo.gov/fdsys/pkg/PLAW-104publ132/html/PLAW-104publ132.htm.

Having initiated the campaign to repeal the AEDPA, PFFUnited has found that thousands of prisoners across the United States have been adversely affected by this law.

WRIT WRITERS

When prisoners do not have the money to pay an attorney to litigate an appeal of their convictions they often begin studying the law themselves, until they become so proficient that they file their own writs. Some prisoners may not feel sufficiently confident in their knowledge of the law to do the legal work themselves. Those prisoners may turn to another prisoner with a great deal of experience fighting their own case in court. These legal eagles, often disparagingly referred to as "jailhouse lawyers," are writ writers.

You may wonder how prisoners can "study the law" while incarcerated. Well, in fact in the traditional sense, they cannot "study law." However, each prison unit is required to have a "law library" specifically for those who may want to file writs to fight convictions. However the materials in the prison law libraries may be old and even outdated and certainly are not of the state of the art caliber as the law libraries attorneys have access to in the free world.

The prisoners must put in a written request each time they wish to go to the law library to review information that may help them overturn their conviction. However, it is up to the prison administration to honor those requests. So, access to the law library is not a given and is often sporadic. Additionally, the prisoner's time in the law library may be limited to only a few hours per week. Some prisoners are fortunate enough to have family members or friends who will scour the internet for legal cases or who will have various law books sent to them in prison. While costly to the loved ones, the personal availability of these books can certainly expedite the prisoner's legal learning curve.

While (as with any attorney) some writ writers are better than others, many have a far greater knowledge of the law than any attorney in the free world. Since they are addressing the law from within the prison, they are obviously primarily filing writs to fight convictions. You may have the occasion to hear prisoners refer to an "11.07" or a "22.54." Those are writs required to be filed in an effort to overturn a criminal conviction.

When a writ writer delves into the transcript of a court case searching for errors upon which to overturn a conviction, they attack the review with a vengeance. After all, whether working on their own case or that of another prisoner they genuinely believe the system has maligned them, as well as others and they actually have an axe to grind. As a result, the writ writer really cares about winning. You can rightly say they would take delight in showing up the system. That would be true for the vast majority of writ writers. But, whatever their motivation, they take great pride in finding credible errors in court transcripts and thoroughly scouring case law to write winning writs.

It usually takes years, but many writ writers have legally fought their own way out of prison; some have won changes in the law—and even changes in the constitutions of their states and even the country! When they return to the free world, some even earn their living by continuing their legal efforts as writ writers on behalf of prisoners for a modest fee. Others become paralegals and a few have even overcome licensing restrictions for felons and have gone on to become successful attorneys.

We can take a very important lesson from these writ writers, because the unvarnished truth is that to really be adequately represented in court, defendants would do themselves a great service by learning more about the law than the attorney representing them, paid or not.

The unvarnished truth is that the court system is actually a "good old boy system." The members of the system look out for each other and when you represent yourself or have a writ writer assist you with legal documents, that takes the money out of a fellow good old boy's pocket and that upsets the equilibrium of their system. However, there is no law that says it can't be done; in fact there is no law that says you can't fight for a law to explicitly say it CAN be done.

A serious word of caution about writ writers: Writ writers who request a fee—especially writ writers living in the community who request a fee should be carefully vetted. While some are extremely genuine and honest, as well as excellent at the craft of writing writs, some writ writers may not be so scrupulous.

As we write this book, one well known community-based writ writer is being investigated and already the investigation has exposed him as a charlatan. It appears that he assumed the identity of a genuine writ writer who the investigators have not been able to locate, although he would be elderly and may have passed away from natural causes.

As the investigation continues, it appears this particular writ writer has bilked numerous vulnerable families out of tens of thousands of dollars by preying on their desperation to have their loved one released from prison. Credible sources believe he has personally pocketed the money and made no effort whatsoever to provide any writ writing services for any of these families, although he is a master at making up what sound to be credible excuses for the endless delays. When confronted with his charlatanism, he lashes out through the social media, accusing his accusers of lying about him and painting himself to be a martyred saint!

Regardless of whether you choose a licensed attorney or writ writer to help with legal matters, always carefully explore their credibility as well as their expertise before handing over any money. If you are paying any amount of money for a service, no matter how small the fee or whether the money is stipulated as a fee or a donation, you have every right to know who they are and their qualifications and capabilities for helping you. If they are legitimate, they will readily provide that information to you. Ask for visible evidence of work they have done. Ask for public notices of cases they have won. Ask for references and for heaven's sake follow up on them!

Chapter II

"THE JOURNEY"

The moment a loved one is convicted of a crime the entire family graduates to the status of a full-fledged Prison Family. There is absolutely no way to sugar coat the experience. The traumatic assaults from the criminal justice system that have been experienced from the moment the loved one was arrested will persist throughout their incarceration and in many ways will continue even through their eventual return to the community and reunification with their family.

WHO IS TO BLAME?

Each member of the family and even the prisoner's close friends are likely to wonder many times over the years ahead how they ever came to this fork in the road on their life's journey. While many prison families have witnessed generations of loved ones entering prison, for many other families this is an entirely new, extremely frightening, traumatic experience. In either case, prison families consist of good people who did their best, as they knew it at the time.

There are no perfect parents; there are no perfect siblings; there are no perfect spouses; there are no perfect families, and none of us regardless of our circumstances live in a perfect world. While we should all be striving to improve ourselves and the world around us, we do the best we know how, with the information and skills we have at the time. Maya Angelou makes this profound statement about our imperfections:

"When we know better, we do better."

Hopefully that means that once becoming a prison family we will learn to do better from the experience. In fact, we can all use this time to improve ourselves and improve relations with each other and within our family.

It is certainly not productive to spend this time blaming the criminal justice system for our woes. If an injustice was done, of course we will appeal our case. But we can also use the time productively, rather than waste all the years it will take for an appeal to slowly grind its way through the courts or for our loved one to serve out their time in prison.

It is also counterproductive to use this time berating ourselves or each other for what we "could have done better." We did our best with what we knew at the time. Now we know better. Now, we must do better. Besides, regardless of our personal efforts, there are numerous other influences on our loved ones besides us in this world.

Sadly, regardless of our best efforts there are monstrous forces outside of our own best intentions that will influence our loved ones and lead them to succumb to temptations. Once they follow these enticers, they find themselves in very sticky circumstances that even Mom and Dad can't fix this time, and now they are facing the dreadful consequences.

Whatever the reason for your loved one's incarceration, unless you personally enticed them to do the wrong thing, you are not to blame—especially if they are an adult! Even youth who stray from the teachings of their parents, knew better. They made their own choices. We only have control over what is inside our own skin. You can provide all the insight in the world; you can provide all of the tools for success; you can yell; you can scream; you can pray. In the end, you can definitely lead a horse to water, but you certainly cannot make them drink it.

REAL FRIENDS & REAL FAMILY

It is often said that you get to know who your real friends are when things get tough for you—when you lose your job; when you lose your wealth; when you lose your standing in the community. Unfortunately, for the prison family that is all too true. When you lose your loved one to prison, you will definitely learn who your real friends are and you will even learn who your "real family" is. Sometimes that means we learn that our real family has no legal or biological relationship to us.

Hopefully you will be among the more fortunate prison families and your current friends and family members will continue to support and encourage you and your loved one in prison.

While some prison families find great support from their old friends, many do not. Not only may those you've thought of as "friends" suddenly slink off and disappear, but even family members may abandon you. In fact, your faith community may even turn its back on you. Far more than one prison family has found that once their loved one was convicted of a crime their long-time house of worship silently spurned them or even bluntly asked them to stop attending.

That may sound shocking and inconceivable, because your house of worship would never do such a thing. We certainly hope not, however, we've heard many stories like that of one young mother who was left penniless to raise four small children alone when her husband went to prison.

The couple had been very successful in their professional careers. They lived quite nicely—nice house; nice cars; traveled abroad every year. But it was all gone within hours of receiving his call that he'd been arrested. By law, she could have kept their home, but now as the sole breadwinner of the family, she had no way to make the mortgage payments or even pay the utility bills, so within a few months she and the couple's four small children were living in their car.

Embarrassed and desperate she swallowed every bit of her pride and went to ask for help from the church that she and her husband and their children had attended for years. They led Bible study and youth programs there. Their children attended Sunday school and summer Bible camp there. Certainly their own church would step forward to help.

She had been so immersed in her husband's legal process while trying to address the needs of her confused and grieving children that she had hardly noticed that she had not heard from anyone at the church since her husband's very public arrest. When she did finally come to that realization, she assumed no one had called because they too were embarrassed and did not know what to say, but she believed the pastor would surely reach out to offer support. She imagined that he would even encourage the congregation to help her get on her feet once again. Maybe life would never be the same; perhaps they would never live in the same luxury they had come to expect, but with their church's support at least they would have a roof over their head and food on their table.

When the young mother finally gathered herself sufficiently to make the trip to the church she was silently ushered into the pastor's office and the door was closed tightly behind her. With the friendliest smile she could muster, she humbly began her plea to request assistance.

Much to her amazement, the pastor actually scowled and looked down at the floor as she was talking, virtually refusing to maintain eye contact with her. Instead of the help she was so desperately seeking she was told, "It would be best if you took the children somewhere else to worship," as though their father's white-collar crime might be contagious.

While certainly not all churches would respond with such callousness, and many would and do reach out lovingly to their congregants in such distress, the fact is that the prison family has been a most maligned, disenfranchised and shunned population for all too long. The shame and embarrassment this type of reception creates for those having a loved one in prison forces many prison families into a self-imposed isolation. Once isolated, they do all they can to keep their burden a secret; even instructing small children to never mention their loved one's incarceration to anyone outside of the family. As a result, we have no idea how many people sitting silently right next to us at places we work, worship or even "play" have a loved one in prison.

Over the years following the conviction of a loved one, with or without the support of the community, things will become more bearable. However, it is highly unlikely there will ever be a full day during which you will be totally free from the reality of being a prison family. Knowing what lies ahead and accepting it as your "new normal" will ease the trauma. Forming a positive support system will ease the trauma, too.

In 2009 Community Solutions of El Paso, a nonprofit organization dedicated to serving the prison family, initiated and hosted the first-ever National Prisoner's Family Conference in our country. We received many calls inquiring about the conference and it soon became evident after a caller had uttered only a few words, which calls were from representatives of organizations serving prison families and which calls were from members of prison families.

In 2009 I answered a call from a woman who muttered in an almost inaudible whisper, "Uh. Uh, I was wondering. I saw this.....Well, there was this small article. It was in our paper. I was…Uh…I was wondering. It said, uh…Well, it was something about a conference."

At that time it took a minute or so for me to realize that the woman on the other end of the phone did not suffer from stuttering. In fact, she could not bring herself to even say the word "prisoner"—even as it pertained to a public conference and she certainly could not openly acknowledge that she was the member of a prison family. The shame and embarrassment of her personal ordeal had sent her into hiding for over eight years, since her son was convicted and began his twenty year prison sentence.

Again in 2010, when the conference was to be held in Florida, I answered another call from a woman who breathlessly mumbled, "I uh…I just…uh…read something…uh… well, it uh…"

More aware now, I interrupted her obvious pained discomfort by saying the dreaded word for her. "Oh!" I said boldly, "You're calling about the Prisoner's Family Conference!"

Her relief was clearly evident as she gasped, "Yes! Oh yes! I had no idea there was anything like this for us."

Amidst many tears for over an hour for the first time she shared that her son had been incarcerated at age 18, and now five years later, he would soon be eligible for release to a half way house. However, for all of those years she lived in shame and embarrassment, keeping his incarceration a secret from her friends and family, including her son's two younger siblings.

Can you imagine the intensity of the stress she experienced keeping all of the secrets necessary to hide his incarceration?

Thankfully, both women mentioned attended the conferences where they found much support from others with similar experiences and even from those community members with hearts to serve the prison family. Today, both are staunch outspoken advocates for prisoners and their families. But how many other families unnecessarily remain in hiding when there truly is support out here?

It takes courage to say those words the first time, but the more we say them and the more we acknowledge the truth about being a prison family, the easier it becomes to talk about it and the easier it becomes to live as a prison family. Those who have successfully survived the prison family journey will tell you that the most liberating way to endure the experience is to avoid fighting the reality by accepting the "new normal" for your family.

Recognize that knowledge is power and seek as much knowledge as possible about your particular criminal justice and prison systems. Learn as much as possible about how incarceration affects you and your family. Learn as much as possible about how incarceration affects your loved one in prison and learn productive ways to support them. Then surround yourself with *only* supportive people. Talk openly about being a prison family and become actively involved with support groups and ministries and other programs specifically for prisoners and their family members. When it is productive and safe, actively advocate on behalf of your loved one in prison. Take an active role in your family and your community. Above all, give yourself permission to smile again; give yourself permission to laugh again--give yourself permission to enjoy life again

Chapter III

"TRAUMA AND GRIEF"

The prison family journey is painful from the outset. It begins with a searing stab in the heart from one single phone call announcing a loved one is in jail. The wound is invisible, but the pain is persistent and deep. You force yourself to push through the pain to manage daily responsibilities compounded by confusing and frightening legal matters compounded even further by a growing secret need to hide the pain.

On the outside you may force yourself to appear cool as a cucumber. But, on the inside you writhe like a boiling cauldron of thick hash. You feel as though you are hemorrhaging from a gaping wound. But, there is no blood! So, you push away the pain and keep on walking. Stuffing the pain down deeper each time it surfaces only intensifies the pain. But you must keep walking, so you keep on stuffing the pain.

Many people do not understand that gaping wounds can be emotional, as well as physical. Although emotional wounds cannot be seen, they can be far more painful and even far more destructive than physical injuries. Unlike most physical wounds, there is rarely a full recovery from an emotional wound. It creates an internal scar that is never fully erased. Because the emotional wound is internal, no one—not even the wounded person can see it. So, it is easy to attempt to keep it hidden rather than to face the additional pain necessary to heal it.

Becoming a prison family is an experience that wounds the heart and soul of each and every person who loves and cares about the prisoner. The wounding goes very deep; so deep in fact that many prison family members are able to hide their pain so well, even they are unable to recognize how severely wounded they really are. Unfortunately, those who keep their pain hidden can never adequately heal, because the first step toward any healing (whether physical or emotional) is to openly acknowledge that we have been injured and are in pain.

Healing from an emotional wound depends in large part on how well we accept and understand the injury and how willing we are to experience the pain of looking at the injury to be able to scrub it clean so that it *can* heal. The wound may leave a scar that we can learn to live with, but we must face the pain to even begin to heal. As excruciating as the pain may be, the more fully we clean out that wound, the faster and more fully it can heal.

There is no time like **now** to take the first steps necessary to heal to begin to actually enjoy life in your new normal. Boldly looking at the trauma you have experienced and pro-actively preparing for the additional trauma you are likely to experience on this journey will begin the healing process.

TRAUMA IMPACT #1: THE ARREST

We won't dwell on the first point of traumatic impact you experience as a prison family, because it is probably clear how deeply traumatized you were by that first phone call notifying you that your loved one was arrested.

The shock of that one phone call announcing a loved one's arrest was probably so stunning that it took days, if not weeks to accept the fact that your loved one was facing very serious charges that could ultimately lead them to prison. Terrifying thoughts of what lay ahead undoubtedly consumed every waking moment and prevented you from performing even mundane tasks. You were traumatized and began grieving. Then, before the trauma of that one phone call had a chance to settle you were thrust into more traumatic experiences like a snowball rolling downhill picking up speed and growing larger and larger.

IT'S GRIEF!

You are grieving. When a loved one goes to prison, the impact is emotionally little different than the loss of a loved one to death. The unvarnished truth is that the incarceration of a loved one may result in an even more profound sense of grief than you might experience with the death of a loved one, because this loss is **relentlessly incomplete. There is never a sense of closure**.

Your loved one is very much alive, but inaccessible—lost to you behind cold impenetrable concrete and steel walls. You can no longer touch them or even talk to them at will. You have no idea what they are experiencing moment by moment. Are they safe? Are they depressed? Are they scared? When will you ever hear from them again? How will they be affected by this experience?

It is as though your loved one has been snatched away to an unknown planet where there are completely new rules to live by and a totally foreign way of life that the entire family must learn to live with overnight. To make matters worse, there are no answers to your questions. Your loved one is out there somewhere in this world with a beating heart and breathing lungs and you don't know when (or even if) you will see them again. You live perpetually with a multitude of new unknowns.

You are grieving your loved one's total absence from your life. You are grieving the total absence of your old and comfortable way of life. The sooner you acknowledge that you are experiencing **grief** the sooner you will be able to relieve some of the pain.

When we grieve, regardless of the reason for the grief, we encounter five predictable stages in a well documented widely accepted Grief Process.

Here's what the Grief Process looks like:

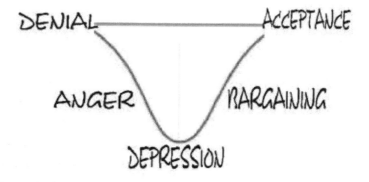

Here's how the Grief Process unfolds:

Denial – When first learning of the "loss" we deny it. "Impossible!" we say. "It's not true!" "This is not really happening." "I just talked to him/her yesterday. They were fine!" "I don't believe it." "This can't be happening." "This isn't happening." "NO!"

Anger – We soon find ourselves feeling very angry and we're usually angry at the very one who is lost to us. "Why didn't they tell me they had a problem?" "What in heavens name would make them do such a thing?" Or even, "I knew this was going to happen if he/she didn't stop ____!" "I told them to stop; why didn't they listen to me?" "How dare they put us in such a position?" "How dare they do this to ME?"

We may even become angry with ourselves for not knowing there was a problem brewing or for knowing there was a problem and not stopping it! And it is perfectly normal to become very angry with God for allowing this loss to occur.

Bargaining – Irrational as it may be, we begin to think of ways to bargain with God to bring our loved one back to us. Since you can only promise God things that you have control over, bargaining with Him indicates you are assuming some responsibility for your loss.

It is very common to assume some responsibility for the loss. We might say things like, "If I had only spent more time with them." Or "I should have taken all of the liquor out of the house." Or, "I should have given them the money they needed." Or, "I should have demanded they get out of that relationship."

Gosh! If you had just fixed all of the problems in their life, they surely would never have gotten themselves into such a predicament— would they?

Well, of course you had no control over your loved one's choices, regardless of your responses to their needs or even their requests and demands. Besides, there is nothing you can do now to make amends with your loved one locked tightly behind impenetrable bars. So you turn to the only one who does have the power to change the circumstances—God.

Who other than God is there to bargain with? Irrational or not you may find yourself saying such things as, "If I just spend more time with the family, God will you make this all go away?" "If I stop _____ (drinking, smoking, procrastinating), God will you please let them come home?" "If I pray harder and more often, God will you let them come home?" "If I promise not to be so selfish, God will you please let them come home?" The "ifs" are endless, and of course the effort is futile.

And by the way, while you are bargaining with God, so are all of the others who love the prisoner, even the small children in the family.

Depression – When the loss becomes very real to us, we sink into deep sadness and despair often expressed by mournful uncontrollable sobbing and wails. We often become so depressed that it becomes painfully difficult to even get out of bed, let alone care for the family or perform our jobs. We want to sleep continually, until we can wake up from this unbearable nightmare.

Acceptance and Resolution – Finally, if we successfully navigate the stages of the Grief Process, we will resign ourselves to accepting the loss and find ways to incorporate the loss into our lives in a manner that allows us to move on and productively continue our own life journey.

We will revisit each stage of the Grief Process time and again throughout the weeks and years ahead. Each time we revisit the stages of grief the intensity of our pain will diminish. That is one of those mysteries about the way we were created as human beings. You can never mentally recreate the intensity of pain or grief you experienced when it first occurred!

Thankfully, while the pain will never totally go away, it will subside more and more over time. While time may improve things and while it is perfectly natural to revisit each stage of the Grief Process from time to time, **it is extremely dangerous to become stuck** in any stage of grief.

If you become stuck in **Denial** and never fully acknowledge the reality of your loved one's incarceration, the numerous challenges and pain associated with having a loved one in prison essentially do not exist for you. Those who get stuck in Denial, live in a dream world where life is unreal. That may sound like the ideal solution to your problems, but it's not.

If you don't acknowledge you have a problem, you can hardly work to resolve it! The actual problem grows larger and larger as you live in a dream state. Thinking logically, how can you possibly help resolve the realities of the crisis for yourself or your loved one in prison, if you won't allow yourself to believe there is a very real problem that needs your full attention?

If you remain stuck in **Anger**, cursing the criminal justice system; seeking revenge at every twist and turn and harshly criticizing those who don't understand your dilemma, not only will you alienate everyone who might be helpful to you in this crisis, but it is also impossible to effectively advocate on behalf of yourself or your incarcerated loved one while madly ranting and raving.

Oh, sure. You can yell into the telephone or write hostile letters. You might even storm into offices of those you feel have offended you and your loved one and give them a loud and vicious piece of your mind. However, to be honest, when you do those things you sound so irrational that no one will listen to you, let alone take the time to try to work through the problems with you. Besides, anger is a very unhealthy place to be—emotionally and physically.

If you become stuck in futilely **Bargaining** with God for the return of your loved one, not only will you be unable to effectively work through the real issues, but you will be unable to establish a healthy spiritual life, which you will definitely need throughout your entire prison-family journey. While we certainly believe in miracles, we also understand the reality of having a loved one incarcerated.

Even though an occasional miracle springs forth from the criminal justice system, in virtually all cases the system as a whole makes decisions about a prisoner's release based on man's law and generally decisions about a prisoner's release will follow those man-made legal guidelines.

Isn't it said that "faith without works is dead?" Doesn't that mean that to achieve the desired outcome it would be necessary to put some brain and brawn into action behind those prayers and pleadings with God? In fact, putting all of your hope in a miracle from a very heartless criminal justice system can leave you hopeless. Without hope, you will remain stuck in depression.

If you remain stuck in **Depression** and can barely force yourself out of bed, you will hardly be able to cope with your routine responsibilities or maintain a job, let alone be able to take an active role in your loved one's complex legal issues or help them cope with the realities of prison life.

Becoming stuck in total **Acceptance** is not unlike being stuck in denial. You either become totally cut off from reality or you become a "Pollyanna," artificially forcing yourself to appear as if life is always a bowl of cherries!

Under no circumstances is life ever a bowl of cherries for anyone one hundred percent of the time, whether they have a loved one in prison or not.

There is absolutely nothing wrong with maintaining a positive attitude. However, even the most positive person encounters a frustration or two from time to time. Pretending that everything is absolutely perfect, or even "just fine" at all times indicates that you have lost contact with your true feelings. Not only is that unhealthy, but it will alienate others who routinely encounter difficulties in their daily lives. Your lack of reality will actually become a hindrance to your loved ones as well, including your loved one in prison, because they are feeling the pain of their loss, and you don't— or more accurately, **you won't**. Your apparent lack of understanding leads them to believe you are unable to help them resolve their pain when you seem not to have any pain of your own.

Research indicates that most people find their greatest source of comfort and strength during times of crisis comes through their faith. Typically people will say that it was their faith that helped them through the crisis. Deeper exploration will generally uncover the fact that initially at least, faith wavered.

It is probably important to know that for many it is often hard to maintain a deep sense of faith when the challenges become unbearably painful. Many firm believers are even known to have lost faith from time to time during the numerous relentless traumatic encounters they've experienced on their prison family journeys. So, if you begin to doubt and lose faith, give yourself time to heal from the wounds. Then you will again be able to find comfort and strength through your own faith.

We believe in a forgiving and unconditionally loving God, who understands that we may say (and even do) unkind things when we are suffering. When you come through the anger stage of your personal grief process it is a good time to seek and find a spiritual connection through a house of worship or through another form of spiritual practice that is satisfying to you.

In addition to turning to God for comfort, strength and even wisdom during times of crisis, one of the greatest sources of support on the prison family journey comes from finding others with similar experiences who truly understand your circumstances and your pain. It is very important to associate with those you can openly talk with about your grief and pain, without fear of being judged.

Unfortunately not everyone will understand. If you find yourself engaged in an uncomfortable debate or even hostile warfare with someone who doesn't understand your distress or even why you would care about anyone in prison (loved one or otherwise), rather than arguing with them or forcing yourself to suppress your innermost thoughts and feelings to avoid such arguments, you may find that to become healthy you must let go of those people in your life who are not fully supportive.

Loved ones may mean well when they try to extract us from a relationship with a loved one in prison. They may truly believe they have our best interests at heart. But, when we have made a firm decision to stand by our loved one through the duration of their incarceration, we find the frequent shouting matches to be more harmful than helpful.

Children especially don't need to hear all of the hostility. After all they are experiencing their own grief and confusion at the disruption in the family. While we will talk more about children of incarcerated parents at a later point, if there are children of incarcerated parents within earshot of such disagreements it is crucial to remember something my parents would say when adult conversations were becoming inappropriate for youngsters to hear:

"Little pitchers have big ears!"

Children are very aware of their surroundings. When they hear adults arguing, even in another room, they become very uncomfortable and listen very intently to learn what is going on. It is especially important to remember that if harsh words are being said about their parent in prison, it becomes another source of trauma for them.

Hearing harsh words about one's parent is hurtful for two primary reasons. First of all, children love their parents regardless of what they've done or where they are. No one, least of all a child, wants to hear negative remarks about someone they love.

Second of all and even more importantly, there is no escaping the fact that children clearly know they are the product of two parents. They see themselves in very concrete terms as "one-half their mother and one-half their father." When you demean one of those parents, you are demeaning one-half of that child. So, when the child hears someone say, "That no good bum in prison doesn't deserve the time of day," the child interprets that to mean, "**I am a no good bum** because my father/ mother is in prison, and these people don't believe **I** even deserve the time of day."

Words are very powerful. We must be very careful with the words we use and the words we allow others to use around children who may hear those words. Like all of us, children need to hear words that help them feel accepted, appreciated, loved and supported.

For some of us finding unconditional support during trying times has meant taking the very painful step of "divorcing" our own family members. Sometimes those rifts in relationships can later be healed, but while you are going through the throes of grief over the loss of a loved one to prison, you must surround yourself with positive, supportive people, rather than those who will drag you down into anger and depression.

In addition to seeking comfort through our spiritual life and surrounding ourselves with positive and supportive people, we may need additional sources of comfort and guidance. One of the most obvious sources of support would be to seek professional counseling.

A word of caution about professional counseling: While professional counseling is certainly an obvious option, it definitely will be most helpful if the counselor you choose is someone who has successfully survived the prison family journey (or is at least very knowledgeable about the journey and sensitive to it) rather than from someone who has no experience with the world of incarceration.

Even the most sensitive of counselors will have difficulty believing your credibility when you share with them the raw and often confounding experiences you encounter on this prison family journey. Even a well seasoned counselor, faith-based or secular will revert to the most typical stereotypes of prisoners and their families, if they have no real familiarity with the issues. This can result in even the most stable of prison family members sounding somewhat paranoid when they are just stating the truth.

In fact, some counselors may be absolutely **dangerous to the mental health** of a prison family member. For example, the wife of a prisoner recently posted this on Facebook:

"ALERT: IF YOU LOVE OR ARE IN A RELATIONSHIP WITH A PRISONER, AVOID GOING TO ANY MENTAL HEALTH PROFESSIONAL! YOU MAY BE DIAGNOSED WITH THIS LABEL: Hybristophilia"

She went on to explain that she had been seeing a therapist for anxiety. She had been in a terrible car accident and had experienced a great deal of anxiety ever since. She had recently been to see the therapist to renew her prescription for anxiety medication. When the therapist left the room the lady happened to glance down at her own case file which the therapist had been writing in and left opened on the desk.

This wife of a prisoner said that she noticed a word the therapist had written that was unfamiliar to her. She was curious about the word, so she jotted it down on a scrap of paper and put it in her purse. She had forgotten about the word until she came across the slip of paper a couple weeks later and Googled the word: "Hybristophilia."

Her Facebook post went on to provide the Google definition of the word.

"Hybristophilia is a paraphilia of the predatory type in which sexual arousal, facilitation and attainment of orgasm are responsive to and contingent upon being with a partner known to have committed an outrage or crime, such as murder, rape or armed robbery."

"The term is derived from the Greek word "hybridzein" meaning "to commit an outrage against someone," and "philo" meaning "to have a strong preference for."

"Unlike most other paraphilias, Hybristophilia occurs almost exclusively in women. In popular cultures this phenomenon is also known as Bonnie and Clyde Syndrome."

Flabbergasted, I responded to this woman's post by posting this comment of my own:

"TO ALL OF MY FRIENDS WHO DEEPLY CARE ABOUT AND/ OR LOVE A PRISONER (OR HEAVEN FORBID, PRISONERS)..... THIS IS ALARMING!"

"Thank you for bringing this concocted 'diagnosis' to our attention. Having worked in the mental health field for the last (I hate to admit it) 40 years, with over 30 of those years in the field of criminal justice with prisoners and their families, I have never heard of such a thing, and obviously I am one!"

"Despite being a mental health counselor, I have always had issues with the mental health community arbitrarily slapping labels on everyone in sight and unnecessarily pushing medications to the hilt. To know there is now an outrageous label for those caring about and/or loving a prisoner is nothing less than alarming."

"There are those who care deeply for the elderly--What kind of deviant sexual perversion is THAT? GEEEZZZZZ!!!! There are those who are passionate about cruelty to animals – is that a sexual deviancy???????....and how about those environmental tree hugger nuts? -- what abhorrent sexual deviancy is that?????"

"While I have my own distrust of the medical community as a whole, I'd say that if you are suffering from a form of anxiety (or for that matter any other form of emotional strain short of psychosis) you'd be far better off going to a medical clinic or general practitioner than any purported mental health NUT!!!"

"If I didn't need my mental health license to do the work I do I'd disassociate (an actual diagnosable mental health condition) myself from the mental health community altogether!!!"

"THIS IS ALARMING!"

And indeed, it is alarming. While there are many very qualified, caring and competent mental health providers out there, avoiding the risk of running into some pseudo-intellectual psycho-analyst such as this one requires that (as with attorneys) you must know as much about mental health as any therapist. When seeking counseling, ask for qualifications; ask about previous experience working with prisoners and their families; ask their feelings about diagnosing—labeling—their clients; ask how often they prescribe medication—ask, ask, ASK!

Labels like this one travel with you for the rest of your life. You don't need unnecessary labeling—especially **erroneous labeling** like this to come back to haunt you one day.

There are several other types of support you might consider in your search for comfort from the trauma and grief you are experiencing, including:

- **Internet websites devoted to providing helpful information for prisoners and their families.** The sites are far too numerous to mention and are from around the world. We have found especially helpful information on sites in the United Kingdom (UK) and Canada (CA). So don't discount them, just because they are in another country. There are websites for specific issues related to the prison family. Simply type in your concern, such as "prison visitation;" "prison gangs;" "prison family support groups;" etc. You will be surprised at the amount of information that pops up! We hope you will include our site, www.pffunited.org in your search.

- **Social media dedicated to prison family issues**. Numerous sites on Facebook and other social media sources such as Twitter are dedicated to prison family issues. There is a difference in the kind of support found from the different types of social media. For example, there is more personal support on Facebook where you can actually engage in dialogue with other prison family members. However, Twitter seems to be a great source for identifying contacts, but the brevity with which you must comment prevents meaningful communication. There are sources for almost every imaginable issue facing prison families, from legal to advocacy issues to substance abuse and family support groups. The social media contacts may lead to finding support or advocacy groups in your hometown or state. These may become excellent resources when you are ready to engage in direct support close to home.

Initially the anonymity of cyberspace allows free expression of your innermost pain. Healing will even increase when you find yourself offering support to others. We do alert you to the fact that some groups seem devoted to wallowing in misery and self-pity, with most posts and comments expressions of complaint or grief. We do not believe these are healthy or helpful groups. It is certainly healthy to ventilate one's feelings, but it is not healthy if that is *all* that is done.

- **Local jail & prison ministries**: Most people who are led to go into our jails and prisons to minister to prisoners are not judgmental and offer meaningful encouragement. They understand that people err, but can be forgiven. While there are ministries from all religions, the most predominate appear to be Christian and Catholic. Whether you actually participate in the work of the ministry or not, you may find comfort in relationships formed with the members of these groups. If you choose not to actively minister, you may find other ways to support the ministry which are also healing.

- **Local prison reform & prisoner advocacy groups**: Not only might you find understanding and supportive relationships within these groups, but you may find that actively participating in improving conditions for all prisoners helps you feel you are actively contributing to helping your own incarcerated loved one. There are few things in life more healing than helping others who are struggling. One well known and respected prison reform group is "CURE," a national organization founded in the 1970's. While the national office is in Washington, D.C. there are many local chapters in most states. This is the CURE website: http://www.curenational.org.

- **Conferences related to prisoners and their families**: Throughout the year conferences are held in various locations throughout the country to address the circumstances of prisoners, especially related to prisoner re-entry. While there is usually a registration fee to attend these conferences, by planning ahead you may be able to attend one held in or near your hometown. Or, you may have time to save up for a trip to an important conference held at a distance from your hometown.

At these conferences you will find ample opportunities to freely talk about uncomfortable topics as you experience what possibly may be your first face-to-face support from truly understanding individuals. You will also find much relevant information for helping your loved one both while in prison and upon returning to the community and family. The annual National Prisoner's Family Conference held the last full week of February each year is the only conference we know of that specifically addresses the unique circumstances of the prison family. You will find details about that conference at www.prisonersfamilyconference.org.

TRAUMA IMPACT #2: THE COURT EXPERIENCE

Immediately after learning your loved one has been arrested, while still in a state of shock you find yourself sitting helplessly dazed and confused in a courtroom. It is the first of numerous court appearances that you and the defendant will experience. Each court date looming ahead; each trip to the courthouse; each court delay; each court negotiation (jury or judge; plea bargain or trial); each court hearing (whether delayed or not) is a source of traumatic impact for every member of the prison family, leaving a thick residue of invisible scars   That same source of traumatic impact affects each member of the prison family differently.

If there are children in the family, you watch helplessly as their school performance plummets and rebellious behaviors erupt from a previously almost angelic child. Adult family members who were formerly social butterflies now refuse to leave home. Former Chatty-Cathys are virtually silenced. Dads who enjoyed a rowdy game of football at backyard B-B-Q's sit immobile for hours staring into space. Moms who were the first to raise their hand to help with the church bazaar stop attending church functions altogether. The family "Energizer Bunny" suddenly sleeps for hours on end, barely getting out of bed and even staying in the same pajamas for days at a time. Those are all signs of trauma. In fact, each family member is experiencing post-traumatic stress.

The trauma impacts come in waves—increasingly brutal waves ceaselessly engulfing each family member. There are no visible signs of the type of trauma prison family members have experienced, yet they have been traumatized no less than a soldier on the battlefield. The soldier's scars may be visible as well as invisible. **All** of the prison family's scars are invisible.

The complexities and frightening unknowns presented by the court process are a series of traumatic experiences the prison family helplessly must endure. Every hearing; every postponement; the trial; the sentencing—each stage of the legal process adds a new layer of trauma. Since the things we don't know frighten us the most, the best way to defend against the ceaseless traumatic assaults is to become as knowledgeable as possible about the legal process to know as much as possible about what lies ahead.

The next best thing that may help endure the persistent waves of trauma is to learn how you personally best cope with stress and then to develop your own stress reduction strategies. It does not matter whether others understand your means for reducing stress; you must use what works best for you. So, whether it's repelling off the sides of mountains or walking ten miles a day or listening to rock and roll music at maximum volume for hours on end or attending daily yoga classes or watching horror shows on TV for hours—if it does not harm you or others—do it, if it works for you. And unless other family members are remaining in total isolation or turning to crime or chemical substances to cope, allow each one to use whatever stress reduction method works best for them, whether you understand it or not.

Many people try to ignore the obvious trauma and force themselves to continue life as if nothing unusual has happened. They are embarrassed and ashamed that their loved one is involved in a criminal matter. After all, theirs is a good family and their loved one's behavior is not typical of someone in their family. So, they try to hide the fact that their loved one was arrested and is now incarcerated.

To avoid talking about what they believe is a shameful experience, many families create "cover stories"—**lies** about their incarcerated loved one: they've taken a job out of town; they are now a long-haul trucker traveling across the country; they have suddenly joined the military and have been shipped overseas or they've joined a ministry and have gone to a third-world country to help the poor and needy—anything but the truth.

Living a lie creates unnecessary stress. In fact, living a life built on pretenses of any kind is unnatural and creates unnecessary stress for everyone. Keeping secrets and hiding from the truth, and certainly living a lie is never healthy. The energy required to suppress the truth and the true emotions about your very real traumatic circumstances is enormous. The fear that the secret will leak out (and it undoubtedly will one day) only adds extreme pressure to your already extraordinarily stressful situation.

Why would you do that to yourself and those you love?

Instead of creating more stress for yourself, find ways to reduce it. The best place to start is by understanding what is happening to you.

TRAUMA IMPACT #3: THE TRANSFER TO PRISON

Convicted and sentenced, your loved one will remain under the supervision of local authorities until without warning they are whisked away and transported to a prison intake unit. It may be several days before you are able to find them again.

Prisons may be slow to enter information into their data entry systems and even slower to post that information on their websites. So by the time your loved one shows up on the prison website they may be long gone from the location that is posted. The data on the website may indicate your loved one is at Unit "A," which may only be an intake or transfer unit. It could take several weeks before they are assigned to a more permanent unit and moved. So, in those first weeks, don't rely solely on the prison website for accurate information.

This is a very scary time for everyone, and especially scary for the family member who is going to prison. They may put up a strong front, but without a doubt they are scared, even if they have been to prison before.

It is not unusual to become frantic with the realization that your loved one is now totally absent and fully under the control of the prison system. The prison now seems to control every facet of your life. In many ways the prison does control your life now, especially as it relates to your relationship with the loved one who is in prison. The reality hits very hard and is traumatic.

There are several critical factors it is now important to know and accept as a prison family:

- Your loved one is now considered to be the "property" of the prison and you have no authority over anything related to them.

- Your loved one needs your support more than ever now, whether they acknowledge it or not.

- You now have a prime opportunity to participate in correcting the problems that took your loved one to prison. Use this time wisely.

TRAUMA IMPACT #4: IN PRISON

There is a distinct difference between local jails and prisons. Perhaps one of the greatest distinctions is that local jails house people before they are convicted of crimes and while they still have hope for soon going home. Prisons house only those who have been convicted and who have lost all hope for returning home, at least for an extended period of time. Perhaps it is this sense of hopelessness that makes prison a much more frightening and even much more dangerous setting than any local jail.

And of course, with the prisoner's transfer from the local jail to a state or federal prison the likelihood of frequent visitation disappears for most prison families. The average prisoner in the United States is housed 500 miles from their home town, making visitation impossible for most prison families.

Your loved one is now confined in a new and frightening unfamiliar culture—the prison culture. It may help to lessen some of that fear to know what lies ahead.

Prison Intake Period - All prison systems have an intake process by which the incoming prisoner is assigned a number and classified according to the severity of their offense and their risk for reoffending and escape. Based on that classification system and hopefully (but not assuredly) any critical medical and mental health needs, the prisoner is assigned to a prison unit that corresponds with their security risk level: high, medium and low security.

We would like to think that the intake process is done in the best interest of "rehabilitating" the prisoner. Unfortunately, the unvarnished truth is that from this point forward everything is done in the interest of the prison system which purports to exist for the sole purpose of protecting the public from its captives. Much of what you and your loved one will now experience (especially related to prison rules and regulations) will seem to have little logic and therefore, will make little sense to you.

During the prisoner's intake it may be difficult, if not impossible for them to communicate with you. They must get their bearings and figure out for themselves how to manage; indeed how to best survive within the confines of a prison. They must first figure out if and when they can use phones. They must first learn how and where and when they can secure writing materials. In other words, they must first learn the ropes and that takes time.

At intake prisoners are (or should be) provided an inmate handbook containing the rules and regulations they are expected to follow throughout their incarceration. Very often the contents of these handbooks are posted on the prison website, so families and friends may also learn the rules. Often this information is not fully current or even fully accurate, but if it is posted it will give you some idea of what to expect.

Think of the irony in this. The "rule-less" will now be totally "ruled." Perhaps this doesn't apply to your loved one, of course, but the vast majority of prisoners lived by their own rules in the free world, which is typically the reason they landed in prison. Overnight they are commanded to "live by the book." That is not easy for many. Those who fight the rule book will pay dearly—unless or until they snap to attention, and "snapping to attention" is not easy in a controlled world where the rules change quickly.

More than one prisoner has told us that rules in prison change almost daily. It is the prisoner's responsibility to keep up with these rapid-fire rule changes to avoid being written up and disciplined for breaking the newest of the rules. While there may be some rules that are uniform throughout a prison system, many rules are set by the warden of the particular prison unit. Therefore different units within the same prison system will operate somewhat differently.

New rules are typically posted in a location that is visible to all prisoners. These rules are not published in the prison handbook that is distributed to all new prisoners at intake. Those handbooks may not be updated for years. Therefore the new prisoner must learn a great many of the rules by trial and error.

While some rules would be considered common sense, such as no fighting or no stealing, other rules are quite subtle and would not even be considered a "rule" by most new prisoners. For example, one prisoner recently told me that in the prison system in which he is incarcerated, some units require the prisoners to remove their jackets (distributed in the cold months and collected and stored in the warmer months) immediately upon entering the building. However, other units within the same system allow the inmates to wear their jackets day and night if they choose; only taking them off when ordered to do so by a corrections officer for a pat-down or strip search.

That may sound like a small thing to those of us in the free world, but inside the prison failure to remove your jacket when it is the rule, can lead to a major disciplinary case. How are new prisoners, or even old-timers transferred between units supposed to know which rules apply where?

In fact, they don't. So, they learn by trial and error. The learning process can be very painful.

While your loved one gets their bearings, try to remember that if you do not hear from them even for several weeks, while it may be unbearably stressful to you, it does not mean there is anything wrong with them. It might be consoling to know that if you are the prisoner's primary emergency contact person, one of the first pieces of information the prison will ask the prisoner is for your contact information. If anything of a truly serious nature had occurred, the prison would indeed notify you.

The best resource to help you during this period will be the prison website. If you do not have access to the internet, the best resource will be your local library which has computers with internet access available for public use. Some university libraries may also let you use their computers to search the internet.

Once on the internet "Google" the name of the prison system. For Federal information, type in "FBOP" (Federal Bureau of Prisons). For State prisons you may need to type in the full name of the system, such as "Oregon Department of Corrections," because "ODOC" could also mean "Ohio Department of Corrections," or your browser may recognize the abbreviated format, such as "TDCJ" which is the common reference for the Texas prison system.

On the prison website Home Page, each prison system will have a link for locating an inmate. Click on that link and enter the information requested. While there may be several people in that prison system with the same name (and all of them will pop up) you will be provided other information by which to identify your loved one. Some prison systems actually post a picture of the prisoner and, of course their offense. Once you click on your loved one's name, you will be able to determine where they are located in the prison system.

By the way, if you can't find your loved one, don't be surprised if the prisoner's name was misspelled in the data entry process! It may *never* be corrected, such as the "Terrence" we know who was entered into the prison data base as "Terrance." After a few years of requesting the "a" be changed to an "e," the effort was abandoned. Now, 4 unit transfers and 23 years later, we just have to remember to misspell his name if we want to find him on the prison website!

You can certainly call the prison unit to inquire about your loved one, but of course you won't be able to talk to them. Most prisons aren't thrilled about outside callers, although it is possible, but not certain that someone at the facility will at least verify whether your loved one is there or not. They probably will not provide you with any additional information. They may or may not be cordial to you; in fact some staff may be downright rude. Regardless of their demeanor or the amount of information they provide, it is important to know that this does not in any way reflect on your loved one's well being.

Learn all you can from the information posted on the website, especially regarding issues that will most directly affect you, such as phone calls, mail regulations and visitation. If you do not understand what is posted, or if you have questions that are not answered by the website, call the prison unit where your loved one is located and inquire.

There is a good reason prison officials are not happy to receive calls from the outside. The prison system is self-regulated. That means there is absolutely no independent oversight of how the prisons operate. **The**

prison system has no accountability for its practices. None! Your call to the prison puts them on notice that someone on the outside is looking in! That makes the prison officials very uncomfortable and it may or may not be a good thing for your loved one. For that reason it is always wise to communicate with the prisoner before intervening or advocating on their behalf.

When mentioning that prisons are self regulated, invariably someone will declare, "There is the ACA!"

The "ACA" is the American Corrections Association. You will find their website at www.aca.org. Check it out. It's an interesting "read." Bottom line: While anyone may become a paid member and we certainly encourage you to do so, the ACA paid membership almost entirely consists of criminal justice officials and prison personnel. We find the ACA training section especially interesting. It would appear from their training focus that their primary concern is "control" of prisoners and avoiding lawsuits for violating prisoners' rights. Experience tells us that while they purport to "audit" prisons, their primary area of auditing interest has to do with technical issues—i.e. Do the toilets flush? Do the locks work? Check out the ACA website, and see what you think.

Phone Calls - While you are not able to call into a prison to talk to any prisoner, most prisons today allow phone privileges for prisoners to call their loved ones. As some prison systems are not yet equipped to provide this privilege, the best we can do is tell you that we know first-hand how difficult it is not to be able to talk by phone.

Texas only installed phones a little over two years ago, as of this writing. Advocacy for phone privileges spanned many decades, before the prison allowed this privilege. It may require some very active advocacy from families and friends of prisoners in your area to have phones installed in your prison system. Having lived for years without phone contact we can tell you that the availability of phones is truly an aid to improving clear communication and even to one's peace of mind. However, as with all wondrous things, there are some drawbacks!

It is notable that these prison phone systems are huge money-makers for the prisons and the phone providers. If prisons didn't profit from the services they allow, such as the phones; e-mail; commissary, etc. it is questionable whether these services would even be available at all, as they require prison staff for monitoring and/or operating. Even the inmate trust fund into which families and friends deposit the money brings in hundreds of thousands (perhaps millions) of dollars each year for the prison system!

Phone charges are often quite high—far more than a typical pay phone and certainly far more than the free long distance services routinely provided with cell phones and most land lines today. Therefore, without careful observance and budgeting, phone bills can quickly run up into the hundreds—even thousands of dollars before you even realize it. Of course it's planned that way—it's a "fund-raiser" for the prison!

As we write, the Federal Communications Commission (FCC) is being flooded with petitions to reduce prison phone rates and apparently the FCC is seriously considering this outcry. Hopefully we will see a significant decrease in phone charges, soon. It is our understanding that in some states one twenty minute phone call costs in excess of twenty dollars. In Texas, with miscellaneous charges (handling; billing; taxing, etc.) twenty minute calls average around seven dollars each. We fully support the effort being made to reduce phone costs and will report any changes on the Prisoner's Family & Friends United website and Facebook page.

To clarify, here we are primarily speaking of State prison phone privileges whereby family members and friends must register for phone privileges via the internet or by phone. Payment is made by credit or debit card on-line or by check or money order through the mail. In the federal system, prisoners pay at the prison. While federal prisoners are paid a few dollars each month for working in the prison, it is quite likely that loved ones supplement their paltry income from which they will pay the phone charges at the prison.

While different prison systems use different phone providers and charge different rates and have different phone rules, there are some common phone practices for all prisoners.

Where phone calls are available, they are a *privilege* and not a right. Therefore, if the prisoner receives any disciplinary action phone privileges are likely to be terminated for a specific length of time—even 3 months or more, depending upon the severity of the restrictions imposed. As it is, prisoners in segregation and on death row currently have no phone privileges.

Consider all phone calls to be monitored and recorded. Therefore avoid profanity and never make any threats against the prison system or each other or anyone else, or phone calls may be disconnected in the middle of a conversation and phone privileges discontinued. Knowing your calls are monitored and avoiding saying the wrong thing may make you feel like you must talk in "secret code!" However, you will gradually become more comfortable with the circumstances.

Some prison systems allow "unlimited" phone time; others allocate a specific number of minutes *per month*. If phone time is limited, you must carefully monitor the minutes used. Not only are those precious allocated phone minutes costly, but once used, you must wait until the first day of the next month to speak again. The waiting time can seem endless. Prison families and friends should clearly inform the prisoner how much they are willing to spend for phone calls each month. The prisoner should be expected to adhere to the limitations imposed by their loved ones.

Phone calls are timed; usually about fifteen to twenty minutes each, before you hear a warning and the call is automatically terminated. To minimize expenses and to avoid unnecessary use of precious minutes, it is good to plan your conversations ahead of time. Even keep a list of everything important that you want and need to say and encourage your loved one to do the same.

Don't become frantic if your loved one does not call as planned. While it is of little use to make that statement, because you *will* become totally distracted when a scheduled call does not come, remember, your loved one has no control over the use of the phone. Usually, the phone system is turned on and off automatically at specified hours. It can also be turned off and on at the will of the prison guards. While the prisoner may "usually" have access to the phones at a particular time of day, things happen on the unit that may or may not have any direct relationship to your loved one, but will affect their ability to make a planned call.

If you were expecting a call that did not come you will find yourself worrying, and as the hours pass the worrying will intensify. When an expected call does not come the **first thing to consider is whether you have paid your phone bill**! We don't say this because we think you are not responsible in paying your bills, but because the payment arrangements for the phone company may be rather unusual. For example, you may register to receive calls with the service provider and not pay a cent to begin receiving calls. The provider may allow your bill to climb to a certain amount—in Texas with unlimited phone calls, phone bills can now climb as high as two hundred dollars without paying a cent—before the phone service is cut off.

Unless you diligently keep a phone log or call the phone provider after each phone call from prison, you may have no idea how high your bill is. Suddenly the service is disconnected and the prisoner can no longer call you, until you pay your phone bill! You have to figure that out for yourself. However, once you do figure it out and pay the bill, within minutes you can receive calls again.

When your bill is paid and you still aren't receiving expected calls, if you just cannot bear to wait two or three days until your loved one can write to tell you they are on lockdown or the phones are out of order, you can call the unit to inquire. However, while some officers will graciously provide you with the requested information, do not be surprised if you are met with a commonly heard sarcastic response telling you, "If they wanted to call you, they would."

Don't become frantic if a call is terminated in the middle of a conversation, even if your loved one does not call back. Calls may be abruptly terminated if the call runs into a "count time" or if there is a disturbance or for absolutely no reason at all. The electronic phone system may even disconnect the call because the prisoners in the dayroom became so loud yelling for their favorite ball team on TV that they disrupt the sound waves enough to electronically make it appear as though you made a third-party call (which is disallowed by most prison phone systems.)

Aside from visitation, phone calls are the most intimate means of communication possible during a loved one's incarceration. Families and friends should make the most of these calls to address critical issues; to work out misunderstandings or to discuss future plans and goals. These precious minutes should be used to know one another at deeper and more intimate levels; to enjoy a laugh together and certainly to verbally express love for one another.

Written Correspondence - Prison is a very lonely place. Despite overcrowding and two people confined to a six-by-eight foot cell or fifty or more prisoners crammed together in a dorm, each prisoner is essentially an island unto them self. Prisoners rarely have true friends in whom to confide while they are incarcerated. It is the "law of the jungle" to never fully trust another inmate. Therefore, being able to correspond with someone on the outside who they can trust with their innermost thoughts and feelings is crucial to the prisoner's emotional well being.

Not only is it important to know someone on the outside loves and cares about them, but prisoners also lose touch with social skills and the realities of the free world, unless those of us on the outside make a concerted effort to keep them posted and involved with life in the free world.

Life on the outside is continually changing, while life on the inside stops and remains stagnant for the prisoner. If you have ever left town for even a few days, you may have noticed that when you return you recognize some significant changes in your community? "They're building an apartment on that vacant lot." "They're tearing down that abandoned building that was such an eyesore." "Look! A new McDonalds is opening!" If that many changes occur over a long weekend, just think of the enormous changes a prisoner will encounter when they return home! To lessen the impact of change, it is critical that someone (or many "someones") from the outside provide a realistic picture of what is occurring in the free world.

Snail Mail: As long as we still have the U.S. Postal Service we can still use old fashioned snail mail to correspond, and prisoners love receiving snail mail. One of a prisoner's greatest fears is summed up in the saying, *"Out of sight; out of mind."* Without contact from the free world, prisoners feel totally forgotten. A friendly letter from the free world is evidence that someone on the outside not only thinks of them, but really does care.

Written correspondence is monitored. In fact prison systems actually hire staff specifically to read incoming and outgoing mail. So, of course there are rules to follow when writing a prisoner, and those rules are established by each prison system and even differ from unit to unit; from day to day; from staff member to staff member! Seemingly innocent things like cute stickers or even colored paper may not be allowed. The use of white-out to make corrections may result in a contraband notice to the prisoner. We once had a letter returned because our agency's pre-printed envelope did not include the name of the writer in the return address—the printed name of the agency was not sufficient!

One of the greatest problems with snail mail is the time lag it presents in conveying information. Because mail is monitored going in and going out of the prison, it adds at least one extra day to delivery of that mail. It takes at least three business days for a letter to be delivered in either direction. The delay in mail delivery creates gaps in time, making it "Time Lag Communication." It is much like the communication we see on television when a news correspondent is speaking from a distant country to a news anchor in the United States. If the reporters are not extremely careful, it results in uncomfortable silences and talking over one another.

Time Lag Correspondence creates the same disorganized interaction. For example, your loved one may write that they are upset about something you said or something that happened at the prison. By the time you receive their letter three to five days later, they may have completely resolved the matter, but unless you've talked by phone in the interim, you have no way to know the matter was resolved. Therefore, you will respond to what they wrote in their letter and worry for another week or ten days before they can write to let you know the matter was resolved two weeks ago.

The use of phone calls and e-mail may help limit any resulting misunderstanding or unnecessary worry. However, if phone calls and e-mail are not possible, you might address this time lag challenge in your letters. Come to an understanding about how you will each handle the time lags between letters. Agree not to write about certain "hot" issues that may create friction or result in misunderstandings.

Be Creative! It may be a challenge to be very creative with letter writing when considering all the rules for sending mail to prisoners, but to keep correspondence interesting it helps to deviate from traditional letter writing from time to time! We can think of a few ways to deviate from the traditional letter. (Be certain to check mail regulations for your particular prison to assure you don't break any rules!)

Electronically copy & insert photos into your letters and provide narratives for each picture. Family photos are always welcome as are photos of activities around the community. Even insert motivational or funny saying or inspiring pictures you see on Facebook. Copy things you believe are of interest or will possibly inspire or motivate the prisoner—or even make them laugh! Send greeting cards, of course. Remember many prisons do not permit stickers; glitter; ribbons or other adornments or musical cards. Occasionally send a post card, if permitted. Clip newspaper, magazine or internet articles about an issue of interest to the prisoner or your family and enclose them with your letter.

If there are children in the family encourage them to draw pictures for their loved one in prison. Typically the use of glue or glitter or other adornments or sometimes even the use of crayon or markers are not permitted, so you may want to photocopy the children's drawings before sending them, just to be certain your loved one will receive them at the prison.

Play games through the mail. While anyone can create or find games to play through the mail, this is an especially good way for children to have interaction with an incarcerated parent. (Such games are provided from time to time on www.pffunited.org.)

FYI: Here is an actual, but typical explanation of writing rules from one facility, including a lengthy list of typical "do not send's" to give you an idea of rules for writing prisoners!

Money (Money orders and checks) will not be accepted at this address, it will be returned to sender if sent. For information on adding money to an inmates account, navigate to the Inmate Money Page.

Sender should include their full name and return address, in case the inmate has been transferred or released. Mail is not forwarded to the inmate, but is returned to sender or sent to the dead letter department at the U.S. Post Office. Legal mail will be opened in the inmate's presence.

Inmates are allowed to receive books, magazines, or newspapers sent from a bookstore (Barnes and Noble, Amazon.com, Borders or directly from a publisher.) and not from any other private company. There is a 5 book maximum that an inmate can receive daily.

Items prohibited from being received through the mail are, but not limited to the following:

- Any items not lawfully obtained or possessed under terms outlined in the Texas Penal Code are considered illegal material.
- Glue, paperclips, clasps, staples, magnets, stickers, tape, plastic, wood, cloth, glass, ribbon, liquids, metal, electronic devices, or any like material.
- Writing materials such as stamps, blank paper, envelopes, pens, pencils, or stationary. [Note: some prisons do allow these items.]
- Unsigned greeting cards.
- Greeting cards larger than 8"x10".
- Greeting cards that contain padding, musical device, metal clasps, plastic, string, ribbon, confetti, glitter, or laminated items.
- Photographs larger than 8"x10".
- Polaroid photographs.
- Photos depicting obscenity, violence, pornography, or of a sexually enticing nature.
- Profanity (on the envelope).
- Tobacco or tobacco products.
- Bus passes, bookmarks, or calling cards
- Perishable items
- Clothing. [Some prisons allow certain items of clothing.]
- Stains or unidentifiable marks.
- Writing/drawing in crayon, marker, or colored pencils. [If children draw pictures for their parent(s) in prison, it is a good idea to copy them and send the copy and not the original.]
- Mail identified as Legal Mail, but containing non-legal material.
- Books that were not shipped from the publisher or the bookstore.
- Any items that by design restricts the ability to perform an effective search.
- Any items that have no value or are of no use to the inmate while incarcerated in this facility.

- Jewelry.
- Any items with a glued surface or backing.
- Any items that may not be readily determined as to their nature or description.
- Items of inflammatory nature described as follows:
    - o Contain information regarding or the depiction of the manufacture or likeness of explosives, weapons or drugs.
    - o Contain material that a reasonable person, could construe as written solely for the purpose of communicating information designed to achieve the breakdown of prisoners through inmate disruption such as strikes, riots or escapes.
    - o If the material leads to specific factual determination that the material is detrimental to a prisoner's rehabilitation because it encourages deviate sexual behavior.

E-Mail: Some prison systems provide e-mail correspondence. While it adds another expense for the prison family, it usually is not more expensive than sending snail mail, although the length of what you can write may be limited, but it certainly simplifies and expedites correspondence. As with all means of communication with prisoners, e-mail is monitored.

Federal prisons use an e-mail system called "Corrlinks" by which you can have relatively normal two-way e-mail communication with a prisoner. The prisoner pays for this service from their trust fund and initiates the e-contact. You will receive a "Corrlinks" notice that the prisoner wants to communicate by e-mail, and you must accept their "invitation." After that, you can e-mail much as you would in the free world—although the system counts your typed **characters** and when the characters are all used up, the prisoner must pay to purchase more characters. To save money, you quickly learn to abbreviate and be succinct with what you have to say!

Many state prisons use a service for one-way e-mailing, such as Jpay. Family and friends must sign up on line for the service from the free world and "buy stamps," using a credit or debit card or mailing a check or money order to the provider. The prisoner will not be able to respond by e-mail. However, even one way e-mailing expedites correspondence. A word of caution about sending photos as attachments on e-mails: not only is the quality of the photo the prisoner receives often poor, but photos are received in black and white.

Other Printed Matter - Even prisoners who never picked up a book or newspaper or magazine before will begin reading once incarcerated. This offers an excellent opportunity to encourage your loved one to develop personal interests in such things as business, hobbies, even the stock market!

Most prisons allow prisoners to receive a wide variety of printed literature sent directly *from the publisher or from major book sellers* such as Barnes & Noble or Amazon.com. Subscriptions to magazines and hometown newspapers provide a steady flow of reading material. Ask their interests; suggest they learn something about your own passions—after all, if you have a passion for something your passion is generally contagious! Send them reading material to pique or expand their interests.

Be sure to follow the rules. For example, some prisons do not allow hard back books; others do. Some prisons do not allow used books; others do. Some prisons have a limit on how many books you can send at one time. If the rules on sending printed material are not on the prison website or are not clear, call the prison unit to inquire—and write down the name of the staff member who provides the answers to your questions. If they provide inaccurate information and you later learn that items you specifically asked about and ordered are not allowed, report the staff member by name. Their unit should train their staff to provide callers with accurate information.

Some prisons ban certain reading materials. Ask if the prison has a *banned book list* to assure you are not sending something that won't be allowed. Sometimes these lists are published on line.

Banned literature is not necessarily that dealing with crime or the occult or pornography or other dark subjects. In fact, most prison libraries are well stocked with such reading materials. But, even self help books; books on religion or certain novels are sometimes banned for whatever reason the prison deems it inappropriate, logical or not. The most frequently banned books however are ones you probably have never heard of or would never consider sending anyhow—books on such things as committing the perfect crime or making weaponry.

FYI: We order all of our reading materials to be sent into prison through Amazon.com primarily because they have an enormous selection of all printed literature and their site is easy to use and track shipments. More importantly, they have proven to be honest about refunds when purchases have been returned for any reason—shipping charges and all! We appreciate their integrity!

About Pornography - We will do our best to be tasteful in providing this information. We would simply leave it out, if this were not an attempt to bring you honest unvarnished information about having a loved one in prison. But the unvarnished truth is that the issue of receiving pornography in prison has been brought to our attention on several occasions, not for its shock value, but in explanation of why inmates do have access to and/or even "need" sexually explicit materials. We will provide the information we've received; you determine how to best address this issue for yourself.

In our society, while "sex" certainly sells, "sex" has been such a taboo subject for so long many hardly talk about it openly, especially within the family. So, when the topic arises, we may tend to skirt the real issues because of long-held beliefs that it is inappropriate for discussion—especially in mixed company. However it is a subject clearly evident in prison and as such it is a topic that clearly needs to be addressed, although it is highly sensitive in addressing here for more than reasons of sex being a long-held taboo subject.

First, there is the issue of homosexuality, because homosexuality in prison is not the same as homosexuality in the free world where individuals have the freedom to choose with whom they will engage in sexual relations. Without any judgment intended we will say that homosexuality is rampant in prisons, but it is not always a welcomed experience.

Second, there is the issue of rape. The harsh reality is that rape is not uncommon in prisons. While rape of any kind is an abhorrent violent act, in prison the cold unvarnished truth is there is only one gender housed on a prison unit, Therefore (unless at the hands of an officer of the opposite gender, which does occur with some frequency) prison rape will be by a same gendered individual—or individuals.

There is a great deal written about same gender sexual abuse and same gender rape. **In the simplest of terms** much of the research indicates that when a person who has formerly considered them self to be heterosexual is raped by someone of the same gender they may begin to doubt their own sexuality. This is reported to be especially true for males who, in addition to being traumatized by the violent act, may also come to believe they are weak, because they weren't "strong enough" to fend off the attack, even when they were gang raped. This leads some to begin to question their own sexuality.

Third, there is the issue of normal sexual drive which is not eliminated by virtue of incarceration. We were created as sexual beings. Sex is a normal and certainly healthy bodily function. It is totally abnormal to think that the prisoner will suddenly become celibate solely because they are isolated from those of the opposite gender or isolated from those with whom they would **choose** to have sexual relations.

When compared to the free world, prison is quite an abnormal environment in many aspects, and sex is certainly at the top of the "abnormal" list in prison. Think of it—over a thousand men or women isolated with only the same gender everywhere they look. Oh, there may be a staff member here and there of the opposite gender—and to be honest, inter-gender relationships do occur in prison, and that too can become very problematic. In fact there have long been questions as to whether it is appropriate for men to work in female prisons, or for females to work in male prisons. Of course we have to deal with all of those labor laws, so we can't discriminate on gender no matter what is "right or wrong" or even what is safe or unsafe for either gender.

So, bearing all of this in mind, there are those prisoners who unabashedly state that pornography has a valuable purpose in prisons and who believe that it may even reduce the frequency of inappropriate and/or violent sexual behaviors that occur all too often in prisons. Therefore, if or when your loved one mentions sending magazines or other printed materials that you may believe are "inappropriate" because they seem to you to be pornographic and of little value, instead of reacting with shock and expressing your belief that the prison would never allow such materials—and even if they did what would the prison staff think of you for sending it—you might want to discuss the matter with your loved one further. In fact, with some specific regulations that are apparently described in prisoner handbooks, "mild to moderate" pornography is allowed in most, if not all prisons.

What Do We Write About? - Not everyone is a budding Ernest Hemingway, so writing does not come easily to many people—including some prisoners. But, the truth is, some prisoners (and some of their family members and friends) just haven't realized their writing talents yet! In fact, many prisoners first realize their real talents while incarcerated.

Currently I consistently write three prisoners, all now in their mid to late 30's who have been in prison since their teenage years. I believe it is safe to say that not one of them had any idea they had any significant writing skills before going to prison. Today, two have university degrees in English literature; one has entered national writing contests and won an award for his writing; another has worked on learning to write grant proposals on behalf of our organization; one, in fact is co-authoring this book with me!

I also recently began volunteering to review creative writing assignments for College Guild, an organization that provides non-credit life enriching curriculum to prisoners across the country. (Actually, College Guild may be a good resource for your loved one if they come to enjoy writing—or through their correspondence with you, learn they do have writing talents! You can find them at www.collegeguild.org.)

Although I don't know any of the prisoners whose papers I review, many of the College Guild writing participants evidence very creative writing skills. Having realized their true talent and even passion for writing since being incarcerated, some actually have submitted scripts that have been seen on television series; others enjoy writing imaginative short stories that have been published in various magazines; one recently even expressed a desire to write a stage play. It is highly unlikely any of these prisoners ever realized these talents and aspirations before someone inspired them to give it a try! Perhaps you will be the one to inspire your loved one to give writing a try!

Unfortunately, I've heard more than one family member say that they are planning to write their loved one in prison *every single day*, but they do not expect the prisoner to write back, because "he/she doesn't like to write." I have to admit that when I hear that, it is difficult not to say anything! For goodness sake! There is so much wrong with that picture that it's difficult to know where to start addressing it! Even if the situation was reversed and the prisoner was doing all the writing and not expecting his or her family members or friends to reciprocate, the picture would be troubling.

First of all, it is hoped that this prison time will be used to build healthy relationships. Healthy relationships are two way mutually satisfying streets. The operative word there is: **"mutually."** It is hardly "mutually" satisfying to endlessly write letters that are never answered. In fact, one way giving or one way taking is never healthy.

In any relationship, when one person does all the giving to another person who is doing all the taking it is not even a true "relationship." The "taker" is being selfish and self-centered and the "giver" is actually enabling the "taker" to remain selfish and self centered. *Neither* is engaged in building a truly mutually satisfying relationship. Each is only fulfilling their own selfish needs. One has an *insatiable need to nurture* and the other has an *insatiable need be nurtured.* One is incapable of comfortably receiving and the other is incapable of comfortably expressing appreciation and love through giving. Because selfish relationships are totally unsatisfying, perhaps (for some people) that type of relationship was in some way instrumental in leading to the prisoner's incarceration in the first place. In any case, now is the time to revise expectations in relationships to assure they are *mutually* satisfying healthy relationships.

While your loved one is incarcerated they are truly a *captive audience.* What better time is there for lessons that seem to have been missed when they were in the free world? Who better to provide those lessons than those who love the prisoner? Not that this time should be used to preach and harp on their bad behavior. Once in prison they clearly know what they did was wrong—even if they don't admit guilt for the offense for which they are incarcerated. So, without any preaching this time can best be used to build and strengthen relationships; to develop strong, positive values; to recognize and develop dormant talents and skills and even to realize enjoyable pastimes and hobbies.

This is a prime time to encourage your loved one to grow in ways they may have never even considered possible in the past. But, be forewarned. Those old "do as I say, not as I do" platitudes just don't fly when you're trying to encourage another person to grow! So don't ask the prisoner to do something you are unwilling to do! Relationships are two-way streets and therefore you may find that you need to make some changes of your own in order for your teaching and encouragement to be well received.

A journey of many miles begins with the first step. The first step is always the most difficult to take, not only because we don't know what lies ahead, but also because we fear we may fail. However, if we never take that first step; if we never write that first word, we will never know where life could lead us. Perhaps this quote may provide some perspective on avoiding that first step out of fear of failure:

> *I've missed more than 9000 shots in my career.*
> *I've lost almost 300 games.*
> *26 times, I've been trusted to take the game winning shot and missed.*
> *I've failed over and over and over again in my life.*
> *And that is why I succeed.*
> *~ Michael Jordan ~*

Whether you like to write or not, writing is now a lifeline to your relationship with your incarcerated loved one. That means that now is the time to develop your own passion for writing. If the prisoner doesn't write, it is your responsibility to motivate and inspire them to have a passion for writing. Write about any and everything that comes to mind or occurs in your daily life. No matter how trivial the matter seems to you, it is a link to connect you to one another.

You can address disappointments and resolve disagreements by writing about them. This does not mean to attack one another, but perhaps you can both read the same book on a relationship issue—an excellent book to start with is "The Five Love Languages" by Gary Chapman. While most people who have heard of this book believe it to be for husbands and wives, in fact it addresses love between *any* two people—even parents and children. By simultaneously reading this or a similar book or even brief articles on issues of concern to both of you, and then discussing it through letter writing, you can move to deeper levels of understanding and resolve issues of conflict.

Discuss—even debate issues of substance, such as race relations; politics; religion—even if these are issues you disagree on. The rules for writing about difficult issues need to assure "fair fighting." This means respecting each other's opinion and no personal attacks; using only "I statements" by taking responsibility for your own thoughts and never finger pointing with "you statements," and absolutely *no name calling*! You will definitely learn much more about one another once you open the door to writing about these typically taboo subjects.

And, definitely talk about family matters, including the issues that landed your loved one in prison. The unvarnished truth is that unless the two of you bring up the subject, the prison experience alone is not going to resolve those issues. Just locking a person away in a vacuum rarely helps them make critical life changes. It's no more effective than locking a lion in a cage for twenty years and expecting it to transform into a sweet adorable kitten! Controlled by iron bars the lion looks so cuddly and even docile while caged, but when the door of that cage is opened and the lion is allowed to roam free, what do you expect will happen?

We don't need to dwell on the possibilities, because most of us know that a caged lion is still a wild and dangerous animal whether in or outside of their cage. Caging the lion may modify its behaviors temporarily, but it will not permanently change its inner workings. It is still the same lion that was caged many years before—perhaps even an angrier lion for having been caged all of those years.

Similarly, a prisoner is typically a troubled human being who is now "locked in a cage." If they receive no encouragement; if they receive no intellectual stimulation; if they receive no insightful input it really doesn't matter how long they remain in that cage. When the cage door opens they will exit as the same troubled human being that went in; perhaps even more troubled by what they have witnessed and experienced from inside that "locked cage."

It is a rare prison that actively inspires or stimulates positive thinking. Until prisons undertake the role of actively, truly rehabilitating prisoners (as we believe should be the case), the responsibility for helping prisoners make positive life changes and healthy choices rests solely on their outside support team. A most effective way the prisoner's support team can encourage and inspire the prisoner is by putting it in writing.

Share Your Burdens - Many prison families believe they should not "burden" prisoners with bad news or difficulties they are experiencing back home. Those family members say that things are already bad enough for the prisoner, so they don't want to "burden" them with more frustration, tragedy and pain.

Too many say, "After all, they're in prison. There's hardly anything they can do to help anyhow, can they?"

The answer is a resounding, "YES! They absolutely can help!"

First of all, if prison families really want to help the prisoner become and/or remain a truly integral member of their family, they will include them as much as possible under the circumstances in all aspects of their family life: the good; the bad and the ugly. By denying the prisoner access to the difficulties facing the family, we *shut them out of the family*. The truth always has a way of leaking out and once the prisoner realizes you have shut them out, not only do they begin to feel like an outsider, but they begin to lose trust in their family. Without trust, it is virtually impossible to build or maintain a healthy relationship.

Here is a "trust issue" that we hear all too often. Many prisoners have told us that their families have lied to them about the illness or even death of a beloved family member or friend. I recall one prisoner telling me that his family had not told him of the death of his grandmother for **eight years**. Instead, they made up a multitude of elaborate lies in their effort "not to burden him" with information they thought would devastate him.

136

The prisoner said that "after the first year of lies," he knew something dreadful had happened to his grandmother or she would at least have sent him a card for his birthday. He said that it was "infuriating" that his family refused to answer his questions honestly, even when he "told them he knew that she was gone."

Years later he would say that he recognized that each time his family lied to him it chipped away at his trust in them more and more, until finally there was an angry scene in visitation when he confronted family members about lying to him. He had even told them himself that he felt he was being shut out of the family when they kept the truth from him about what was happening at home. Their refusal to tell him the truth about his grandmother, and apparently some other unpleasant issues at home, ultimately created a rift between them that never was fully repaired.

Give your loved one a chance to be a valuable member of your family. Simply share your burdens with them as you would with anyone else you feel you can trust with your burdens. Share the every day annoyances such as flat tires and plumbing problems and computer crashes. Share the challenges you face such as disagreements with the boss or difficulties paying the bills. Share the painful experiences such as your best friend moving away, losing your job or the death of a loved one. Sharing these experiences keeps the prisoner connected to the family and strengthens the relationship and builds trust.

After all, isn't that how we build relationships with anyone? We share a little and they share a little, so we share a little more, which leads them to share more with us at a deeper level. That sharing builds trust. The more we share from our hearts, the greater the trust that builds between us. There is absolutely no reason to lie to a prisoner (or anyone for that matter) for any reason, especially if your goal is to strengthen the relationship. It is impossible to build healthy relationships on lies or even half-truths.

There is certainly no reason to lie if your goal is to strengthen the prisoner's capacity to cope with life's challenges in the most healthy and productive manner. In "counselor-talk" shielding an adult loved one from the realities of life is called "infantilizing." Infantilizing is a process by which one adult treats another adult like a child, leading them to feel child-like and helpless and incapable of undertaking adult responsibilities or making adult choices and decisions.

If it is your intent to help the prisoner become a healthy and productive adult, you must treat them as the adult they are. Throughout life, all adults face difficult and painful experiences. *Healthy* adults learn to cope with these experiences in healthy ways. Isn't that what you wish for your loved one? If it is, and especially if you are unable to visit the prisoner in person or talk with them by phone, at least communicate the truth about difficult situations through written correspondence.

As for believing prisoners are in no position to help with the challenges facing their families, that is absolutely not true. Give them an opportunity to show you that they can help.

If you are facing a difficulty, let the prisoner know what it is and ask their opinion on how they might resolve the situation. Not only may they come up with a creative solution you've never considered, but they will be able to encourage you as you walk through the challenge. By sharing the difficulties with them you let them know that their opinion is valued—that they are valued as a human being and valued as a member of your family. By letting them join in resolving the problem, perhaps they will also learn some important life lessons about problem solving. Whatever the outcome, sharing challenges and difficult times will help build trust and develop a deeper understanding of one another.

Visitation - Understandably, but unfortunately visitation is "off limits" for many prison families. There are those who tire of their loved one cycling in and out of the revolving prison door and there are those who have been directly harmed by the family member in prison. So those families are likely to refuse to visit the prisoner.

There are also prisoners who are forbidden by law to visit or even communicate with family members. Whether anyone desires to visit or not, if they are forbidden to do so by law the prison is provided that information and will assure there will be no visits.

And, there are also family members who have not yet and may never forgive the prisoner for whatever they've done that led them to prison and therefore they refuse to visit the prisoner. While unforgiveness is an unhealthy state for anyone to remain in, it is understandable that those who have not forgiven the prisoner will refuse to visit them. However, it is unfortunate when these circumstances occur, because during a time of incarceration so much can be done to right the wrongs in relationships and what better way to do that than by direct face-to-face dialogue, which can only occur through visitation?

Fortunately many families do want to visit their loved one in prison, and that is a very good thing, because visitation is the only opportunity for a semblance of true understanding and intimate communication while a loved one is incarcerated.

For all prison family members a visit to see a loved one in prison is a highly emotionally charged ordeal.

As we prepared for the 5th annual National Prisoner's Family Conference I received a call inquiring about scholarships for prison family members. Struggling to sound nonchalant, the heartbroken grandmother burst into tears as she told of her sixteen year old grandson's incarceration in the adult prison system in their state, five years before. The family had just visited him the previous weekend for his 21st birthday.

"People don't realize how hard it is, going to visit," she cried. "The four hour drive there is filled with fears of what we'll find. There's a bruise on his face and he tells us 'it's nothing.' How do we know the truth? You strain to smile and enjoy your time together and it drains all of your energy, because on the inside you're in agony and you're doing everything you can not to let him see it."

The grandmother digressed to let me know that when the bailiff escorted her then sixteen year old grandson from the courtroom after his conviction he was barely five feet three inches tall and weighed just one hundred pounds. She said the family was horrified for him. Their family had no previous experience with prison before and now this small child was to be placed in a prison with grown men, most of whom had done some terrible things. She added that while her grandson had grown over the past five years he was still rather small in stature.

"Now we see signs that he's being abused, but he won't talk to us about it," she stammered bursting into sobs.

She continued to sob while telling me of her fears for her granddaughter, who refused to even talk about her only brother being in prison. "She lies; she tells everyone he's away in college, but after five years her friends are pushing to understand why he's never returned home in all of those years. She says she just cannot bring herself to say that her only brother is in prison. She's eating herself up over this."

Her sobs grew louder. She apologized for breaking down. I attempted to be consoling, but knew in my own mind that the excruciating pain she was experiencing would never totally go away. I encouraged her and her granddaughter to come to the conference where talking openly about loved ones in prison is safe and comforting and very healing.

She worked to calm herself until she was finally able to speak again. "The pain of leaving him behind when we visit him is unbearable. I can't even describe how empty I feel turning my back and leaving him behind."

For families who deeply love and care about their prisoner family member there is absolutely nothing to celebrate about visiting them in prison. It is an extremely emotional and even physically challenging ordeal in all aspects.

First of all, for those traveling any distance to the prison there are preparations to make and expenses to plan for. The family may need to rent a car or make plane reservations. If staying overnight, there will be motel reservations and e xpenses. If they have children or pets they must make proper arrangements to leave them behind or plan for their travel.

Will they take food with them, or plan to have meals out—or both? The expenses keep mounting!

Depending on the prison's visitation policies, extended visitation time may be requested. It may not be granted. In Texas you are required to call the prison on the Monday preceding the planned visit to request a "special visit" for the following weekend. In that phone call, you are told, "Call back on **Friday** to see if it's approved." In the meantime you begin packing for a journey that may or may not result in an extended visit, or any visit at all. To arrive in time for visitation, many families must begin their car trip—or even fly out before they even know if the special visit is approved. It's a risk they are forced to take if they want to visit at all, and besides—they've already made all the arrangements.

For all prison visits there is the worry that the entire unit may be on lockdown when you arrive, and you won't even be able to visit at all. You can call or check the prison website before you begin your travels, but the prison may not have posted it—or a lockdown may occur *after* you call! In other words, you will not know if visitation has been cancelled until you are standing at the prison gate. However, the energy has been expended and the financial cost remains whether you get to visit or not.

Even calling to confirm whether your special visit has been approved offers no sense of security, because you can arrive at the prison and the paperwork has not been delivered to the gate. If the prison's office is closed for the weekend, and it probably will be, you can argue with the guards until you're blue in the face, but without that paperwork with the warden's John Hancock on it in their hot little hand, they won't honor that special visit. So, "It was a clerical error," and there's not a darn thing you can do about it. You accept the brief "regular" visit, or have no visit at all—and if you argue too long or too loudly the officer at the gate may deny the visit altogether and ban you from future visits!

So, you drive up to the prison unit already filled with anxiety and stress that continues to escalate. Procedures differ from prison to prison. At some, you simply park your car and lock it. At others the guards will stop you to search your car. They may be friendly—they may be all busi-ness; they may be curt and even disrespectful. You won't know until you roll down your window or they ask you to step out of the car to open your trunk and hood.

There may be a very long line waiting to get into visitation. I've waited in the hot Texas sun two hours to even be processed in for a visit. Others have waited longer.

The anxiety continues to escalate while you are cleared by the metal detector and the pat down search and electronic wanding and lifting each bare foot so they can see you have nothing hiding there. It is not until you begin nervously gathering your shoes and jacket and belt from the bucket on the conveyor belt that you can even begin to breathe nor-mally. Even then there is no sense of assurance that you will see your loved one until they are actually sitting right there in front of you.

No matter what the length of the visit, it is never long enough. There may be a few restless moments; perhaps some difficulty knowing what else to talk about, but those moments are fleeting and in your heart you never want to leave until they can walk out of the prison gate with you.

Then there is the searing pain of saying goodbye. Fighting back tears and attempting to appear casual as you pass guards and other visitors on the long walk out of the prison. Walking to your car is painfully depress-ing and you still face the long trip home. Each mile – No! Each inch you move away from the prison rips at your heart just a bit more. It takes a day or two to settle back into your daily routine. A deep sadness engulfs you as you stop occasionally throughout the following days to reflect on the visit.

Despite being extremely stressful and highly emotional for every-one, above all else prison visits are exceptionally prized by prisoners. Knowing someone cared enough to go through the rigors and scrutiny required to visit them is indescribably heartwarming to them. It is also painful for them to watch you leave; so painful in fact that the next time you plan a visit they may very well tell you not to come. They may even pick a fight so that you won't come, just so they can avoid that excruciating pain of departure. After all, there is no place for tears inside prison walls. However, when weighing the facts, most prisoners come to realize the visit itself is worth the residual pain they too experience for days, even weeks afterward.

Those who live closer to the prison or are just fortunate enough to be able to travel to visit frequently usually do not experience the same *intensity* of emotions that the long-distance-special-visiting-family might experience. However, they will experience all of the same emotions.

Unfortunately, most prisoners receive few or no visits during their entire period of incarceration regardless of the duration. First of all, the average prisoner in our country is housed 500 miles from their hometown. This makes visitation a virtual impossibility for most prison families. There are also personal reasons why a prison family may not visit, including anger at the prisoner for being incarcerated in the first place or for taking them on this prison family journey over and over again. There are also those family members who actually believe their loved one when they say they don't want the family to visit while they are in prison. So, they just don't go.

And, then there are sadly those families that are so desperately trying to meet their own needs that they just don't have the time or energy to share themselves with the prisoner.

There is a state prison unit just outside our city and several years ago, as a volunteer I had the opportunity to provide counseling there on a weekly basis for inmates who requested it. (That ended when a new warden arrived and put the kibosh on all volunteer programming.)

One prisoner I counseled was from the same city and when he provided his mother's address, I realized it was less than five miles from the prison unit. There were 1,100 prisoners at that unit, but on visiting days maybe only thirty or so had visits. However, since his family literally lived just down the street, of course I expected that they visited often.

"They have never been here," he said with obvious sadness.

"Why do you think that is?" I asked, trying to hide my surprise.

"They're really busy with their own lives. They don't have time," he said reciting a litany of busy activities essentially excusing his mother and various extended family members for their failure to drive up the street to visit him.

"Do you tell them you'd like them to visit?" I asked.

"No. I don't want to bother them," he said. Then he added with a tone of sarcastic anger, "It wouldn't matter if I did, they're just **too busy** to take the time to come **all the way out here**."

All the way out there! Five miles down a freeway? Three exits from their home? Too busy?

I had to wonder if they were too busy to visit the Wal-Mart located almost across the road from the entrance to the prison. What effort would it take them to turn left instead of right and drop in at the prison on occasion—even once a month? How busy could a family be?

In counseling, when things go wrong in a family it is important to look for the common denominator to the problems. If you can "fix" the common denominator, perhaps the problems can be minimized! So, of course I fished to learn more about his background.

In this young man's family there were four adult children. One brother was sentenced to prison for life for a murder in a drug deal gone wrong; another brother had just been released from prison after ten years for an aggravated assault, also the result of a botched drug deal; their sister had been in and out of the county jail for years for drug related offenses and the young man I was counseling was incarcerated for the third time for robberies—stealing to feed his drug addiction. Their father had been in and out of prison all of their lives for various offenses—most drug related. And the mother?

While I learned the young man's perception of his mother while he was incarcerated, it was not until he was released and I'd offered to take him to enroll in the local community college that I got a broader picture. His mother was totally oblivious to her role as the enabler in the family. This is the short version.

Although probably in her mid to late fifties, his mother was very youthful and attractive in appearance. She seemed intelligent, possibly well educated; dressed to the T's; beautifully coifed; nails done, etc. She actually had a well paying respectable job; lived in an upscale middle class neighborhood. Her home was very well appointed. But, despite the fact that all four of her children struggled with drug addictions and spent extensive time incarcerated, she avoided any mention of that fact and had never engaged them, let alone herself in any treatment program or counseling. She simply went about her life as though she had not a care in the world and the young man told me on our way to the college that his mother had arranged for a family celebration on the night he returned from prison. Despite having never visited her son in prison during his two year confinement, she celebrated his return by taking the whole family out to "Margaritas," a rowdy nightclub where beer and liquor were flowing. The young man later told me that his mother's live-in boyfriend had a plentiful stash of hard drugs and marijuana in their house.

It was fairly predictable that this young man returned to drugs soon after his release and he also returned to robberies and shoplifting to feed his drug habit. As a result, of course before a year was up, he returned to prison.

While certainly all families do not have the extreme dysfunctions as this young man's family, let's be totally honest: **all** families have troubles. If we take an honest look at our families, we can typically find the common denominator for those troubles and the common denominator is **not** always crime-related!

Let's take a side-trip on our prison family journey and look at who is in prison, and possibly why they are there, as this is the best time for a family assessment.

THE ROLES WE PLAY IN OUR FAMILY

In his play "As You Like It," William Shakespeare famously wrote:

"All the world's a stage. And all the men and women merely players."

So it is that each of us plays a role on the stage of life and all those around us are playing their own roles. No one is being real—not totally.

It is impossible to be all that we truly are at any one given time. Each of us plays a different and distinct role for every aspect of our life—our student role; our recreational role; our business role; our consumer role; our church role; our volunteer role—we even play a unique role in our own family whether it is our child role or our parent role or even our aunt or uncle role or grandparent role. In fact, we usually play our biggest role in life in the one place we should logically feel safest and most comfortable fully being our genuine self—in our own family. Each role we play fulfills a personal need. We acquire and play out our family role for a **self-serving purpose**. If we take an honest look at our families we can find the reason for that.

There is one universal truth about all families: a family is a system not unlike the system that runs our car. When one part of the system breaks down, it affects every other part of the system. For example, if the water pump blows up, the entire car stops running! One broken spark plug may allow the car to sputter and clunk along, but at a much slower than optimal pace. It's the same with our family.

Whether the one broken part of the family system is only in bed with the flu for a few days or whether they are in prison with a life sentence, *that broken part* of the family system slows down or even stops the *entire family system*. So, when one family member is broken all of the other members of the family system find themselves limping around in

146

an attempt to move forward while adapting and responding to the affects and needs of the broken part.

Another hard fact about systems that we often don't want to admit is that individual parts of that system typically break down due to **long term neglect or overly harsh handling**. The individual parts of the family system, just like our car's system, are less likely to break down if they are handled with care and regularly maintained. Isn't it interesting that some of us are more likely to devote the time and energy and even expense to maintaining our **cars** than we are willing to devote to maintaining our families?

The good news is that if the system breaks down, it can usually be repaired, although repairing it can be much more costly and often take much more time and effort than it would have taken to have regularly kept it maintained in the first place. But, it's better late than never. Maybe next time we'll do what it takes to keep the system in good repair!

The prisoner is only one member of that complex inter-related family system and their incarceration does affect every other family member—directly or indirectly. However, when a loved one goes to prison it is an opportune time for a family tune-up. It is a critical time to assess how well your family has functioned as a system and to repair what may be broken. This has nothing to do with blame. As adults, family members are responsible for their own decisions and choices of behavior. However, in all families there is always room for improvement.

***

In all families, prison families or not, each member of the family system plays a role to help them cope with any dysfunctions or *perceived* dysfunctions in their family. The greater the dysfunctions, the more evident the individual roles become. There is a distinct purpose for every role.

The Family Joker: This family member is a jokester! They seem to be really happy, because they are joking and laughing and making everyone else laugh all of the time. They are often the class clown and the life of the party! They are a barrel of fun, but in reality they are using their sense of humor to cleverly avoid intimacy. They may have loads of friends, but rarely do they have a healthy intimate relationship with anyone. By turning almost every situation into a joke they keep others from ever knowing their genuine thoughts and feelings. If they can keep laughing, and keep everyone else laughing they won't have to experience their own pain. They perceive their family as their source of pain; an unsafe place where the family members inflict pain on each other. The purpose of their role in the family is to lighten up the heaviness and discomfort and pain there. Ultimately, the Joker often turns to drugs or alcohol, self-medicating to ease their own pain so they can keep on laughing.

The Family Idol: This family member is a high achiever and often a perfectionist. From a very young age they assume serious responsibilities. As children, they rarely require correction and are admired and praised for their responsible behaviors. They excel in school and acquire responsible positions, such as becoming the class president or captain of the football team. As adults, they are successful in their occupations, often climbing the corporate ladder with apparent ease. They perceive their family as unhealthy and dysfunctional, and the purpose of their role is to make the family look good. The higher their achievements the more dysfunctional they perceive their family to be. They put so much pressure on themselves to "look good" and to single handedly make their family "look good" that they often snap when they can't handle the pressure any longer. Self medicating with drugs or alcohol is common to avoid feeling their pain and the strain of self imposed pressure to be perfect.

The Invisible One: This family member works very hard to make them self virtually undetectable by burying them self in their studies or gluing them self to the television or computer. While they may be a good student and a valuable employee they avoid interaction with others and definitely prefer pets to people. They recognize from a very young age that animals and inanimate objects won't hurt them the way people do. As a child on a school field trip or family vacation this is the one who is occasionally left behind, because no one even knew they were there in the first place. The purpose of their role is to keep peace in the family by avoiding any action or interaction that may lead to conflict. They find this is best accomplished by remaining silently invisible. They avoid confrontation or even the slightest disagreement by withdrawing and isolating from the family. They rarely state an opinion or even make a comment. If directly asked a question they will typically respond, "I don't know." They continually stuff their feelings placing them at risk for exploding from the growing internal pressure. In their attempt to avoid emotional pain they are likely to become workaholics and often alcoholics or drug addicts.

The Family Rebel: Of course the Rebel is the most visible and easiest to identify of all family roles. This is the acting out child who is constantly in the principal's office and often expelled or transferred to the alternative school. They talk back and fight and break all the rules often leading to breaking the law. As juveniles they may spend time in detention; as adults they often land in jail. They are the squeaky wheel in the family that gets all of the attention—all of the *negative* attention. They are risk takers and rough-housers and loud mouths who disrupt the classroom or rage angrily at their co-workers and bosses. They have a hard time keeping a job. The purpose of their role in the family is to distract everyone from the **real** family dysfunction by acting out the family pain. Quite often they become addicts and alcoholics and possibly verbally abusive and physically assaultive in their fruitless effort to manage their own emotional pain.

While the Family Rebel seems to be the most obvious family member to become incarcerated, **all** of the foregoing family members are at risk for incarceration. The Family Joker frequently becomes the addict or alcoholic involved in multiple DUI incidents, even killing others with their irresponsible behaviors. The Family Idol would be likely to pilfer from the cash register at work or commit white-collar crimes; embezzling or committing fraud to acquire needed funds to maintain their façade of perfection. However, the pressure from trying to maintain the perfect façade can also lead to explosive violence. The Invisible One stuffs their feelings to the point of explosion too, and in doing so they are at risk for addiction or alcoholism or even aggravated assaults and murder. All are seething with anger and rage. All are at risk for incarceration.

How do these family members become so terribly out of control?

The culprits may be found in two additional dominant roles in the family. Either or both are the likely common denominator.

The Family Enabler: Typically when you take a really close and totally honest look at the family system you will find at least one member who enables and even encourages these family roles to continue and escalate. The Family Enabler may actually look OK to outside observers. They may hold a responsible job and make a decent wage. However, they frequently whine and complain about how hard life is and how much they have to do, while at the same time continually picking up the pieces of their broken family and hiding the truth about their family from the outside world.

They are likely emotionally abused by other family members and may even be physically abused. However, they consistently cover up for the failures of other family members by making excuses for them: they create excuses for why a child's homework wasn't turned in; they fabricate reasons why an adult family member didn't show up for work and if worse comes to worst, they keep bailing them out of jail and may hide the fact that they were ever in jail in the first place.

The purpose of this role in the family is to create a façade of normalcy for the outside world and to maintain a semblance of equilibrium within the family system by not rocking the boat and by not allowing anyone else to rock the boat either. This family member may excessively use prescription drugs or alcohol in an effort to stabilize their emotions, possibly becoming addicted in an effort to manage their internal pain. It is not unusual for the Family Enabler to become a workaholic to achieve a degree of esteem and certainly to avoid being drowned in their own emotional pain.

The Sleeping Elephant: When things go wrong in families it can almost always be traced to a common denominator that is very evident to everyone, but never discussed inside or outside the family. It is like an enormous elephant is asleep on the easy chair smack in the middle of the living room. No one wants to wake it up by acknowledging it is really there, right in the center of their lives.

It might be a family member who is clearly an alcoholic or drug addict or one who is cruel and physically abusive. But it may also be a member of the family who is chronically ill or aged and frail, requiring constant daily care. It could be a situation that the family perceives (often unnecessarily) as highly embarrassing, such as a bankruptcy or the incarceration of a family member—or multiple family members. Very often, it may be a family secret that is generations old! The secret may only be known to some, but not all of the family members and whoever it is that is insisting on maintaining the secret is the real sleeping elephant. Whatever it is, while it may not seem to be such a big deal to others, it is a huge deal to the family members so they never mention it to anyone, not even to each other.

Keeping the secret requires that all of the family members tiptoe around the huge elephant sleeping in that easy chair in the middle of their living room. Everyone clearly knows the Sleeping Elephant is there, but no one has the courage to wake it up. Everyone who keeps the secret becomes a co-enabler.

As a note of explanation, family roles are distributed according to family size. In very small families the members may carry out multiple roles in any combination. For example, the Joker may also be the Family Idol and the Invisible One can also be the Joker. In fact, an only child in a dysfunctional family will play out all four roles, simultaneously. In larger families individual members assume one primary role, but to a lesser degree may evidence behaviors attributed to other roles. In exceptionally large families there will be a duplication of roles.

While there is usually only one primary Enabler, all family members play a role in enabling the Sleeping Elephant to remain asleep. While there is usually one primary Sleeping Elephant in the family, there are often multiple smaller Sleeping Elephants. For example, the primary Sleeping Elephant may be a raging alcoholic; however the family may also experience severe financial hardship and catastrophic illness and loss of jobs all at the same time. Those are smaller sleeping elephants, however they are usually the result of the effects of the primary Sleeping Elephant on the entire family—the actual common denominator for the family dysfunction.

You can decide whether the descriptions fit or not, and if you agree they do, it is then up to you to muster the courage to wake up the Sleeping Elephant and change the family dynamics by openly addressing it. It does take courage to wake a Sleeping Elephant, but if no one ever does, nothing will ever change. It often helps to have support, so you may want to seek professional help to wake and address any Sleeping Elephant you may find in your family.

———

When a family member is incarcerated there is the danger of placing **all** of the blame for family problems on the one in prison. After all, if they hadn't gotten themselves into such a mess the family wouldn't be suffering. However, it is very important to recognize that the one in prison may **not** be the family's *primary* Sleeping Elephant at all. In fact, their behavior that landed them in prison is quite likely to be a **symptom of the family dysfunction** that has been created by the real Sleeping Elephant and encouraged by the Enabler.

When a family member is incarcerated it becomes an opportune time to make an honest and fair assessment of where things went wrong and what improvements are needed in the family system. It is an opportune time, because the prisoner really is a "captive audience," and by the virtue of their incarceration all of the other family members can no longer deny that there is a real problem in the family. Now is just the time that family members may listen to some wisdom they refused to hear before. It is also an opportune time for other family members to make an assessment of their own role in the family and to determine how healthy it is or not to maintain that role.

Again, this is not a matter of blame. Incarceration of a loved one happens in all types of families—in all socio-economic classes; all races; all religions. Incarceration happens in fairly well functioning families, as well as seriously dysfunctional families. The point is that if incarceration occurs and the prisoner is actually guilty of the offense whether they or anyone else acknowledges guilt or not, something is wrong somewhere. Now is the time to find the crack in the family system and to work together to repair it so it won't break down again.

VISITATION PRACTICALITIES

Prison visitation is the one extended period of time the family has for face-to-face communication with the prisoner. It is the best time to address tough and uncomfortable issues and commit to working together to improve them. Therefore, if visitation is a possibility for families and friends, it is important to assure that nothing interferes with it. Like phone privileges, visitation is a privilege and not a right for the prisoner. By the same token visitation is considered a privilege, not a "right," for the family and friends of the prisoner. Following are some practical issues and guidelines to help keep the prison visitation door open for meaningful family interaction to take place.

1. Correct Information!

Be certain the prisoner has **accurately** placed you on their visitation list. If you are not on the prisoner's visitation list at all, when you show up at the prison you will not be allowed to visit. If the information on the visitor's list does not match the information on your driver's license or state ID, you will not be allowed to visit—certainly not without a huge hassle. So, Women! If you change your name on your ID because you get married, be sure the prisoner makes the change on the prison visitation list! Many women have married *the prisoner* and excitedly changed their name on their driver's license. Then, when they went to visit they could not get in to see their *now* husband, because that new name was not on the prisoner's visitation list!

In some cases visitation lists are also used to approve phone calls. If you are not on the prisoner's visitation list you may not be able to receive calls from them. If you change your name, the same thing also applies here. We've had numerous calls from recently married women who could not register to receive calls from the prisoner, because they were trying to register for phone service under their married name, when the prison visitation list showed their former name. The same holds true if you move and change your driver's license to reflect your new address. The address on the license must match the address on the prisoner's visitation list. Always double check the accuracy of the information entered into the prison's computer system. Everything must match!

Making changes on the prisoner's visitation list is not a simple task, because the prisoner must make the changes. They cannot simply pick up a phone and call the prison office and ask that the change be made. They must submit a written request and wait for the prison to make the requested change. This may not hold true for every prison system, but in Texas, while prisoners can put in a name or address change on their visitation list at almost any time, they can only change *who* is on their visitor's list every six months!

2. Special Visits

If you live a great distance from the prison you may be able to receive permission for special visits. Generally the distance must be at least 300 miles or more between your home and the prison unit before being considered. For some prisons it's 500 miles or more!

Special visits are longer than regular visits and they may extend to two days rather than only one. In Texas special visits last four hours, rather than two and may be allowed for two days, rather than one. However, we know a family that visits their loved one in Colorado, and they actually have two full eight hour days for their special visits! Some prisons even allow weekend visits, providing trailers where biological or legal family members may stay overnight a few times a year.

If you live far outside the stated distance and are fortunate enough to be able to visit frequently you may be *denied* special visits. One husband who was able to travel almost 700 miles to visit his wife every other weekend had been approved for the longer special visits. However, he arrived at the prison gate one Saturday where he was coldly informed his special visit was being "denied because he **came too often.**" Of course he argued the point, but to no avail. He said, "They say family visits are really important and that they 'encourage families to visit,' then turn you away like that! Just how important is *family* to the prison anyhow?"

The unvarnished truth is, "family" is of absolutely **no** importance to the prison. They can espouse niceties all they want, but the reality is that "family" is at best a *nuisance* to the prison. If the law did not provide for visitation, it is highly likely there would be no visitation, regardless of how important family is known to be to the successful reintegration of any prisoner.

Having said that, if you can visit only once or twice a year—regardless of distance, perhaps due to medical problems or lack of transportation, it won't hurt to call and ask about "special visits." Some prisons have made exceptions for elderly grandparents or terminally ill relatives, whether they live a great distance from the prison or not. It certainly cannot hurt to ask. The worst they can do is say "no!"

3. Know the Rules and Follow Them

Carefully read and adhere to all prison policies about visiting. Those rules are usually posted on prison websites and in the prison visitation area. There will be a limit to the number of visitors that can visit at one time and that number may or may not include visiting children. If only two adults are allowed at the same time, any additional people who travelled to see the prisoner must wait in the car or find another way to occupy the visitation hours. Some prisons allow "split visits." Half of the visitors may go into the prison for half of the visitation period and then leave, so the other half of the visitors may go in for the remainder of time. Always check the prison website first or call the prison unit for clarification.

4. Vehicles Searches

Always expect your car to be searched—under the hood; in the trunk; in the glove box and even underneath. Rules change from day to day, so although there may have been no vehicle searches the last ten times you visited, the next time they may be searching cars. Just plan for it and you won't have a problem. Some prisons may request your vehicle insurance before you can drive on the property. Take it with you, just in case. Always have your driver's license with you.

5. Follow the Dress Code.

Do not test the dress code. If it is not followed you won't be allowed inside the prison. Most prisons do not allow visitors to wear the same color clothing as the prison uniforms. Besides, prisoners see nothing but that color day in and day out, so give them a treat by wearing something bright and cheerful!

Women need to dress modestly. In Texas women cannot even wear sleeveless shirts, let alone plunging necklines or shorts or mini skirts. For goodness sake! What are some women thinking? They are not going to a night club; they are going to a prison! They may know their loved one is not going to think any less of them and won't cause them any harm, but consider the fifty or so other prisoners and their visitors who will be in the visitation area! These women don't know them and certainly don't know the taunting their loved one will receive from the guards and other inmates when they leave. It is best to dress in business casual clothing and you cannot go wrong.

Open toed shoes or sandals may not be allowed for men or women. This not only relates to modesty, but (according to the prisons) it also refers to "safety" in the event there is a need to move quickly, or run (although in 30-plus years of working, visiting and volunteering in prisons, I've never had that experience)!

Clothing should not be ripped or have holes in it no matter how stylish it is! T-shirts should be free from logos representing chemical substances, cults or violence or even rock groups that could be interpreted as a cult or promoting violence. Just wear a plain T-shirt and avoid the hassle. Women! Jeans do not need to be so tight they cut off your circulation and men—you too need to be dressed appropriately and sagging pants are **not** appropriate for a prison visit.

6. Keys, Driver's License and Allowable Money, Only....unless...

Adults and teens, take ONLY your car keys and driver's license or state ID with you when you enter the prison. Pre-teen children usually do not need an ID, although it is our understanding some prisons require a birth certificate proving the child is yours.

Empty all of your pockets. Lock purses and wallets and other possessions in your car trunk.

If you bring a baby or very young child, check the prison website to learn what you are allowed to take in for them. Most prisons allow a couple paper diapers and a bottle or two, but that is not uniform at all prison units. If the website is not clear, call the unit to ask what you can bring in for the baby.

If the prison allows cash to be taken in, often you may only bring coins for vending machines—no paper money. In other prisons you may only bring in one dollar bills! There is also a limit on the amount you can bring in to the prison, and by the way, in virtually all prisons, prisoners are not permitted to have cash, so **never** hand them the money—coins or bills.

Of course the prison makes money from the vending machines, so they are happy for you to stuff your quarters in their machines. Just be aware that the **machines don't always work**, and often will not return your money, and there is usually **no refund policy**.

I once watched (and heard) one father pounding away on a vending machine located about eight feet from where I was sitting for my visit. Apparently the machine had eaten the three dollars he had inserted for a dry, tasteless sandwich. The door he wanted would not open and so he began trying every other door; none would open.

We are not allowed to speak with other visitors, let alone prisoners, but he must have pounded on the machine for five full minutes; it was becoming annoying. So I turned around from my visit and told him, "It's not going to work; just consider it a donation."

When he asked, "Can I get my money back," I told him, "No," and asked if he needed more change for another machine.

There is really no reason to waste precious visitation time arguing with a dysfunctional machine. Consider your priorities for being there—are they to eat, or to visit? Just take more money with you than you expect to spend, in the event a machine eats some of your money.

Also, you might take in extra money to have pictures taken with your loved one. Prison staff picks up a few extra dollars to hold their annual Bar B Q or holiday party by taking pictures of you and the inmate. They may only do that once a month. You can call ahead to see if pictures will be taken while you are visiting and ask how much they are. You will probably be permitted to give the cash in bills to an officer upon entering the facility and they will later come around with the camera during your visit to take your picture.

If you take more money with you than permitted, you will be denied entrance and have to return to your car to dispose of the additional money (or bills if they are not allowed) and you must start the entire visiting process all over again. I watched a mother race to her car as I was entering the prison the last time I went to visit. She soon returned and cut in front of me in line. She turned to me and said, "I had a dollar bill in my pocket I didn't know was there; they told me to get rid of it or I couldn't come in, so I had to take it to the car." One dollar! Check those pockets.

7. Plan to be Searched—Pat Down and All

Body searches upon entering the prison are much the same as we are searched today at our airports. In all likelihood you will walk through a metal detector and be asked to remove shoes, jackets, belts, jewelry, etc. and put it all on a conveyor belt. You will likely even undergo a pat down search. There should be both a male and a female corrections officer available to do pat down searches of visitors of the same gender. They may ask you to show them the bottom of your (bare) feet. Some prisons require you to shake or run your fingers through your hair!

After doing that little barefoot dance and jumping through a few more hoops and possibly walking three city blocks to another building, you will finally make it to the visitation area! It will probably take a good while before your loved one comes into the visitation area. If you wait more than fifteen or twenty minutes, go to the visitation officer and ask (nicely) if they can check on your loved one. Sometimes, they will.

8. Don't talk to strangers!

Unless given permission do not talk with other visitors or prisoners. While it just seems like common courtesy to talk to someone else sitting alone and waiting for their visit, and it's certainly a nice way to pass the time while waiting, the prison does not allow you to talk to anyone in the visitation area other than the person you are visiting. While they may kindly remind you to stop talking, they have been known to toss out unrelated visitors who were talking to each other and **give their loved ones a case.** Just don't chance it!

9. Contact Visits or Through the Glass

Most prisons allow only biological or legally related relatives to have contact visits with prisoners. Non-relatives must visit through the glass, which may require talking on a phone receiver for the entire visit unless there is wire mesh or tiny drilled holes to speak through. That can become tedious. You may leave with a painful ear, but it's better than no visit at all!

If you have a contact visit, take care not to make any gestures that can be misinterpreted as passing items between yourself and your loved one. Countless numbers of visitors, including spouses have been banned from visitation for **years**, because they "*appeared* to be passing contraband." Of course no contraband was ever found, but nevertheless, if the officers even *think* you are doing something wrong, they can banish you from visitation forever, if they so choose. I've known many people who fought for years to get back in to see their loved one after being erroneously banished. In some cases the inmate was given a major case for some "misbehavior" **attributed to their visitor!** It's a nightmare you want to avoid at all cost.

If you have a contact visit, follow the rules about touching which generally allow a hug upon arrival and again when leaving, but may not allow you to touch one another any time in between (although some prison units actually allow hand holding). Just make certain. You don't want to be banished to non-visitor status because you patted your loved one on the hand. Maintaining visitation privileges is a much higher priority than to sacrifice that privilege for a pat on the hand.

10. Interaction with the Officers

While we certainly believe we all have a right to speak up for ourselves, there is usually a right way and a wrong way to do that. We need to remember the old adage: "You get more flies with honey than with vinegar," or better yet—"kill 'em with kindness"—when addressing the officers at the prison.

Let's preface this information by saying, "respect (usually) begets respect." Typically, if you have a question and ask it nicely, while it may not be so true for the inmates, as a visitor the officers will typically respond in kind. In fact, on several occasions I've even seen officers rush to aid elderly persons who fainted or passed out in visitation, which tells me that all of them are not totally heartless.

However, to be totally honest, I have had the opportunity to meet and interact with a good number of officers over the years and it quickly became clear that the majority seemed to either despise their jobs or to be so fearful of the inmates that they never smile or let their "bully face" guard down for even one second—even with volunteers or visitors. My thought has always been, "If you hate your job so much, go find another one. No one's forcing you to stay here." Good heavens! We spend the majority of our lives in the workplace. Why would anyone insist on remaining in a job that makes them miserable, unless they secretly enjoy misery?

On the other hand, there have been a handful of officers, both male and female, who clearly enjoy their jobs and interact in an appropriately amiable way with both inmates and outsiders. They seem quite capable of maintaining a professional posture that lets everyone know that they will treat you with respect, as long as you act in a respectful manner.

If you have a question, ask it politely with a smile and you are likely to receive a kind—or at least polite response in return. It may not be the response you were hoping for, but at least it will come to you respectfully.

If, despite your own kind and polite efforts, an officer becomes rude or hostile (and that does happen) **do not escalate the disagreement** into all out warfare. Note their name, which should be on their uniform, say their name so you will remember it and the following workday report their rudeness to the warden. Perhaps the warden will be able to answer your question or resolve your problem. However, if you create a scene in visitation, you will likely be asked to leave and may not be permitted to return.

If worse comes to worst, and you can find no resolution to your problem through the prison personnel, seek outside support through an advocacy group such a Prisoner's Family & Friends United (www. pffunited.org) or take the matter to your own State Representative. Sometimes it only takes a call or letter from an outsider to resolve problems incurred with officers or the system.

11. Rules Change

And finally—don't be surprised if the rules change with the wind once you arrive at the prison. What was acceptable last week may not be acceptable this week. What was acceptable with one officer may not be acceptable with another. If visits are important to you, simply go with the flow and adapt quickly.

Always remember that the visit itself is top priority and above all else, use visitation time productively and enjoy your time together as much as is possible.

TRAUMA IMPACT #5: GOING HOME

Who would ever have believed that the final step of your prison family journey would be almost as traumatic as your first?

All of these months and years of waiting, anticipating, praying this unwanted journey would end and now that the end is here, each member of the prison family is again filled with fear, anxiety and confusion. The announcement of the prisoner's release date takes everyone back to square one; as though you've just received the call informing you that your loved one was arrested and is in jail! Shock and disbelief are soon followed by inexplicable new fears and sudden tears of relief and joy not far behind. The feelings are totally unexpected; it seems irrational, but the feelings are very real. Try as you might, you can't shake them.

One father who had been a strong supporter and advocate for his son throughout his years of incarceration, eagerly counted down the days before his son was to return home. Proud of his son's accomplishments while incarcerated, he frequently announced his hopeful plans for his son's future to everyone who would listen.

When the actual date for his son's release was finally announced, he said, "I should be so excited, even relieved, but I feel more doubt and fear than excitement. I don't know what lies ahead for him. I don't know what lies ahead for us as a family. I'm actually scared for him and I'm even scared for us. I don't know what's happening to me. What happened to all of my excitement that he would soon be coming home?"

In another family, several weeks before her husband was to return home, one wife e-mailed almost desperately, "I don't know why I'm crying all the time for no reason. Last week I was jumping with joy when we received his discharge date. Today I was so depressed I could hardly get out of bed this morning. What's wrong with me?"

One former prisoner, out of prison only six months at the time, told me, "After ten years in prison you'd think I would have been ecstatic to be leaving it behind, but let me tell you, when I heard the electric gate slam behind me for the last time, I desperately wanted to turn back and go to the place of safety I'd created for myself on the inside."

Anxiety and doubt about the prisoner's return to the family and community are common emotions for **all** prison family members.

CHAPTER IV

"RETURNING CITIZENS"

Let's discuss using "politically correct terminology." At the most recent Prisoner's Family Conference one attendee confronted me with using the word "prisoner" to refer to—of all things—prisoners! I was told with some apparent coolness that there is a movement afoot to "call them PEOPLE."

OK!

There was certainly never any doubt in my mind that prisoners are "people!" However, in explaining various circumstances there are particular times that it seems necessary to use descriptive words to advance your point. Therefore, without intending any disrespect, I typically explain my concerns for people confined in houses of incarceration by using the descriptive word "prisoners."

Similarly, several years ago I was informed that people returning to the community from houses of incarceration (prisons) are now to be called "returning citizens" and not "reintegrating prisoners."

Oh my! Are we going too far with this political correctness; with attempting to coddle the feelings of all people at all times?

How then do we distinguish who we are discussing? After all, soldiers returning from war in a distant country are, in fact, "returning citizens." People who have traveled abroad for vacation are, in fact, "returning citizens" when they come home again! So, how will you know who I am talking about when I use the most recent politically correct term for a "person" who has been incarcerated in a prison and is returning to their hometown and family, if I simply refer to them as "a person?"

No offense is intended, but in the work I do I find it necessary to call a prisoner "a prisoner" and a "returning prisoner" seems to best describe those who have ended their prison stay and are returning to the community! I know those **people** are, in fact, **returning citizens**. I hope you will understand, if the most recent politically correct terms are not used.

When you consider all of the facts it really is not surprising that community re-entry and family reunification is another source of trauma for the entire prison family. In fact, fear and apprehension about the prisoner's return is completely predictable.

Now that you have learned to live as a prison family, you must rearrange your lives all over again to live as a free world family. Just the thought of that can be overwhelming. Now that each of you has learned what to expect as a prison family, you must start to live with all of the unknowns once again. How has everyone changed? Will he/she revert to former behaviors? How has prison affected him/her? Am I ready to share my life with him/her on a daily basis—24/7? The questions themselves become overwhelming, because they are questions with no answers. Living with all of the unknowns begins again.

Regardless of how well each of you has prepared for re-entry and reunification *before* the prisoner's release, you will experience this emotional turmoil when the reality of the release date is before you.

Rather than belabor the topic, we want to present you with one of the best and most accurate resources we have come across in thirty years on the topic of "re-entry." It is from the prisoner's perspective, but the information is absolutely accurate and **something all prison family members should prepare for**.

The following data was developed by Boston College: School of Theology and Ministry – Prison Ministries Initiatives. It appears this data was distributed at a 2010 conference on prisoner re-entry. We wish we had actually been at this conference, but didn't learn of it until two years after the fact when this information appeared on Facebook! Not realizing at the time how valuable the information would be, regrettably we did not maintain the link. However, we are grateful to Boston College – Prison Ministries Initiatives for their obvious commitment to prisoners, and thereby their families.

We believe this information is of such value that we insert it here, exactly as we found it.

PSYCHO SOCIAL PROFILE OF NEWLY RELEASED PRISON INMATES

1. Post-release shock and disorientation (no fixed bearings)
2. Lack of Continuity/follow through (flaky behavior)
3. Suppressed hostility (seething rage and undifferentiated hate)
4. Lethargy: often extreme social withdrawal and psychological denial
5. Deep-based depression (frequently chronic) resulting in mal-adaptive behavior
6. Financially destitute with a growing sense of anxiety and desperation
7. False expectations and illusions on a multitude of personal and social levels
8. Intense range of fears: personal failure, social and vocational rejections, etc.
9. Severe alienation (man from Mars); often intense, long-term social isolation

10. Cultural shock: cannot relate or adapt to social change and new tempo of life
11. Poor to non-existent problem solving and conflict resolution skills
12. Engulfed in the prison value system; kindness is weakness
13. Personal and cultural inferiority complex ("branded and banished")
14. Compulsive neurotic behavior; minimal stability (addictive mentality)
15. Hunger for instant gratification: "All I want is EVERYTHING, NOW."
16. Poor self esteem/hungry for approval (often actively resistant to disapproval)
17. Compulsive drive to "catch up and catch back"; extreme impatience
18. Confused and frustrated sexual roles, values and identities
19. Emotionally and perceptually distorted view of self and others
20. Limited employment related skills and out of touch with current market needs
21. Frequently displaying self-destructive attitudes and actions ("bad attitude")
22. A fragile and vulnerable grip on life itself!

As your family moves through the re-entry process, you all will recognize most, if not all of these behaviors. While each and every item on this listing is vital to prepare for, we want to emphasize a few of these items, because our experience tells us they are most disturbing and frequently the fuel for many other items on this list. Therefore they become the primary cause for recidivism.

#3. Suppressed hostility (seething rage and undifferentiated hate)

To earn parole; to avoid danger; to just survive in prison, prisoners must suppress their emotions. Year after year the prisoner conditions them self **"not to feel."** On the outside they may have created an appearance of calm, even stoic tranquility, while on the inside they are "seething" with rage, hostility and hatred fueled by years of humiliation, inequity and injustice at the hands of less than caring often inhumane administrators of the prison system. They have witnessed gruesome brutality and often experienced the humiliation and downright savagery of other inmates as well as prison administrators. Much of what prisoners have seen and what they have experienced has never been shared with anyone. Of necessity, they have buried a plethora of emotions, just to survive.

Once the prisoner returns home, although their expression of these horrid emotions is most likely not intended to be directed at you, *you* become the AVAILABLE target. The INTENDED target (the criminal justice system; other prisoners; prison officials) is not available to them any longer. Therefore, YOU will witness **and receive** the brunt of these emotions.

It is important to always remember that prisoners see and experience things that most of their loved ones will never see or experience in a lifetime. While they may share what seems like a lot about their prison experience, they can and will NEVER share it all. Even if they do tell us of having witnessed a vicious and bloody assault or repugnant sexual act, we will never be able to comprehend the repugnance of what was actually witnessed. Because these dreadful acts occur so frequently, prisoners literally emotionally deaden themselves, becoming desensitized to these horrific acts. What they are unable to tell us remains bottled up within them like a vat of nitroglycerine ready to explode at the drop of any perceived accelerant—or even with no accelerant at all.

What we must keep in mind is that prison is a very dark place. Not that we should feel sorry for our loved one; not that we should coddle the prisoner or the returning prisoner because things were so bad for them—that kind of sympathy only serves to infantilize them and make them helpless and dependent. But we must maintain a healthy degree of empathy (NOT sympathy) to avoid interpreting their anger personally.

Empathy is the expression of objective and helpful caring.
Sympathy is caring too much,
So much that you become part of the problem.

#4. Lethargy; often extreme social withdrawal and psychological denial.

We are so excited to have our loved one home we want to share everything with them—everything we've wanted to share with them all the while they've been gone—and we want to share it with them as quickly as possible, in hopes that they will "catch up" quickly with us and with the free world.

The returning prisoner is also eager to get started on their second chance at life, and although many know it is unrealistic, most have a burning desire to make up for lost time. That is **impossible** and to even attempt to achieve it sentences the returning prisoner to failure. Social immersion is **absolutely the wrong thing** for a newly released prisoner. In fact, it is **dangerous**.

One former prisoner we know had been out of prison about seven years when we invited him and his wife to a social gathering. While he appears to have fairly well reintegrated into society—he's married; he's working; he's clearly intelligent and articulate and even appears pleasantly sociable—but, he responded to the invitation by saying, "I appreciate that you want me to join in these activities, but to be honest I'm just not ready for large groups of people; I prefer one on one or a couple of people, but not a crowd. I hope you understand."

Good for him! He has learned his limits; he has learned to stay within his safety zone and he has learned to speak up for his limitations in an appropriate manner.

The gentleman mentioned above is actually an exoneree. That means he spent over twelve years in prison for a crime he did not commit. Therefore, he obviously did not return to the community with the same stigma of an ex-convict, a felon, as other returning citizens do.

He also did not have the burden of being released from prison on parole or probation, requiring extraordinary demands in addition to the typical throes of reintegration. Never-the-less, having spent over twelve years in the confines of prison his adjustment to the free world has been quite similar to that of any felon returning to the community. His wife once mentioned that when he first came home he would barely venture outside their back door for months. Therefore, he's clearly come a long way in the past seven years, moving ahead at his own, steady but slow pace

Unfortunately, "steady and slow" is not possible for those released from prison on parole or probation.

The absolute unvarnished truth is that the criminal justice system itself is designed to set up returning prisoners for failure. Within 24 business hours of release, the newly released prisoner is ordered to report to their local parole or probation office. (State prisons release prisoners on "parole;" the Federal system releases prisoners on "probation.")

Upon reporting to their assigned officer (who typically has an unmanageable caseload of one hundred or more parolees or probationers) the newly released prisoner is inundated with demands—unrealistic expectations including the immediate – YES, IMMEDIATE necessity to find a job. After all, they have fines and fees that must be paid, and it is the officer's duty to assure they get paid. From the immediate outset it becomes clear that the officer and returning citizen, as well as their family are on entirely different pages with entirely different agendas, the disparity of which is often the recipe for failure.

EVA'S REALITY

Having come upon an article espousing "Five Tips" for helping spouses of incarcerated individuals prepare for reintegration. I e-mailed the article to Eva, a counselor and long time friend, whose husband, Ray had returned from prison a couple years before, to inquire how helpful these tips might be for reintegrating couples. Her interesting and informative responses are copied exactly as she responded—typos and all! This is "Eva's Reality." It is likely most reunited families will find it much like their own reality.

On Fri, 30 Jul 2010 16:03:20 -0700 (PDT) Eva E <lp@xxx.com> writes:

my responses are in **this bold font!**

Eva K. LPC

Five Tips to Keep from Becoming Divorced after Your Spouse is Released
By ALEX KECSKES

So how do couples survive the prison experience? How do they stay married and raise a family when all the odds and statistics are stacked against them? Here are five tips to survival for ex-cons who want to keep their marriage alive while they rebuild their lives.

1. Have realistic expectations.

Don't go on a trip to Disneyland, throw a big party, or dwell on all the great sex you're going to have. Concentrate first on helping your spouse prepare for life outside of prison. Remember, they're used to a slower, controlled, regimented life, where food, shelter and medical care have been taken care of. **If you have never been involved in an inmate returning home, you have nothing but unrealistic expectations, because somewhere in the back of your head you're thinking, yes, but, not me, not my spouse. We are unique, we are different. no one is prepared for the changes that takes place in their loved one while being incarcerated. ray and i were in constant communication, wrote to each other faithfully, the man that i got to know while in prison was not the man that came home. Neither of us was prepared for the anger and rage that he experienced weeks, months, and even years after release. i did not plan any big parties for him, in fact i told everyone to stay back and give him a chance to adjust for at least the first year. we went very slow about his meeting friends and family and it was still overwhelming for him. i was told that the first thing he would want upon release was a big fat steak, so i was prepared to take him out for steak. He wasn't even interested. In fact he couldn't make up his mind what he wanted to eat. So he let me choose and without even thinking we went to a buffet. it was too much for him. By the time we got thru the salad and entree and on to dessert he said, "you pick something"**

2. Get them organized.

Your newly released spouse will need help with things like entitlements, even before they embark on a job search. Help them find a case manager who can get all the paperwork together and filed. Don't try to get them a job, case manager, apartment, enrolled in school, and buy a car all in the same week. **The Parole officer was the one that wanted sixty things done all at once. She had him on an ankle monitor before he ever left the facility, we had 4 hours to get to his mother's house and report in, I had never driven from Huntsville to Dallas before. I didn't know the directions or how long it would take. Of course there was construction and detours. Things had changed since Ray had last been out. So we were late and that created tension. the next day we had to report to his PO and she hit him with a big bag of ugly, started barking orders and making demands, had so much time to get everything done and still be in on time, find work attend meetings, provide random monitoring, all this without transportation.**

3. Help them find a job.

There are many public and private resources you can both use to help your spouse find gainful employment. Encourage them to participate in every worthwhile program offered by public and private resources. Make sure they keep appointments for job interviews. If they can't be there on time or they need to cancel, notify the person they were scheduled to see. **We were given the names of a couple organizations to contact, but if men won't ask for directions what makes a person think they will ask for help? i had to leave him in Texas to fend for himself and return to Colorado for work. so i was not available to help with the organization and appointments**

4. Don't get paranoid about people finding out your spouse was in prison.

There is no central file in some all-knowing computer with everything about your spouse. DOCS, Medicaid, their doctor — all have separate files in their computers, but these computer systems are not linked together, and each has information that they can't share with the others. Ordinary people who have a computer can't access this information. **My support system knew Ray had been in prison, I had no problem with it but he sure did. I can't help but think it's the former inmates that think worse of themselves than perhaps the general public. Most everyone i talked with had at least one family member that had been incarcerated and understood that it happens to eveyone. a former inmate i had been counseling told me she was a felon, i said you mean a former felon and she said no i will always be a felon. That kind of mentality is detrimental, she refused to think of herself any other way.**

5. Don't let your spouse revert back to the criminal lifestyle.

Always encourage them to be the best person they can be. Keep your spouse away from the unsavory characters they hung around with just before they broke the law. Be ever vigilant of drug or excessive alcohol use. And don't let your spouse violate parole. **i did everything i could to encourage ray to avoid the old people, places, and habits. but in the end, the individual will do what they want and there was very little i could do to stop it. no amount of persuasion, arguing, screaming, threats, leaving did any good at all. it's been 2 1/2 years since ray was released and he is looking at a year in county for another DUI, and has been inpatient twice this past year.**

In summary, I'd have to say, the theory is good, but theory doesn't always work out in real time. Will things be better when he comes home again? Time will tell. I support gradual reintegration with massive family counseling but even then, you can take a horse to water...........

Reality!

Eva's experience is so very typical. Fortunately, it has been over five years now since Ray was released. He did relapse several times; he spent more time in jail and treatment programs. The last year has been better. Parole demands have lessened, which helps greatly.

Returning to the Boston College profile for newly released prisoners. This is another area of exceptional concern:

#11. Poor to non-existent problem solving and conflict resolution skills. (In some ways this relates to #12, about being engulfed in prison values – kindness is a weakness.)

Prisoners make very few decisions during their confinement. Their days begin when the prison says they begin; their activities are determined by the schedule, rules and regulations of the prison; they eat when told to eat; they work when told to work; they don't even open a door on their own, and yes, humiliating as it is they even go to the bathroom as determined by the guards in the prison. They have few, if any options to choose from. Creative thinking may occur, but it is not encouraged by the prison. As a result it may require deviancy to resolve problems simply to meet needs. **If prisoners learn anything in prison about problem solving, it is to keep their mouths shut and to avoid expressing their feelings.**

Effective problem solving and resolving conflicts requires having options and being creative. In the free world "creativity" would mean that successful problem solving and conflict resolution would necessarily remain within the bounds of written and unwritten laws and **there would be options to choose from**! However, if you have no options, as is usually the case in prison, there is no decision to make and you either do nothing about your problem and learn to live with it, or you risk doing something devious and if found out, get punished for it.

As Eva notes in her e-mail response, Ray was overwhelmed by even making a choice about food in a cafeteria. For years he had eaten the one option served or he didn't eat at all. Once in the free world the returning citizen is inundated with a multitude of choices and as though life were one enormous cafeteria, the options become overwhelming. It will take a great deal of time for the returning citizen to even begin to learn how to weigh options and make good choices.

RECIDIVISM

Despite prisoners' persistent vows to never return to prison again, recidivism across our country has remained at an average of 65% for eons and shows no sign of improving. While the failure of our prison system to "rehabilitate" prisoners in any form or fashion is the primary culprit for the extraordinary number of prisoners who return to prison, another culprit is the entire prison family's lack of understanding of what to realistically expect when a prisoner returns to the community and the family.

The Boston College School of Theology and Ministry – Prison Ministry Initiative data provides a very honest and realistic view of what the reunified prison family can expect over the **FIVE (5) YEARS following the prisoner's re-entry.**

PREDICTABLE STAGES OF POST RELEASE ADAPTATION

1-2 weeks	Multilevel shock, grief & mental disarray!
3-6 weeks	Lost in dense fog; numb; passive attitude
7-12 weeks	Bouncing off the walls; high-stress level
3-6 months	Body out; mind in; very frustrated
6-12 months	Daily life on a runaway roller-coaster

12-18 months	Just hanging on; sick of being out of control
18-24 months	Building a house of cards; a fragile construct
24-30 months	Finally free, now what? What source of power?
30-36 months	Hungry for progress, but fearful and uncertain
36-42 months	Three year itch; another major turning point
42-48 months	Leap of faith...afresh commitment to the future

60 months forward – Begin shift from mere survival to quality of life

The unvarnished truth is that our **prisons fail on an average of 65% of the time**. To put that in perspective, consider this:

If surgeon lost 65% of their patients each year for decades, what would you expect would happen to that doctor?

In a less life-threatening realm, if a teacher failed 65% of their students each year for decades, what would you expect would happen to that teacher?

We're sure you get the picture! In fact, we all know that neither the surgeon nor the teacher would have been allowed to continue working, and it would never have taken decades to terminate them. However, we have allowed our prisons to fail 65% of the time for decades, and we have **rewarded** them by actually paying them (via our taxes) to grow larger and larger so that they can continue to fail 65% more of the time.

Because our prisons fail 65% of the time, the most prevalent statistic is that the majority of released prisoners return to prison within three years of their release. In part, much recidivism occurs due to technical violations of parole/probation (missed or late for appointments; not finding employment; not paying fines and fees; dirty UA's; violating curfews, etc.) and not for committing a new crime. However, when we consider that at one year out of prison the typical newly released prisoner is still on an emotional roller coaster and by two years has not established a firm foundation for life in the free world, we can understand their continued fear and uncertainty at *three years* places them at continued risk for reoffending.

Lack of community support plays a huge role in prisoner recidivism.

Of the more than 315-million people living in the United States, almost seven million adults were under the supervision of corrections in 2011. (U.S. Census and U.S. Bureau of Justice statistics.)

We can presume that those seven million adults—at least the vast majority of them, came from families. For example, the Federal Bureau of Prisons estimates that fifty-four percent of all prisoners have children. Using the typical 2.5 children per family estimate, that would indicate that over seven million children have parents who are incarcerated in local jails and state and federal prisons.

Just counting prisoners and their children, 14-million people in this country are directly affected by incarceration! But, what about the untold number of parents, siblings, spouses and other relatives of prisoners? Mathematically speaking I can already see that this is way out of my league! But, suffice it to say that a very large portion of our population is directly impacted by incarceration. However, an even larger portion of the population is not.

Those who have not (yet) been impacted by incarceration rarely give prison/prisoners/prison families a single thought, unless called to jury duty or unless faced with the (frightening) dilemma of housing or hiring a returning prisoner. Then, suddenly they snap to attention.

I guess I've been fortunate in that we have owned our own home since I became an adult. However, about twelve years ago I moved from Colorado back to Texas on very short notice and was faced with renting a place to live. I contacted a realtor who showed me several places and when I finally settled on one, she stated, "Well, if the background check clears, we'll make out the rental contract."

"Background check?" I questioned.

"Oh yes, my dear," she came back firmly, "All rental companies, and certainly public housing have to carefully assure we aren't renting to felons, you know."

Of course I knew that, having worked with those "felons" for over twenty years at the time. But, to hear it so blatantly stated was stunning.

So, where do "felons" live when they are released from prison? Surely a realtor would know the answer.

"Well, where do felons go to live when they are released from prison?"

"Who cares?" she snapped back. "As long as they don't live in our rentals, I could care less."

OK. So, all returning felons can sleep under bridges. The State of Florida had a scandal on its hands not so long ago when the media exposed the fact that hundreds of ex-offenders were holed up in free-way underpasses and even more were setting up lean-to communities on vacant land outside of major cities. Of course there was no electricity or plumbing, but felons surely don't need lights or toilets, do they?

If not under bridges, surely returning citizens can all live in homeless shelters.

So, what about employment for ex-offenders? Surely they must work, or how do they get food and clothing and even medication if they become sick?

I will say that federal probationers (at least in our city) do have some positive support. Our federal probation office even holds job fairs by actively seeking local employers who are willing to hire ex-offenders. Federal probation also offers employers a bit of liability insurance, if they will hire a returning prisoner. As I recall, it was $5,000.00 coverage for six months in the event the felon they hire takes off with inventory or tools or cash! In fact, the federal government even gives tax breaks to employers who hire returning prisoners (state or federal prisoners). However, even with those perks, most employers are too frightened to hire those with felony records.

It is interesting to note that in a survey provided by Prison Fellowship some years ago, they learned that the primary reason employers are fearful of hiring felons is *not* out of fear that they would steal or even cause them any physical harm. The survey results indicated the primary reason most employers were fearful of hiring ex-offenders was that they would not have the *appropriate social skills* to interact with their customers! That fear of course was followed by the fear of stealing and being physically harmed by the ex-offender.

This past year a former prisoner who had been successfully working in the community for over a year decided to move to a new community for family reasons. With a good work history and an excellent reference from his current boss, he felt fairly confident that he could land a job in the new community with little difficulty.

Months later I was receiving discouraging e-mails from this young man. He was finding, of course, that potential employers seemed very impressed with him until he handed them a completed application on which there was always the question, "Have you ever been convicted of a felony?" He knew it would be grounds for immediate termination if he falsified the information by checking "no," so he tried writing, "Will discuss in person" on the applications. Of course this statement was a dead give-away that the actual answer to the question was "yes."

Fortunately, this young man had family support in his new town, so at least he wasn't homeless as he continued his frustrating search for work.

Then one day he excitedly called me and announced that he had just been interviewed for the **second time** by one man who actually seemed to be seriously considering him for a position. He had told the potential employer to call me for a reference, and wanted to give me a heads up in the event that the man might actually call.

The next day, the employer did call me. It seemed he was not so interested in the young man's qualifications or capabilities for doing the job. In fact, he informed me that the young man was "overqualified" for the position he had open. He said he was calling because he was "afraid" the young man would "explode unpredictably" and "run off all of our customers." He was seeking reassurance that this would not happen.

I suppose my inability to stifle laughter at his question did no harm, as after about an hour on the phone with this employer, he made the bold decision to hire the young man, who has now remained employed without incident for almost a year.

This employer is "one in a million." At least he was willing to remain open to the possibility of hiring an ex-offender. At least he was willing to ask questions and learn. Most employers are not so willing. Therefore employment opportunities for returning prisoners are exceptionally scarce. Most returning citizens find their best resources are day labor jobs, for which many are exceptionally overqualified. Rarely does a returning citizen find a job that matches their true capabilities.

Recently someone e-mailed me a lengthy list of potential employers who stated they were open to hiring ex-offenders. Excitedly I began reviewing the list. There were at least 100 companies listed on the attachment. Surely these companies deserved to be applauded for opening their doors to hiring former prisoners. Then I noticed that all of the businesses listed were enormous conglomerates having head offices in major metropolitan areas and numerous branches throughout the country.

As I reviewed the lengthy list, my eyes caught the names of some companies that had branches in our community and I recognized that these were businesses that had adamantly refused to hire ex-offenders in the past. So, I began reading the *question* that had been posed to the head offices of these large companies. It read, "*Will your business consider hiring those with felony records?*"

Well, of course! Of course they would **consider** it, but actually **doing** it would be a far different matter! So the head offices sounded quite gallant in their "willingness" to hire ex-offenders. However they weren't the ones doing the actual hiring! The local branches which had the actual hiring responsibility were certainly not so fearless!

Shunned by the community; unable to find housing; unable to acquire employment and almost definitely unable to find *satisfying* employment, of course the majority of former prisoners lose hope and resort to returning to former lifestyles just to survive, ultimately returning to prison in record numbers.

POST-TRAUMATIC STRESS

While we typically want to believe, "When the going gets tough, the tough get going," for the former prisoner who recognizes they aren't as tough as they thought they would be upon returning to the community, when things get tough and seem to take forever to come together for them, they are prone to give up and say, "What's the use. Nothing is working."

This does not mean we should all be walking on egg shells for six or seven years. However, as unpopular as some people might find this, the facts should remind us that the prisoner is not unlike the soldier returning from war. While the nobility of the "mission" is distinctly different, *the trauma is the same.* In fact the entire prison family suffers from post-traumatic stress as the result of their loved one's incarceration. Prison is the prisoner's "war zone" and their family is experiencing their "soldier" returning from a very private war. The entire prison family is experiencing "post-traumatic stress."

Post-traumatic stress or as it is called in its most severe form, post-traumatic stress disorder (PTSD) is a very real diagnosable mental health condition that while treatable, vestiges will remain for a lifetime.

This is what the National Institute of Mental Health (NIMH) has to say (in part) about PTSD:

WHAT IS POST-TRAUMATIC STRESS DISORDER, OR PTSD?

PTSD is an anxiety disorder that some people get after seeing or living through a dangerous event.

When in danger, it's natural to feel afraid. This fear triggers many split-second changes in the body to prepare to defend against the danger or to avoid it. This "fight-or-flight" response is a healthy reaction meant to protect a person from harm. But in PTSD, this reaction is changed or damaged. People who have PTSD may feel stressed or frightened even when they're no longer in danger.

WHO GETS PTSD?

Anyone can get PTSD at any age. This includes war veterans and survivors of physical and sexual assault, abuse, accidents, disasters, and many other serious events.

Not everyone with PTSD has been through a dangerous event. **Some people get PTSD after a friend or family member experiences danger or is harmed.** The sudden, unexpected death of a loved one can also cause PTSD. (Emphasis added.)

WHAT ARE THE SYMPTOMS OF PTSD?

PTSD can cause many symptoms. These symptoms can be grouped into three categories:

1. Re-experiencing symptoms:

Flashbacks—reliving the trauma over and over, including physical symptoms like a racing heart or sweating

Bad dreams
Frightening thoughts.

Re-experiencing symptoms may cause problems in a person's everyday routine. They can start from the person's own thoughts and feelings. Words, objects, or situations that are reminders of the event can also trigger re-experiencing.

2. Avoidance symptoms:

Staying away from places, events, or objects that are reminders of the experience
Feeling emotionally numb
Feeling strong guilt, depression, or worry
Losing interest in activities that were enjoyable in the past
Having trouble remembering the dangerous event.

Things that remind a person of the traumatic event can trigger avoidance symptoms. These symptoms may cause a person to change his or her personal routine. For example, after a bad car accident, a person who usually drives may avoid driving or riding in a car.

3. Hyperarousal symptoms:

Being easily startled
Feeling tense or "on edge"
Having difficulty sleeping, and/or having angry outbursts.

Hyperarousal symptoms are usually constant, instead of being triggered by things that remind one of the traumatic event. They can make the person feel stressed and angry. These symptoms may make it hard to do daily tasks, such as sleeping, eating, or concentrating.

It's natural to have some of these symptoms after a dangerous event. Sometimes people have very serious symptoms that go away after a few weeks. This is called acute stress disorder, or ASD. When the symptoms last more than a few weeks and become an ongoing problem, they might be PTSD. Some people with PTSD don't show any symptoms for weeks or months.

HOW IS PTSD TREATED?

The main treatments for people with PTSD are psychotherapy ("talk" therapy), medications, or both. Everyone is different, so a treatment that works for one person may not work for another. It is important for anyone with PTSD to be treated by a mental health care provider who is experienced with PTSD. Some people with PTSD need to try different treatments to find what works for their symptoms.

If someone with PTSD is going through an ongoing trauma, such as being in an abusive relationship, both of the problems need to be treated. Other ongoing problems can include panic disorder, depression, substance abuse, and feeling suicidal.

HOW CAN I HELP A FRIEND OR RELATIVE WHO HAS PTSD?

If you know someone who has PTSD, it affects you too. The first and most important thing you can do to help a friend or relative is to help him or her get the right diagnosis and treatment. You may need to make an appointment for your friend or relative and go with him or her to see the doctor. Encourage him or her to stay in treatment, or to seek different treatment if his or her symptoms don't get better after 6 to 8 weeks.

To help a friend or relative, you can:

Offer emotional support, understanding, patience, and encouragement.
Learn about PTSD so you can understand what your friend or relative is experiencing.
Talk to your friend or relative, and listen carefully.
Listen to feelings your friend or relative expresses and be understanding of situations that may trigger PTSD symptoms.
Invite your friend or relative out for positive distractions such as walks, outings, and other activities.
Remind your friend or relative that, with time and treatment, he or she can get better.

Never ignore comments about your friend or relative harming him or herself, and report such comments to your friend's or relative's therapist or doctor.

HOW CAN I HELP MYSELF?

It may be very hard to take that first step to help yourself. It is important to realize that although it may take some time, with treatment, you can get better.

To help yourself:

Talk to your doctor about treatment options.
Engage in mild activity or exercise to help reduce stress.
Set realistic goals for yourself.

Break up large tasks into small ones, set some priorities, and do what you can as you can.

Try to spend time with other people and confide in a trusted friend or relative. Tell others about things that may trigger symptoms.

Expect your symptoms to improve gradually, not immediately.

HOW CAN I HELP A FRIEND OR RELATIVE WHO HAS PTSD?

If you know someone who has PTSD, it affects you too. The first and most important thing you can do to help a friend or relative is to help him or her get the right diagnosis and treatment. You may need to make an appointment for your friend or relative and go with him or her to see the doctor. Encourage him or her to stay in treatment, or to seek different treatment if his or her symptoms don't get better after 6 to 8 weeks.

To help a friend or relative, you can:

Offer emotional support, understanding, patience, and encouragement.

Learn about PTSD so you can understand what your friend or relative is experiencing.

Talk to your friend or relative, and listen carefully.

Listen to feelings your friend or relative expresses and be understanding of situations that may trigger PTSD symptoms.

Invite your friend or relative out for positive distractions such as walks, outings, and other activities.

Remind your friend or relative that, with time and treatment, he or she can get better.

Never ignore comments about your friend or relative harming him or herself, and report such comments to your friend's or relative's therapist or doctor.

HOW CAN I HELP MYSELF?

It may be very hard to take that first step to help yourself. It is important to realize that although it may take some time, with treatment, you can get better.

To help yourself:

Talk to your doctor about treatment options.
Engage in mild activity or exercise to help reduce stress.
Set realistic goals for yourself.
Break up large tasks into small ones, set some priorities, and do what you can as you can.
Try to spend time with other people and confide in a trusted friend or relative. Tell others about things that may trigger symptoms.
Expect your symptoms to improve gradually, not immediately.
Identify and seek out comforting situations, places and people.

Chapter V

"THE CHILDREN OF PRISONERS"

Undoubtedly you did not actively seek the role of caregiver for a child or children of a prisoner. However, if you are a caregiver for a child of a prisoner, you are not alone.

- Over 2.5 million children in the United States have a parent in prison.
- 1 of every 7 children in the United States' classrooms has a parent or parents in prison or on probation or parole.
- The vast majority of children of prisoners are cared for by their remaining parent (usually the mother) or by relative caregivers—grandparents; aunts and uncles.

As this country moves more and more into privatization of prisons, more and more parents will be incarcerated. As a private industry the prison system will only increase in size to ensure its investors make a profit at the expense of many families. As the caregiver of a child or children of a prisoner you are encouraged to join advocacy groups fighting to stop the growth of the prison system before more children are traumatized, because the incarceration of a parent (or any other close loved one) **is traumatic** to children.

Incredibly, 70% of children of prisoners will ultimately become prisoners themselves. This tragedy is rarely the result of poor parenting. This tragic statistic is primarily the result of the children having been traumatized by the incarceration of their loved one.

This is what happens to the vast majority of children when their parent goes to prison:

- They mourn and grieve the absence of their parent; even infants grieve.
- They realize the stigma related to "prison" and withdraw and isolate in shame.
- They feel rejected and abandoned.
- They feel powerless and helpless.
- They begin acting out their fears and pain.
  - o Their school performance plummets;
  - o They become truant from school;
  - o They begin to disrespect authority figures, especially law enforcement;
  - o They join gangs for a sense of belonging;
  - o They turn to alcohol and drugs to numb emotional pain;
  - o They resort to violence to express their outrage.
- They experience post-traumatic stress like the rest of the prison family.

In some ways the prison family experience is much more difficult for children than it is for adults. This is because children are all too often left out of the loop when families discuss serious issues and the incarceration of a loved one is definitely a serious issue that is rarely discussed openly with children.

When children are left out of discussions they can only resort to *imagining* what is being said behind closed doors. As with most of us children's imaginations conjure up visions far worse than the reality probably is. When children are not offered the opportunity to openly discuss this serious issue, they have no way to appropriately relieve themselves of their frightening and painful emotions. Their fears and frustrations grow to mammoth proportions, fueled by their growing imaginations.

The grief of losing a parent to incarceration is traumatic enough, but being mysteriously rushed out of the room, only to hear the frantic whispers and frequent crying of adults in the next room adds further trauma for children of all ages. The children's trauma often goes unnoticed because the adult family members are lost in their own pain and grief. The children's pain also goes unrecognized because adults often believe "children are too young to understand," when in fact children of all ages do understand and need a healthy outlet for their scary feelings. They need to talk about it; they need reassurance and understanding from the adults in their lives.

Here is what the National Institute of Mental Health has to say about trauma in children:

PTSD – Do children react differently than adults?

Children and teens can have extreme reactions to trauma, but their symptoms may not be the same as adults. In very young children, these symptoms can include:

- Bedwetting, when they'd learned how to use the toilet before
- Forgetting how or being unable to talk
- Acting out the scary event during playtime
- Being unusually clingy with a parent or other adult.

Older children and teens usually show symptoms more like those seen in adults. They may also develop disruptive, disrespectful, or destructive behaviors. Older children and teens may feel guilty for not preventing [the traumatic event.] They may also have thoughts of revenge.

HELPING CHILDREN COPE & HEAL

The responsibilities inherent in raising a child or children of a prisoner and addressing their traumatized reactions are a challenge for all caregivers. However, if caregivers take time to effectively address the children's grief and fears, it can actually make their job much easier. First, caregivers must understand what the child is experiencing.

- **Feelings of Abandonment** – Children typically believe parents are all-knowing and all-powerful. As a result, children *of prisoners* have difficulty understanding that there could possibly be a valid reason for their parent being absent from their life. After all, in their minds parents can fix anything and there seems to be no good reason why their parents can't fix this problem! Therefore, telling a child that their parent has "no control" over their absence due to their incarceration is not a believable, let alone a satisfying answer. While you may repeatedly explain the circumstances as honestly as you know how—and as you should do—the children may never believe you.

- **Fear of Being Further Abandoned** – In the child's mind their parent has left them for no valid reason. Therefore, they will begin to question what will prevent you or other possible caregivers from disappearing as well, leaving them totally vulnerable and alone. As adults, we know there is no guarantee of tomorrow. Children figure that out, too! With so much chaos and confusion surrounding them since their parent's absence—chaos and confusion that wasn't there before the parent was incarcerated, why would a child believe you will still be there tomorrow? They live in perpetual fear that you will abandon them also. Their incessant thoughts of their parent's sudden absence are terrifying and make it nearly impossible to satisfy their need for feelings of security.

194

- **Feelings of Guilt** – Children, especially very young children have a "magical" way of thinking. When they learn their family is experiencing a difficulty they actually believe they must have done something awful to create the problem the family is experiencing. So, the child will look to them self for the reasons their parent has "disappeared" and "abandoned" them. They will reflect on every moment of their own misbehavior that they can possibly recall, especially their misbehavior just prior to their parent's disappearance from their life. When they recall their misbehavior the children begin to blame themselves for their parent's absence.

  As irrational as it may seem to adults, these feelings of guilt are very real to the child—so real in fact that they begin to believe that if they had the "power" (the "magical power") to make their parent disappear, there must be something they can do to make their parent reappear. Of course, that is impossible and these futile thoughts only add to the child's frustration and fear and feelings of powerlessness.

- **Feelings of Shame & Embarrassment** – Children are quite aware of the stigma associated with "jail" and "prison." Even from television they know that the "bad guys" are the ones who are incarcerated. Additionally, adults project their own sense of shame and embarrassment with their actions. The children may overhear the adults actually talking about their embarrassment or calling the prisoner-parent names and vowing to disassociate from them. Perhaps adults tell the children never to let anyone know their parent is in prison. The children may observe the adults withdraw from their own former activities to avoid having to tell others the truth. Each of these actions projects a sense of shame and embarrassment. Children are extremely sensitive and intuitive. They **feel** everything in their environment. These behaviors of the adults in their life tell them there is something to be ashamed of.

Another source of shame and embarrassment for children comes from other children, especially classmates. Bullying is tragically so prevalent in our schools. It wouldn't be unlikely for another child who has learned of a classmate's parent being incarcerated to taunt that child by making hurtful comments about their parent in prison.

Children also know that they are the ones who are supposed to get in trouble, not parents! So, unlike other children whose parents may be absent due to divorce or death, children of prisoners feel shame and embarrassment over their parent's absence due to their parent's "misbehavior."

• **Disrespect for Authority, Especially for Law Enforcement** - Regardless of what a parent has done children love their parents. Experts tell us that even those children who have been horribly abused by their parent still love that parent. Most children also believe their parents can do no wrong, so *despite even admission from their parent* that they did do something wrong and are now paying the consequences, many children refuse to believe it and blame law enforcement officials for their parent's absence. In the children's minds the police have wrongly arrested their parent and the jailers are wrongly confining them. In the children's minds, the prison guards are keeping their parent from them. Having come to the conclusion that their parent is wrongfully being held by law enforcement, the children develop a deep disrespect for law enforcement and ultimately project this disrespect onto almost any adult in a position of authority.

• **Lack of Trust** – In a child's way of thinking, if all-knowing/all-powerful parents and law enforcement officials cannot be trusted, no one can be trusted. So whoever is charged with caring for a child of a prisoner will not be trusted either. It is very difficult to help someone who doesn't trust you.

- **Inability to Adequately Express Thoughts & Feelings** – Children, especially very young children sense the emotions related to their experiences, but they most often do not have the understanding or the language skills to adequately express what they are feeling. In addition to their inability to express what they are feeling, children of prisoners do not trust. Therefore, even if they had the ability to express themselves, they would withhold their innermost thoughts and feelings, because in their minds there is no one they can trust with whom to share their painful thoughts and feelings.

  Instead, children bottle up all of their pain and anger and frustration until they cannot hold it inside any longer. That is exactly why children of prisoners are at such high risk for engaging in delinquent behaviors. When they can no longer manage the increasing intensity of their bottled up emotions they must release it in some way. Therefore, they "explode" and act out their emotions.

  Even adults will "act out" when they have no appropriate outlet for their emotions. Adults may overeat or overspend or begin gambling or using drugs or alcohol when they are unable to express themselves. Children will begin fighting or bullying other children or disrespecting authority and engaging in delinquent behaviors or even running away from home when they cannot verbally express themselves adequately.

- **Exceptional Need for Reassurance** – For all of these reasons, children of prisoners need consistent meaningful assurances that they are OK; that their parent in prison is OK; that no more harm will come to the family; that they will be cared for without fail as long as their parent is unavailable to care for them. They need constant assurance that they are and will be safe. Unfortunately, there can never be sufficient assurance to satisfy these needs, which leaves the children feeling frightened and vulnerable.

———

Despite what may seem like insurmountable challenges—challenges that place seventy percent of prisoner's children at risk for their own incarceration, there are ways to improve the odds for these children to become healthy, productive and successful adults.

First of all it is important to remember that thirty percent of children of prisoners do well. In fact, some do exceptionally well, such as the child of a prisoner we know who is now a district court judge. There are others we know who are college professors and counselors and business owners. Many have become excellent parents to their own children. These "success stories" confirm that children of prisoners have excellent potential to excel.

Second of all, there are steps caregivers can take to improve the odds that a child of a prisoner will succeed. Following are suggested ways caregivers can improve the odds for children whose parents are incarcerated.

1. Never allow children to hear any condemnation of their incarcerated parent.

WHY? No matter what you or anyone else thinks about the parent in prison, **irrefutably a child is one-half their mother and one-half their father. When anyone criticizes or shames either parent they are criticizing and shaming half of their child.**

When anyone calls the parent a derogatory name in the child's presence, they are calling the child the same name, as well. Whether it is intentional or not, **that is how the child will interpret it**. Never think that pointing out a parent's flaws to a child will prevent the child from

198

engaging in the same behaviors that led the parent to prison. It will only shame the child. Allow children to know their parent. Children are smart; they can make their own decisions about their parent based on what they actually come to know.

We also want to teach children to appropriately let go of their own anger about their parent's incarceration. **As adults we must model forgiveness**. How else will the children learn to forgive?

HOW? To provide loving and supportive care to the child of a prisoner the adults in their life **must first resolve their own feelings** about the incarcerated parent. If anyone wishes to say bad things about that parent, they **must never say it where the child can hear it and they absolutely must never say it directly to the child.**

If the adults in the child's life need counseling to overcome negative feelings about the parent, they need to **seek counseling**. If money is an issue, local family service agencies generally have low cost counseling and many churches provide counseling for free or for a small donation. If it helps to talk to a friend about anger at the parent, invite them for coffee while the children are away in school and ventilate those feelings. Speak with a clergy-person about forgiveness and ask them to help you find forgiveness in your heart for the parent in prison. Above all, caregivers must **avoid displaying or allowing others to display disdain and disrespect** for a child's parent in front of them.

2. Encourage the children to talk about their feelings.

WHY? Children need to express their feelings without fear of being judged or rejected.

When children do not feel safe in expressing their feelings, they will begin stuffing those feelings deep down inside. When any of us, adult or child, stuff too many feelings and we have no room to stuff any more we will *act out* our feelings. As adults when we don't express our feelings and stuff them until we have no room to stuff them any longer, we may overeat or turn to alcohol or start gambling. It is the same for children who have no appropriate safe outlet for their feelings.

Children especially act out their feelings when they don't know how—or are not allowed to talk about them. That is when they begin having problems at school or start disrespecting their caregivers at home. Maybe they start fights with other children; join a gang or start using drugs.

HOW? To avoid the risk of children's emotions building up until they explode into troubled behaviors, **you must assure them that it is safe to air their feelings with you.** If you do not make yourself totally available to listen **without judgment**, the children will turn to other sources to relieve themselves of their uncomfortable feelings.

You must lovingly teach children how to express their feelings appropriately. Even though you are busy and burdened with the extra responsibilities of caring for a child or children of a prisoner, **you must make time to listen to them**. In the long run it will save you a great deal of time and distress.

Before you can help children talk about their feelings, you must become comfortable talking about your own feelings. It is impossible to teach children to do something we as adults do not know how to do, or are unwilling to do.. Only when you are comfortable expressing your own feelings without becoming emotional and judgmental will the children feel safe in expressing their feelings to you.

The rules for sharing feelings should include: no interruptions—only listen; no judgment—only words of encouragement and praise.

Children should not be expected to share your same feelings and they should never be condemned for the feelings they express. Each one of us has a right to feel as we do whether others agree with our feelings or not. By refraining from criticizing the child's feelings, you will let them know that you are a safe person to talk to about their feelings!

Also, learn to separate the situation from the person. When people misbehave (whether adult or child) the reality is that we don't dislike the person; we dislike the behavior they have exhibited. Lovingly express that sometimes you are sad, frustrated or even angry about the **situation** (not at the parent.)

If you absolutely cannot talk with the children about their feelings without becoming emotional or judgmental, visit the school counselor and tell them that the **children need someone safe to talk with about their feelings**, because they are hurting about their parent being in prison.

3. Involve the children in life-enriching meaningful activities.

WHY? To become healthy, productive and happy adults, all children need to know that they are valued and important—NOT JUST SOMEONE TO HELP WITH CHORES. While there are certain activities that are their expected responsibilities, such as making their bed or helping with the dishes, children also need to be involved in responsible family decision-making and worthwhile community activities to let them know that they are important to the larger world. They need opportunities that show them that **they matter**.

HOW? Help the children find community service projects that are meaningful to them. If they enjoy animals, ask the local animal shelter or local wildlife rescue agency if the children can volunteer. If the children care about the homeless, ask the local shelter if the children can volunteer once a week. Perhaps they care about the elderly or sick children or even about a certain social issue such as bullying or even prison reform. If they do, find a local organization that addresses that problem and encourage the children to become involved in it. Perhaps you can even get them interested in a project of particular interest to you? It may require some driving to get them to meetings or scheduled volunteer activities, but it will do so much to improve their self esteem and it will definitely help them build character. In the long run, it will make the job of raising them SO MUCH EASIER!

4. Provide the children with opportunities to develop their faith.

WHY? We all need to believe in something larger and more powerful than ourselves; something that will protect us and care about us unconditionally. Most of us call that "God." In troubled times we need our faith more than ever and children are no exception. Children need to feel the safety and comfort that only something bigger than themselves can provide.

HOW? Providing faith opportunities is probably the easiest thing to accomplish on this to-do list! Take the children to your house of worship at least once every week. Enroll them in Sunday school. If there is a youth program there, enroll the children and take them to the activities the youth group provides. Provide the children with age-appropriate inspirational books and other faith-based reading materials written for their age group. Take time to discuss what they have experienced or read about "faith."

5. Give the children ample opportunity to "just be kids."

WHY? Children of prisoners are often thrust into adult responsibilities well before their time by feeling the need or even being required to absorb some of the responsibilities formerly managed by their now absent parent. They may take on major responsibilities for running the household or caring for younger siblings. We have even known of teenagers taking responsibility for keeping a family business running during their parents' incarceration. Those are heavy burdens that prevent a child from enjoying their childhood!

The truth is that as the normal progression of child development goes—or is supposed to go—"play" is actually the "work" of children. Through play, children learn to become responsible adults. Play teaches them communication skills; social skills; leadership skills. Play teaches skills for sharing and teamwork and fair play and so much more. When children miss the opportunity for sufficient play time, they miss opportunities to sufficiently develop these important life skills.

HOW? Simply let the kids play! Recess at school is **not** adequate, especially because it is usually structured. Electronic games are **not** a substitute for "play," either. Kids need both verbal and physical interaction with other kids. Children need time to just be silly and to goof off with family and friends and especially with those who are their same age. Get them involved in children's activities at the "Y" or at your church or the community center. Those activities are usually provided at nominal cost and some may be free. Scour your local newspaper for children's activities. You may be surprised at what your community offers and you may also be surprised at how much *you* actually enjoy some of these activities as much as the children do. We all have a silly kid inside us who needs to be nurtured and just have fun!

6. Support and encourage the children to maintain contact with their parent in prison, or provide them with a valid reason *why they cannot have contact.*

WHY? All children need to experience the love of **both** of their parents. It doesn't matter how you feel about the parent in prison or where their parent is or why they are there. The children still need to experience their parent's love. That is simply **a basic human need** and deprived of the fulfillment of this need children begin to feel unwanted and unlovable which leads to acting out behaviors and poor relationship experiences in later years.

While not all parents are capable of appropriately expressing their love, when they are capable, it is the responsibility of the children's caregiver to assure the children are able to experience their parent's expressions of love for them. When a parent is in prison, the children **cannot have that communication without their caregiver's support.**

HOW? Of course, under the circumstances visitation would seem to be the ideal way for children and parents to maintain communication. However, not only is this not feasible for many families, but visitation does have its drawbacks and may not necessarily be in the best interest of all children.

A former employee of our agency that serves children and families of prisoners had previously been a corrections officer at a state prison unit. Unfortunately, he became involved in some of the unscrupulous behaviors some prison guards get caught up in when they recognize the financial gain to be made by smuggling in contraband to the prisoners. More unfortunately, he began using some of the drugs he was smuggling into the prisoners and ultimately landed in prison himself.

Years after his release from prison he began working with our program. At one of our weekly staff meetings the issue of children visiting their parents in prison came up. Our stance had always been that if a child desired to see their parent in prison they should have that right fulfilled if at all possible. However, this gentleman interjected a new perspective for us.

He said, "Actually, when children visit the prison it's all fun and games for them. They get treats out of the vending machines; they giggle and laugh for hours. In some prisons they even provide games for children to play with. When I was assigned to visitation when I was an officer I always wondered what message those children were getting when they came to visit at the prison. For them, prison certainly wasn't scary at all and it certainly didn't seem to give them the message that it was a bad place to be."

That one statement definitely gave us pause to reflect on the messages we send our children when we attempt to make prison visitation a social activity no different than going to a birthday party!

This issue is very challenging. On one hand we would like the child and parent to actually enjoy seeing one another and we certainly don't want to fill children with fear. On the other hand we certainly don't want the child to believe prison is a fun place to be! The challenge is to impress upon children the seriousness of incarceration while allowing them to enjoy a time of meaningful interaction with their parents.

Visitation should be used as a time for parents and children to talk about important issues such as school or friendships or even values and beliefs. At the same time there should be opportunities to share a laugh together and especially to share love for each other in a thoughtful way. If that healthier balance cannot be achieved in visitation, perhaps phone calls would serve the parent/child relationship much better than visitation.

If phone calls can be arranged, even if only once a month, it is important to provide the calls consistently. Be certain the children understand if the costs will limit phone time. Help them make a list of things they want to share with their parent when they call, so they don't waste time trying to remember and then feel badly when they forget to tell their parent something that was very important to them.

Writing is not only a good way to communicate with parents in prison, but it is a GREAT way for children to learn to express themselves. Provide ample writing materials and envelopes and stamps that the children have ready access to whenever they feel a need to write their parent. Even schedule a time one night a week for letter writing to assure the children know you support the contact.

If the parent does not reciprocate readily by writing back, it is the caregiver's responsibility as the adult (regardless of how they feel about the parent) to let that parent know how important their letters are to their children and how disappointing it is to the children not to receive responses to their letters. Caregivers should kindly, but boldly confront any "poor me, it's too painful" excuses from the parent for not writing. That type of excuse (which occurs all too often) is downright childish and selfish. Let them know that excuse is unacceptable.

WHEN CHILDREN ARE LEGALLY PREVENTED FROM HAVING CONTACT WITH A PARENT, THE CHILDREN HAVE A RIGHT TO KNOW WHY.

Occasionally there are legal reasons a parent in prison cannot have any contact at all with their children. Whether we agree with those reasons or not it is important for the caregiver to be honest about that fact with the children by explaining it in terms they can understand at their ages. If the Court ordered that there be no contact, state just that. Do not elaborate with editorial comments about the parent or the Court.

7. Surround children of prisoners with caring non-family adults.

WHY? All children are very aware of the stigma and shame attached to prison and prisoners. They know very well that the community no longer respects their parent in prison, and they need reassurance that the community does not shun them as well, just because they are the child of a prisoner. As adults we must show them that as children of prisoners they do not need to carry that shame and disrespect.

Also, the children may actually understand the reasons *you* remain in their life and why *you* support and love them. The real concern is that they learn that other adults who are not related to them will accept them, as well. By providing the children with caring and supporting unrelated adults in their lives we are able to tangibly demonstrate that they *will be* accepted in spite of their parent's incarceration.

HOW? Enroll the children in programs that provide interaction with unrelated adults, such as mentoring programs. Enroll them in programs guided by positive adults such as sports teams or creative arts programs (dance; drama; music; art) with adults as coaches and instructors. Environmental groups, such as local Sierra Clubs often have nature programs for children that are led by adults. Of course a great source for engaging the children with unrelated adults would be to enroll them in Boy Scout and Girl Scout troops in your community.

If money is an issue, look for a YM/YWCA or community center that offers free or low cost adult led activities for children. Churches usually charge nothing for children to attend Sunday school or youth group activities with adult leaders.

Take the time necessary to enroll the children in age-appropriate activities with adults as the leaders. In the long run it will save you time and ultimately make your life easier, as the children's lives become far more productive and satisfying.

CAREGIVERS NEED SUPPORT, TOO

Children of prisoners need energetic, emotionally and physically healthy caregivers. Unless you take care of yourself you will not have the physical or emotional stamina to take care of anyone, least of all a traumatized child of a prisoner.

Just by serving as the caregiver for a child or children of a prisoner you are experiencing excessive stress. In addition to former responsibilities you now have the responsibility for caring for additional children or caring for your own children alone or assuming the care of children well after your own children have left the nest and you were looking forward to enjoying your golden years of retirement. Any of those conditions adds extraordinary stress to your life.

You also are likely to have the additional responsibility of providing some sort of support for your incarcerated family member. Whether that is devoting time to writing letters to them or whether it is managing complex legal matters for their appeal, it adds even more stress to your life.

When we are forced to assume additional responsibilities there is the danger of attempting to fool ourselves into believing we "can do it all" and we can do it all without changing one single thing about how our life operated before the new challenges were added to our plates. This tendency to ignore new stressors and attempt to carry on "as usual" unfortunately creates further stress, because it is so very unrealistic.

To cope with the additional responsibilities you are likely to eventually realize that something has to give. That realization in and of itself adds even more stress to your life! You may necessarily have to sacrifice some former pleasures like weekly dinner or a movie with friends or bowling league on Monday nights or quiet times to enjoy prayer and meditation. The sacrifice adds even more stress, because no one wants to give up activities they enjoy to do something they did not *choose* to do.

To best survive and even thrive as an individual, it is crucial that caregivers take care of their own needs. Let's look at some ways to get the support needed to be a positive and loving caregiver.

1. Surround yourself with only encouraging people.

This may be tough to do, so hopefully that won't make you wait too long to do it—or avoid doing it altogether, because this is one stress reducer that many prison families have found to be an absolute necessity.

No one needs or even wants to be around negative people, especially when times are difficult! It may be hard and it may even seem rude (at first), but you must let people know (including your own family members if necessary) that you will not entertain their negative thoughts and comments. THEN DON'T. Don't allow it to continue. You only have two options:

- You can allow negative people to stay in your life and continually drag you down with their negative comments, or

- You can eliminate negative people from your life and replace them with positive supporting people who will help you overcome obstacles and achieve your goals.

There is no middle ground. Trying to find positive support by hanging on to negative people is like straddling a picket fence. It will only result in discomfort and pain.

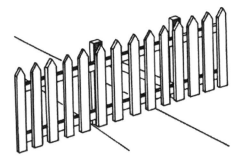

You can say calmly and politely, "I love you; I care about you, but during this difficult time I really need people in my life who I can count on to support me. If you cannot support me and my decisions I am very sorry, but I must ask you to leave." Once you've told them the truth, *they* will have two options:

- They can change their tune and start being supportive, or

- They can move on.

The choice is theirs! It doesn't matter if they are upset with you. If they don't understand your need for **positive** support, they are really not a very supportive family member or friend to begin with. At times like this you need truly supportive friends and family members.

2. Get involved in enjoyable <u>adult</u> activities.

As adults we need to associate with other adults. It is stifling being with only children all of the time! In fact, it is not healthy! Just as children need interaction with other children their own age for healthy growth and development, adults need interaction with other adults to live healthy lives, too.

Even if you don't feel like it, DO IT! Join a Book Club; join the church choir; enroll in a class at the community college. See what activities the community center or "Y" has for adults that you might enjoy—maybe an arts and crafts or woodworking class or perhaps a dance or exercise class one evening a week.

Even if you have to force yourself to go in the beginning, GO! After you get there you will see how much better you feel and how much the contact with other adults energizes you. Unless the experience is totally dreadful to you—go again. It is likely that you will enjoy it more the second and third time, as you become more familiar with the other adults. Hopefully you will even find yourself making new friends.

3. Seek help to answer the children's questions.

With one in every seven children in the U.S. classrooms having a parent in prison or on probation or parole, there should be a great deal written about the needs of the caregivers of children of prisoners and the prison family as a whole. Unfortunately while we are finding more information and story books *for the children*, this is not the case for the adult prison family members. However, there are some good *children's books* that can help you answer the children's questions. One such book is *"What Did I Do?"* compiled and authored by Joy DeSomber, herself a single mother of a child of a prisoner. The website for this book is www. whatdidIdobook.com.

What we can tell you right now is that the best answers to children's questions are always:

- Given with love.

- Provided in words the child will clearly understand at their age.

- Honest and forthright, but avoid negative comments about anyone, including the parent(s) in prison.

As new resources are reviewed by PFFUnited and found to be useful, they will be listed on the www.PFFUnited.com resource page and of course you may also search the internet for new information. If you find exceptionally good resources, please let us know about them, so we can share them with other caregivers. Our e-mail address is info@pffunited.org.

4. Ask for help with routine needs.

Often *"we have not because we ask not"* and all it would take is a simple "please" to elicit the help of friends and family and even the children in your care. When you allow yourself to become overwhelmed by routine daily responsibilities, now compounded by the additional responsibility of being a caregiver to a child or children of a prisoner, you may easily snap and instead of asking for help lovingly you may become critical and harsh and angry—**demanding** help, instead of asking for it.

We only need to put ourselves in others' shoes to consider which we would respond to more readily: a pleasant "please" or an angry "do it" demand! Don't allow the burdens to pile up to the boiling point. Simply say to the children calmly and with love, "Kids I really need your help!" Then clearly, but kindly define the chores you believe they are capable of doing.

Do not expect perfection from children. Demonstrate how the job needs to be done; praise them for their effort to do the job and thank them for their help—and **do not re-do their work**. Re-doing their efforts only tells children they are inferior and incapable and it hurts their self esteem. They will retaliate by becoming rebellious and not helping you at all. Simply say, "Great job! Thanks for helping." With practice their skills will improve.

If you think they could have done a better job at their particular age, you might say something like, "Great job!" and offer an example of how they might improve their skills, such as, "You know what some people do to make this job easier is to tuck the bottom of the sheet in first and it makes it easier to pull up the top. Thanks so much for helping." *(period)* Or, "Super! Do you know what I heard? I heard some people put the glasses and cups upside down so they can dry faster. Thank you so much for helping." *(period)*

Never criticize, only encourage. It's amazing how much kids want to please us when we praise them for their efforts—even if the final result of their work isn't as perfect as we would have done it.

By the way there are a number of churches that offer special assistance through ministry work for house and car repairs. If your own house of worship doesn't have such a ministry, call around until you find a church that does. They usually provide the work for free and even in some cases provide some of the materials for the repairs. It can't hurt to ask for help.

5. SCHEDULE breaks for yourself.

Very often we don't take advantage of opportunities to enjoy life when those opportunities are right in front of us, because we don't SCHEDULE time for ourselves. There is an old adage that says *"if it isn't written it didn't happen."* The truth is that when we fail to write down our goals, they won't happen. If your goal is to keep yourself as healthy as possible, you must write down the steps you are going to take to assure you achieve your goal. That includes writing those healthy actions on a calendar—scheduling time for *you*.

If you are caring for school aged children, make it a habit of *scheduling* at least one full hour a week (or more) while the children are in school to do nothing except that which you totally enjoy. If you have little one's at home, *schedule* at least one day a week to set your alarm and get up an hour early, before the kids are stirring and just enjoy the peace and quiet with your first cup of coffee. Even if you only do it once or twice a week it will energize you. But SCHEDULE IT & DO IT—REGULARLY!

A number of churches offer a weekly "Mother's Day Out" babysitting and child care ministry. Call around to find one and drop the kids off for a few hours to minister to YOU and ONLY YOU! Very often the child care is offered for free or for a small donation.

Think about what you really enjoy and DO IT—meditate and pray; read a novel; work in the garden; soak in the tub; visit with a friend; take a class; go to the gym. Whatever makes YOU feel good—do it! You have a right to your own pleasures. There is no reason to feel guilty because one day a week you spend one full hour watching your favorite TV show in peace!

INVOLVE THE CHILDREN'S PARENTS

When parents go to prison, they are still parents. Unless there is a *legal* reason why a parent in prison is not permitted to have contact with their children, it is healthy for the parent and it is healthy for the children to maintain as much regular interaction as possible. **But they will need the caregiver's help to remain actively involved in each other's lives.**

Whether or not the parent has been an active and involved parent before going to prison is not the issue. That was then; this is now and *now* is an excellent opportunity for them to build their parenting skills and to demonstrate their love for their children. Some parents may not know how. Others may be so saddened at being away from their children that they can't think of ways to be a part of their children's lives from a distance. In either case, **it is up to the children's caregiver to encourage them to be a loving and involved parent from afar.** That may require helping the parent learn to parent effectively from afar.

Since most caregivers are unprepared for teaching parent skills to a parent in prison, here are some suggestions that caregivers can share with the children's parents to help them interact in a meaningful way with their children. Once showing them how, you must keep the door wide open to allow the parents consistent access to their children.

- **Send photos** of the children to their parent(s) in prison. One of the biggest problems *children* cite is that their parent always thinks of them as "littler" than they really are. If the parent does not visually see the child aging, they continue to treat the child as if they are the same age as when they left. Help the parent visually watch their child grow and mature.

- Encourage parents to **ask** their children about their special interests and suggest that they **ask** their children to teach them about things they enjoy or even something interesting they learned in school. Suggest that they might find articles in newspapers or magazines related to their children's interests to mail to their children—or if they can't cut out articles, they can write about the information they've found. This will show the children that their parent is listening to them and cares about their interests.

- There is no reason parents in prison cannot **share their own values and beliefs with their children**. Suggest they write and even

214

talk with their children about what they've learned from this experience and how it has changed their own values and beliefs. It is interesting to note that regardless of why a parent is in prison they typically present their children positive values and beliefs.

- Children enjoy hearing WHY we love them. **Suggest the parent find something very special about the child that makes them loveable** and tell the child what that is. Perhaps the child has a great sense of humor or is very caring about less fortunate people. Those are unique qualities in that child, and they appreciate it when others recognize those qualities. **Help the parent identify these unique qualities in their child**, so they can praise the child for their special gifts and talents.

- **Remind the parents that their children need to hear them say THE WORDS, "I LOVE YOU."** If the parent is unable to call, they certainly can write those words in letters or cards.

- **Let the parent know that you will not serve as a "middle man"** by allowing them to have YOU tell the children they love them. **Encourage the parent to tell the children of their love directly.** Then assure the door remains open for the parent and child to communicate as often as possible.

While it may not always be necessary, sometimes it may be helpful to provide parents in prison with creative suggestions for making contact with their children meaningful. Here are some ideas to share with the children's parents in prison to help make contacts with their children more meaningful.

- Reassure the children you will have contact with them while you are away. Give immediate proof of your intention to stay in contact – a phone call or a letter – and remain consistent in carrying out this promise.

- Write each child something special about THEM. Perhaps a story about a special time the two of you spent together; a silly poem about something funny the child did or said when they were very young; use each letter of their name to say something special about that child—i.e. "Tommy" – Terrific; Obstinate! Magnificent; Magical; Young—turn that into a poem or even a short story. Be creative!

- If it is allowed by the prison, draw them a picture of where you live so they aren't so fearful about where you are. If you are not able to provide a diagram, perhaps you can provide a verbal description of where you live. Reality is often far less frightening than what is conjured up in a child's imagination.

- If you can draw, the children would love receiving your art work as gifts. They will appreciate those gifts the most, and the gifts would far better sustain the relationship, if the drawings specifically relate to that particular child. So, even if you're drawing Bugs Bunny or Sponge Bob, put a ballet tutu on them if your daughter loves ballet or a baseball bat in their hand if your son loves baseball!

- Never forget a Birthday! Write a special birthday letter or create a card yourself. Use the number of years of the *new* age to tell them as many things that are special about them. You can title your list "The 8 Special Things about Michael" or "The 12 Special Things about Sarah."

- If you can, call your children on special occasions or set a regular time for their "special call." Be sure to explain to them clearly that there may be times you are unable to call because of the rules at the prison. But, let them know that if you are prevented from calling you will be thinking of them at the time you're supposed to call and that you will call or write them as soon as you can—and then, do!

- Children love to receive mail, so write as often as you can. Avoid always preaching and teaching in your letters. Parents mistakenly believe preaching and teaching proves they are good parents. It doesn't prove anything of the kind! It only makes you sound critical and disapproving of them. Just write about your thoughts of them or maybe something interesting you read or saw on TV or even something you talked about with another prisoner, especially if it reminded you of that particular child.

- If you have more than one child it is important to write each one separately. Each child desires to be uniquely recognized and valued for their unique qualities. Writing letters addressed to "Dear Everyone," even if you do list each of their names, indicates you do not recognize each child as a special separate and unique human being.

- If your children are able to visit you, be prepared for changes – new habits; new likes and dislikes. Let each child know you recognize how they are growing and changing. Praise them for specific good things you see them doing.

- Let your children know you miss them, but reassure them that you are OK, so they don't feel guilty about your loneliness or worry about your safety. Surprisingly even very young children engage in "role reversals" with parents in prison, believing it is their responsibility to cheer their parents up! It's great for children to learn compassion, but children should be allowed to be children. Parents are adults who should cheer their children up when they are sad or lonely or hurt.

- Encourage the children to be active in the community; to get involved in activities like sports or music classes or to go to the library and read to learn new things. Even suggest activities for them to become involved in, such as going to the park or church camp and just having fun with other children or even volunteering to help others. Let them know you want them to learn all they can and to have fun and that you want to hear everything they do.

CHAPTER VI

"PRISON FAMILY RIGHTS"

The unvarnished truth about the prison family journey is that prison family members and friends of prisoners have absolutely *no rights* when it pertains to their loved one in prison. However, there has been movement toward establishing "rights" for members of the prison family. Those efforts have been thoughtfully crafted and documented into two Bills asserting expected rights for children of prisoners as well as expected rights for prison families.

While these bills are not legally enforceable, they can and should be actively used as advocacy tools in efforts to improve circumstances for children and families of prisoners, as well as prisoners themselves.

You are encouraged to share these bills with other prison families and advocacy groups supportive of prisoners and their loved ones. Share these bills with legislators and even prison officials. Let them know that these bills assert realistic and meaningful expectations for how prisoners' children and families should be respected.

On the following pages you will find both documents.

CHILDREN OF PRISONERS
BILL OF RIGHTS

Quite some time ago the *San Francisco Children of Incarcerated Parents Project* drafted a Bill of Rights for children of prisoners, with the input of many children of prisoners who offered thoughts about how they should be treated. The document actually speaks to the "needs" of children of prisoners.

1. **I have the right to be kept safe and informed at the time of my parent's arrest.**
2. **I have the right to be heard when decisions are made about me.**
3. **I have the right to be considered when decisions are made about my parent.**
4. **I have the right to be well cared for in my parent's absence.**
5. **I have the right to speak with, see and touch my parent.**
6. **I have the right to support as I face my parent's incarceration.**
7. **I have the right to not be judged, blamed or labeled because of my parent is incarcerated.**
8. **I have the right to a lifelong relationship with my parent.**

"PRISON FAMILY RIGHTS"

Prison Family Bill of Rights
As affirmed at the 2012 National Prisoner's Family Conference and
As Adopted at the 2013 National Prisoner's Family Conference

A Coalition of prison family members and representatives of secular and faith based organizations serving prison families from across the United States in attendance at the 2012 National Prisoner's Family Conference affirmed the following:

The Prison Family has the right to be treated with respect and dignity by any and all representatives of the prison system at all times.

The Prison Family has the right to expect and be assured the utmost care is established and maintained to provide a healthy and safe living environment that promotes effective rehabilitation, reintegration and parole planning throughout a loved one's incarceration.

The Prison Family has the right to be treated and integrated as a positive resource in the process of rehabilitation and reintegration preparation and parole planning of an incarcerated loved one.

The Prison Family has the right to receive consistency in the enforcement of rules; regulations and policies affecting a loved one's incarceration.

The Prison Family has the right to receive consistency in the enforcement of rules; regulations and/or policies affecting visitation and/or all forms of communication with an incarcerated loved one.

The Prison Family has the right to be informed in a timely, clear, forthright and respectful manner of any changes in rules; regulations and/or policies affecting visitation and/or communication with an incarcerated loved one.

The Prison Family has the right to be informed within 24 hours and in a compassionate manner regarding the illness; injury and/or death of an incarcerated loved one.

The Prison Family has the right to extended visitation during the hospitalization of an incarcerated loved one.

The Prison Family has the right to be informed within 24 hours of the security status change and/or transfer of an incarcerated loved one to a new facility.

The Prison Family has the right to be provided specific written and evidenced-based reasons for a loved one's security status change; clemency denial and/or parole denial.

The Prison Family has the right to have their incarcerated loved one housed within a distance from their permanent address that provides reasonable access for visitation and/or to facilitate serving as a resource in the rehabilitation and reintegration preparation and parole planning of their incarcerated loved one.

The Prison Family has the right to be provided the current specific name or names and direct phone numbers of prison officials to contact for questions about their incarcerated loved one.

The term "Prison Family" is herein defined as including, but not limited to a blood or adopted relation, spouse, domestic partner and/or trusted friend designated by an incarcerated person upon or during a period of confinement as one who will serve as an outside contact on his or her behalf for the relaying of any communication regarding the medical and mental health, security status and location of the incarcerated person and/or for making critical decisions on behalf of the incarcerated person in the event of his or her incapacitation.

For further information:
www.prisonersfamilyconference.org or FaceBook Prisoners Family Conference page

CHAPTER VII

"THE PRISON SYSTEM"

While it is certainly important for those left behind when a loved one goes to prison to learn as much as possible to effectively manage the prison family journey from the *outside* of prison, it is also critical to understand the environment in which the loved one is living on the *inside* of the prison.

The prison culture is no less complex than any foreign culture. As a prison family you actually have a member of your family living in a foreign environment. The language they speak and the rules they live and play by in their new culture will be unfamiliar to you. In some ways their new lifestyle will be adverse to your values and beliefs. In fact, some aspects of the prison culture are likely to be offensive to you. To understand your loved one as they adapt to their new culture and to be best prepared to help them make positive choices and live most productively while incarcerated, you must first understand the environment in which they live.

By far, the United States has the largest prison population in the world.

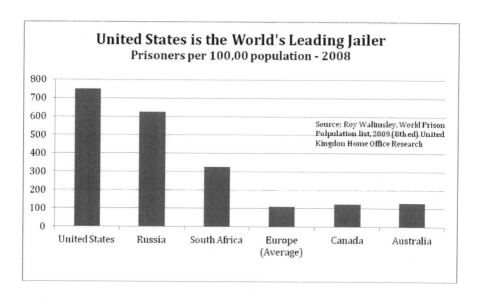

United States is the World's Leading Jailer
Prisoners per 100,00 population - 2008

Source: Roy Walmsley, World Prison Polpulation list, 2009 (8th ed) United Kingdon Home Office Research

With 5% of the world's population, the U.S. confines almost 25% of the world's prisoners. There are several factors fueling the mass incarceration in our country, not the least of which is the extraordinary profitability of the prison industry.

Prison was not initially conceived of as an economic enterprise that would amass fortunes for a select few. Until the mid-1970's U.S. prisons were largely viewed as housing facilities in which to detain (and/or punish) those who were thought to require consequences for having committed serious offenses against society and its citizens. Because the behaviors of those confined to prison were considered "deviant" there has always been a stigma attached to incarceration.

Deviance was abhorred. Therefore, very few citizens took an interest in the prison system as a whole let alone cared about what occurred behind the concrete walls. Prisoners were considered the dregs of society and became outcasts even to their own families. Citizens gladly paid taxes to assure these misfits were safely locked away. Complacent in the belief that society was being kept safe, those citizens turned a blind eye leaving the entire responsibility for keeping society safe to the few who were paid to do so. To this day, there is no independent oversight of our nation's prisons. Operating in total autonomy with no accountability for its practices, the prison system has radically changed.

The radical change began in 1971:

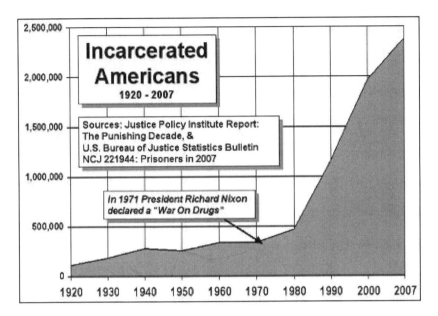

Before 1971 apparently neither our states nor our country nor its citizens conceived of prison as having the potential to become a "money maker." However, with the advent of the "War on Drugs" by 1980 that vision was set in concrete, and the growth of our prison system has escalated unabated ever since.

Today, the vast majority of prisoners are incarcerated for drug related offenses, and despite widespread knowledge that the War on Drugs has been an utter failure no one—at least no one in a position of power wants to stop that "war," because it assures our states—and it assures some very powerful people that large sums of money will assuredly be amassed. Thus, today **private** prisons are adding fuel to the fiery explosion of our prison population.

Private prisons are by their nature competitive economic enterprises that have invested millions of dollars in lobbying to assure their consistent economic growth and profitability. Thus, today operators of private prisons contract with the states with the firm stipulation that the states must keep prisons beds filled at a *minimum* of **ninety percent capacity** at all times for the next **twenty years** to maintain those contracts.

The only concern for private prison operators is "profit," and of course it is impossible to be profitable without cutting corners, especially in a poor economy. Cutting corners to assure profitability has resulted in a prison industrial complex that does not sustain a "corrections" mentality intent on preparing offenders to become safe, productive citizens upon returning to the community. In fact, some prison systems have removed the word "corrections" from their name.

The Texas prison system was formerly referred to as "TDC," which stood for "Texas Department of **Corrections.**" The name actually implied that corrective intervention for the rehabilitation of prisoners was occurring within the system.

Over twenty years ago the name of the prison system was changed to "TDCJ" and it is now referred to as the "Texas Department of Criminal Justice" and exceedingly little "corrective" rehabilitation occurs within the system any longer. For example, despite the fact that the majority of prisoners are either convicted of a drug related offense or committed their offense while under the influence of a chemical substance, when budget cuts were necessitated in the 1980's to balance state budgets, the first programs to be cut (in the midst of that "War on Drugs") were the prison's drug prevention and education programs. Those programs have never been replaced, and in some cases even totally volunteer provided programs such as Alcoholics Anonymous or Narcotics Anonymous are denied entrance to some of the prison units.

Whether privatized or not, today all prisons are profitable. In addition to taxation, state prisons rely on hefty federal funding to supplement their budgets and of course that hefty federal funding comes from tax dollars. Unfortunately for our states, the recent national economic crisis meant prison budgets became strained as the feds cut funds to the states while trying desperately to balance their own budget. So prisons had to do with less. In their wisdom, they made some very interesting cutbacks. Here's an interesting place to cut costs of prison operations:

Well, of course! Feed a prisoner on ONE-FOURTH the cost of what the average American spends to eat! Perhaps this means the average American only eats steak and lobster on a daily basis.

While no one expects prisoners to have a diet that contains *any* steak and lobster, the fact is that no human being, no matter how frugal could stay healthy—or perhaps even stay alive on less than $2.50 A DAY!

Prisons appear to assess "healthy diets" **not** by nutritional value, but by "sufficient calories." Thus, prison diets largely consist of cheap starchy and fatty foods, resulting in many health problems for prisoners, not the least of which is (excuse the indelicacy) constipation—leading to a virtual epidemic of hemorrhoids! So, of course prisoners having any outside support rely on family and friends (taxpayers themselves) to kindly supplement their diet by regularly depositing funds into their inmate trust fund accounts so the prisoner can trek to the prison commissary to purchase items to keep them alive! Do you know that the only sem-blance of a "fresh vegetable" in prison may be found in a commissary pickle (when it is in stock), which the prisoner's family paid for? God help the prisoner with no outside support.

OK. So prisoners don't need an adequate diet; maybe they don't even deserve an adequate diet, but how about adequate medical care? Following Florida's lead (and possibly the lead of other states) here's what Texas did to cut their budget: Texas passed a bill **assessing each prisoner $100.00 a year for using the infirmary** at the prison.

That's a great idea for balancing the state budget! And, after all it's *only* $100.00 (a year) and besides, prisoners should be responsible to pay for their upkeep. There's only one problem with that. In Texas, while prisoners are *required* to work and provide every imaginable service to operate the prison from mopping floors to repairing plumbing to cook-ing and serving the food to maintaining the landscape to painting the buildings to manufacturing the furniture to sewing the prisoners' uni-forms and even their underwear to everything in between, they are **paid absolutely nothing** for their work.

Of course, prisoners should take care of their living facility! The only problem is that because they are not paid for their work—not one red cent—their **family and friends** (taxpayers) must pay the $100.00 medical fee (tax) each year—and if the prisoner should walk (or be carried uncon-scious) into the infirmary for any reason, the prison assures it receives that payment by automatically taking it out of any monies family and friends deposit into the inmate's trust fund account, **before** that money can be used for pickles or any other semi-nutritious substance at the commissary!

To avoid having their families pay this medical tax, many prisoners are refusing to receive any medical care, often jeopardizing their health (especially those having chronic medical conditions such as diabetes or heart disease). And, by the way, those prisoners who have no outside support are taxed this $100.00 a year (if they use the infirmary for any purpose) and the accumulated amount is billed to them upon release from prison. So, indigent prisoners leave prison already financially in debt to the state.

Of course the state says they have lessened the need for inmates to go to the infirmary by stocking the prison commissary with a larger variety of over the counter medications. So now, prisoners can "shop" for their own medicine, using money from their trust fund accounts which of course their FAMILIES AND FRIENDS deposit into their accounts. Perfectly logical! Except for one thing, when prisoners "shop" for over the counter medicine in the prison commissary they are not purchasing name brand items, although they are paying name brand prices. In fact they are purchasing what appears to be generic medication, some of which appears not to yet be approved by the Federal Drug Administration (FDA), dispensed by the prison pharmacy.

OH! And about that commissary—the commissary is no different than Wal-Mart. It is a business. It is a prison-business and it is profitable—for the prison. This past year, I had the opportunity to talk with the administrator over the operation of the commissaries and inmate trust fund for our state prison system. We were at a "conference" of sorts intended to appease families of inmates and we were told we could ask any questions we wanted. So this is about how that conversation went:

Me: "Hi. I've been wondering how the commissary works at the prison. Do all prisoners have access to the commissary?"

Administrator: "Well, sure. As long as they have funds in their trust fund to cover their purchases and aren't on a commissary restriction, they sure do."

Me: "So, how do you all decide on the prices for commissary items? I've heard the prices are pretty high."

Administrator: "Don't know who told you that, but our prices aren't any higher than Wal-Mart. We barely make a cent off of the commissary."

Me: (incredulous) "What? Wal-Mart may cut prices, but at the prices they charge they certainly make a killing off of their sales."

Administrator: "Well, I mean we don't make a cent more than Wal-Mart makes off of similar items."

Me: "So then, how about the inmate trust fund. How much do you all make off of that each year?"

Administrator: "Absolutely nothing! We don't make money off of the trust fund. That's the inmates' money?"

Me: (incredulous!) "What? You all have millions of dollars in that fund at all times. You all don't invest that money?"

Administrator: "Well, it's the inmates' money."

Me: "I know it's the inmates' money—at least their families put the money in their accounts. But it seems to me that it would be unwise—even wasteful, if the prison wasn't investing it in some way to help offset the prison budget."

Administrator: "Well, maybe the prison makes a few bucks off of it, but it's not 'invested.'"

Me: (incredulous glare) "Really?"

Administrator: "I don't think we made more than $44,000.00 off the trust fund money last year."

End of conversation.

For far too long, we have turned a blind eye to the autonomous operation of our prison system. Operating with absolutely no accountability, the system is now broken and out of control as over 2.5 million are incarcerated in a secret and very dangerous culture. Here, with unvarnished candor is a rare glimpse at the culture of the broken prison system we have allowed to materialize in our society.

Chapter VIII

"PERSPECTIVE FROM INSIDE PRISON"

PRISON GANGS

When it comes to prisons, most likely the first thing that comes to mind for most prisoners' families is the safety of the prisoner. Of course one of the most common stereotypes portrayed in movies and on TV is that of the dangerous prison gangs. Since it is likely that will be the first thing that will come to mind when you learn your loved one is going to prison, let's take a look at prison gangs.

Some "not too pretty" things occur behind prison walls. The prison system is a culture all its own. Having been transferred between several prison units in my state, I could also say that each prison *unit* has its own culture—its own unique environment which is pretty much created by the inmates who are housed there. Knowing the answers to "who is who" and "what is what" on each unit becomes extremely vital to each individual inmate's welfare and even survival.

Before discussing prison gangs in detail, I would like to assure you that in no way am I on board with my assignment in writing as the PFFUnited Advocacy Director to simply bash the system. I personally believe there are at least two sides to every story and I believe my role is to provide the most relevant information in as unbiased a manner as possible.

The fact is that during my years in prison I have witnessed problems from both inmates and from the prison administrators. In truth, the difference between the two in regard to character and behavior seems to be very little. The greatest difference is perhaps that there are far more prisoners than there are officers and administrators. So there are more prisoners to do more wrong things, which may therefore happen with more frequency but no less malicious intent.

I hope I have become a person who thinks with logic and responds with common sense. I say that to preface stating my opinion about "gangs," because I believe that one of the biggest mistakes an inmate can make is to join a gang or "prison family." (In prison, the term "prison family" means the same as "gang" and **no matter what any inmate might tell you**, if an inmate is part of a "prison family" that particular inmate has joined a "gang." They are not "pals"; they are not "friends" or even "close friends." They are a "gang.")

Although I have never been a member of any gang whether inside or outside of prison, I have had many opportunities to witness gang mentality and even to interact with gang members, and in all honesty I can only find two words to describe all gangs: "bad" and "evil."

There is absolutely nothing of substance that comes from being a part of a gang or even from associating with individual gang members. Gangs do not love or even care about those individuals they recruit as members, and gangs certainly aren't designed for the personal growth and development of anyone. Gangs don't recruit new members because they love them and want to educate and elevate them to new heights; they recruit new gang members because they know there is strength in numbers. Every new member means more strength for their gang—physical strength, that is. Gangs only exist for the following two purposes:

- grave manipulation and deception

- violence and sexual misconduct

When inmates are new to the prison environment their conduct and disposition shows that they are new to the prison way of life. They can't help it. They have no idea what the prison culture is all about, and they certainly don't know how to act and react within the culture. So everything they do from the way they walk, to the way they talk or even the way they wear their prison uniform is a dead give-away to their newness in the system.

Inmates who have been incarcerated for five years or longer refer to new inmates (five years or less) as being "green" or "lame." The terms "green" and "lame" of course refer to the fact that inmates are new in the prison system; they have no idea of what prison life or the environment is all about and that makes them **extremely vulnerable to become prey** to grave manipulation and deception.

Whether new inmates know it or not they are constantly being watched; they are being observed from every possible angle from the minute they enter the prison system. They are scrutinized for their potential vulnerability for potential recruitment into a gang and as potential prey for the manipulation of financial resources and sexual favors.

Gang members have devious indirect ways of learning information about potential recruits. Gang members will sit and observe new inmates for hours and watch for how much mail a potential recruit receives; how often the potential recruit receives visits; how often the potential recruit goes to commissary (the store); how often the potential recruit uses the phone; how physically fit and tough the potential recruit seems to be and they actually assess the potential recruit's overall personality, character and criminal conviction.

Once gang members acquire all of the necessary information they believe is needed to have an adequate understanding of how the potential recruit can benefit the gang's "cause," gang members develop a strategy of how they will approach their potential recruit.

There are two primary strategies I've witnessed gang members implement in their efforts to recruit others to join their gangs. The first strategy I will call: "The Fear Factor" and the second strategy I will call: "Grave Manipulation and Deception."

The "Fear Factor Strategy" is often implemented after the gang members investigate and learn the potential recruit is incarcerated for any of the various sexual offenses. Once they learn the new inmate is incarcerated for a sex crime, the gang members' strategy is to use the "Fear Factor" to intimidate them into joining their gang. They intimidate by emphasizing the inmate's exceptional vulnerability to physical harm and stressing that joining their gang will provide the new inmate "protection." They tell the new inmate that joining their gang is for the recruit's own safety.

In reality, inmates who succumb to the fear factor strategy are actually being intimidated to join the gang to be used for their financial resources and to engage them in inappropriate sexual behaviors. The gang members will falsely embrace the new recruit for their own personal gain, protecting the unaware prisoner until the well runs dry and the new recruit has no more resources to share with the gang members. The truth is that the new prisoner was never intended to really be part of the gang. The gang members only wanted to use him. When the new recruit is no longer of any benefit to the gang, the gang members will turn their backs on him—even attacking him themselves.

The "Grave Manipulation and Deception Strategy" is used to recruit potential gang members by using insincere expressions of friendliness to manipulate and deceive potential recruits for selfish gains. In other words, if your incarcerated loved one joins a gang by succumbing to grave manipulation and deception strategies, they will actually be used as a crash dummy to further someone else's cause.

Gangs aren't administered over by individual members who can *think*. Gangs are administered over by the individual members who can *fight* the best. All of the other members are simply "crash dummies" who do what their gang leader bids them to do, because they are either afraid of the leader and have no backbone to stand on their own or because they have no cognitive abilities to think on their own.

The bottom line is always this: If your incarcerated loved one is not a part of a gang, it is vital that family and friends strongly encourage them to remain free from gangs. If your incarcerated loved one is already affiliated with a gang it is equally important that family and friends strongly encourage them to *discontinue* any and all association with the gang regardless of the cost. In the long run your loved one's decision to disassociate from gangs will serve them well.

In 2001 I myself was new to the prison environment. Having witnessed gang members in the free world and knowing they were up to no good and were of no benefit to anyone, I made it my number one personal rule—a commitment to myself to never join a gang! My rationale was that since I wasn't a gang member before entering prison, I wouldn't become a gang member now that I was in prison.

It seemed to me that those who waited until they came to prison before deciding to join a gang only joined gangs for protection. Because the vast majority of the prison environment is so infested with gangs, it takes a strong-minded person to say "no" to gang affiliation knowing that the odds are against them for going it alone. I told myself (and a few others) that I would rather fight to my death before becoming a gang member. Yes, there is definitely fear associated with saying "no" to the gangs, but to conquer that fear one must make a stand and face that fear head on.

While I was still a new prisoner and housed at one of the system intake units I saw a few other inmates that I had known from the county jail who had **not** been gang members when they arrived in prison. I witnessed one of those inmates doing what gang members call "perpetrating" ("pretending") he was a part of a particular gang.

Out of concern for this particular inmate (because I knew him from the county jail) I periodically pulled him aside and told him that he should not be acting like a gang member when he was not one!

The reason I admonished this inmate was not entirely unselfish, but was because I knew that when events associated with being an actual gang member came his way (such as, violence) I would instinctively feel the need to help him and thereby might risk my own life by intervening to stop a physical altercation. I wasn't willing to do that.

Why would I want to put myself in harm's way as the result of someone else's foolishness, especially if they refused to listen to my advice? Is that fair to me or to those who love and care about me? So I figured that if this particular inmate did not care enough about me (or himself) to accept my advice, after giving him fair warning that I would not be there to help protect him if he chose to continue his charade of pretending to be a gang member, then I would not feel any guilt about not risking my own life when he found himself in trouble.

I learned a good lesson from the choice I made to not get involved with gangs. That choice has served me well during the ensuing years in prison. In the end, regardless of my efforts to influence that "perpetrating" gang member to stop pretending to be a gang member, he continued throwing gang signs like it was cool.

About a week later the real gang members found out this inmate I'd known from the county jail was not a gang member and was only trying to masquerade as one. They were angered at having been fooled into including him as a member of their gang. They reacted the way gangs usually do; they beat and stomped the perpetrating inmate unconscious. Adding to the humiliation of the beating, not only was the perpetrating inmate lying there, bleeding uncontrollably on the floor, but he urinated and defecated on himself while unconscious, for everyone to see.

It is a myth when people say it is "impossible to get out of a gang." In fact I know many prisoners who renounced their gangs and have been free from gang affiliation for many years.

238

To aid and assist your own incarcerated loved one in preventing gang association and gang affiliation, tell them to say a firm "No" whenever approached to join or participate in gang activities. When saying "no," saying it **firmly and consistently** is key to avoiding problems. If your loved one is consistent in reaffirming they want no part of a gang, over time (for the most part) gang members will stop trying to recruit them.

However, there are times when saying "no" to gang affiliation just isn't enough and gang members will persist in trying to intimidate other inmates to become a part of their gang by using physical force. When gang members (or anyone else for that matter) threaten to use physical force to make inmates comply with inappropriate requests (i.e. financial or sexual favors) it is extremely important that your loved one is able to protect them self against those potential threats.

Unfortunately, **you cannot depend on the prison administrators to protect inmates**. The unvarnished truth is that the administration could care less about what happens to inmates and that becomes the primary source of problems within the prison system. In fact, there is absolutely no protection to be had from administration when it comes to the safety and welfare of prisoners. The prison administration only sees its role as protecting society from us; not protecting inmates from each other. Therefore, to be protected against gangs or any threat within the prison system, inmates must learn how to protect themselves.

I want to share something that is highly against the prison norms and the inmates' code of conduct, but if implemented inmates will be as safe as can possibly be expected within these prison walls. If there is an imminent threat to an inmate's safety; the inmate needs to do one of the following:

• Try to remove them self from the threatening situation, or

• Fight back

If inmates are able to remove themselves from an imminent threat, the removal is only a **temporary** resolution and in time they will once again be confronted with the threat. Therefore, it is vital that inmates carefully **document** that threat.

Documentation is not a popular resolution to problems in prison. However, anyone with any common sense knows that documentation provides a paper trail as a form of protection for the threatened inmate in the event that, despite outcries and warnings of imminent danger the administration leaves the inmate in an unsafe and threatening environment, and the inmate is continually forced to physically defend them self against those potential physical threats.

Assuming not all new inmates are well versed in maintaining paper trails, it will be up to you as their outside support to inform them of the importance of maintaining paper trails, and possibly they will need your help in guiding them in what to document.

Encourage them to send their documentation to every top official and relevant department in the prison system and even outside of the prison system. Typical documentation protocol is to write the warden of the prison unit, or any ranking officer using grievance forms provided by the prison, but **also** encourage your loved one to write to the Office of the Inspector General for their unit; write to the Chaplaincy Department; write to the Chief of Classification; write to the unit Case Manager; write the Safe Prisons Department; write the Unit Safety Coordinator's Office and write the Security Threat Group (STG), even write the local Sheriff and District Attorney of the community where the prison is located. The whole point is to let everyone know that there is an imminent life threatening problem and the prison is doing nothing to protect the inmate.

Writing each and every one of these officials and departments and explaining the potential threat demonstrates that the inmate is attempting to resolve the problem. Tell your loved one to **always make several copies of all documentation**. They should keep copies for their own records and send *additional copies* to you for safe-keeping in the event the proof of their paper trail is needed at a later date.

Family and friends can aid in the prevention of potential threats that incarcerated loved ones are experiencing by contacting the warden of the unit; by contacting the ombudsman (or the community liaison for the prison system) and/or by contacting their state representative's office and explaining the situation. The unvarnished truth is that regardless of how the prison attempts to minimize the danger of the potential threat or even attempts to intimidate those reporting the potential problem, families must persist in reporting these potential threats until the prison acts to protect their loved one or the prisoner will be forced to do something to protect himself or become a victim of violence at the hands of other prisoners.

Documentation is definitely **not** the norm in prison. The vast majority of prisoners would rather physically fight against a threat than to document the threat. The reason for that is that inmates don't want to be labeled as a "snitch." But, I've witnessed so many inmates physically fight against a physical threat and in the process of defending themselves kill the other inmate, earning themselves longer sentences and even the death penalty. Other inmates that observed the killing had no problem testifying (just another word for "snitching") as to what they observed in exchange for early parole or a reduction of their prison sentence. The prison officials and District Attorney will readily use every available resource (including "snitches") to assure the inmate who defended himself gets life in prison or the death penalty. Therefore, it is just common sense to officially document threats in the event the person is forced to defend them self.

———

A word about "Fighting Back": Fighting back is always the last resort, but every person has the right to defend them self against an imminent threat of physical harm. If inmates can remove themselves from potentially harmful situations, they should. And, inmates should officially document the situation afterward. However, if inmates are in imminent danger of physical harm and cannot safely remove themselves from the situation, in my opinion they have no other choice and should fight back.

THE PRISON GRIEVANCE PROCESS

Speaking of documentation—there are ample opportunities to "document" in prison that are definitely within the norms of the prison culture. The primary source for accepted documentation is the prison grievance system.

Although many innocent people are incarcerated, most people in prison have done something wrong and are guilty of the offenses for which they have been incarcerated. However, what some people seem to forget is that guilty or innocent those who are in prison are still human beings. It was always my understanding that we are sent to prison to become *better* human beings. Unfortunately, the prison environment is not always so conducive to becoming a better person.

As one would expect, there are problems in prison. Frequently things go wrong. Frequently people don't do what they are supposed to do. When things go wrong in most large organizations, there is usually a formal internal process by which to "resolve" those problems. In prison that process is called: "filing a grievance."

I have been incarcerated for over twelve years during which time I have filed several grievances. While I am incarcerated in Texas, I am fairly certain the grievance process is similar in other states. I do my best to use the grievance process as little as possible and I personally reserve grieving for what I consider truly serious matters, such as matters of physical safety or inadequate medical care.

With 111 prison units (several privately contracted), Texas currently has the largest prison system in the country with over 160,000 prisoners.

The grievance process is administered uniformly throughout the entire prison system. There are two stages of the grievance process that must be exercised before justifying the filing of a Federal lawsuit against the prison system.

When an incident occurs the inmate requests a Step 1 Grievance form, sometimes referred to here as an "I-127." In a "Step 1 Grievance" the inmate is asked to describe the matter being grieved and also to give their own statement regarding how they want the matter resolved. The "Step 1 Grievance" is placed in the unit truck mail and delivered to and answered by the warden or assistant warden of the unit on which the prisoner is housed or where the incident occurred.

If an inmate is not satisfied with the response to their Step 1 Grievance, they can then file a Step 2 Grievance which is answered on the regional level by the Regional Executive who is responsible for overseeing the operation of several prison units in one geographical area. The Step 2 Grievance basically asks the inmate to explain why they are not satisfied with the determination made on their Step 1 Grievance. They may provide additional information and are asked to state how they would like the matter resolved.

At the outset, I will say that the grievance system is totally ineffective. However, to provide a fair and balanced discussion of the grievance process, I believe that it is vital to discuss both of the following topics:

- The Prison Environment

- The Structure of the Grievance Process

The prison environment is designed for two types of people. The *first* are those individuals who break the law by committing crimes and are prosecuted, convicted and sentenced to prison. The *second* are those individuals who are supposedly law abiding citizens who administer over the prison system. In my opinion, prisoners and officers are not all that different when it comes to character and conduct.

Throughout my incarceration, I have witnessed many unpleasant acts of cruelty demonstrated by inmates that are simply outrageous and in all honesty "stupid." Gang violence is extremely rampant; extortion and rape happens all too often, as do many other devious acts. I am sure that many of these acts of cruelty demonstrated by inmates are not surprising to many people. I only mention these incidents to say that there is definitely a need for the governance of prisoners.

However, what might surprise many people is the character and acts of those individuals who administer over the prison system. As I have witnessed with inmates, I have also witnessed officers and even upper level prison administrators engage in many acts of cruelty that are also outrageous and "stupid." Officers routinely abuse their power by acts ranging from belittling and humiliating prisoners to violently attacking and sometimes killing inmates.

In addition to the many acts of cruelty, I will say that the prison system is operated in the manner it is because of the method of management and the character of those who administer over the *entire* prison system. As with virtually all organizations, the day-to-day operation of the system is a reflection of the top administrators, for how they govern is how the lower echelons operate. So, how do cell phones; drugs and money (all considered to be contraband) get into circulation in the prisons when there are supposedly stringent checks and balances at every level of the system?

It does not require extraordinary intelligence to know that officers either bring these items into the prison themselves or officers allow these items to enter the prison through specific checkpoints.

Another question: Why would an officer engage in an inappropriate intimate relationship with an inmate, sometimes marrying the offender and thus risking their entire career and livelihood and even risking going to prison them self?

In addition to the fact that many of the officers are just as contaminated and corrupt as prisoners, the overall operational structure of the prison system is to blame for the ineffectiveness of the grievance system.

The structure of the grievance process is identical to the structure of the overall prison system in that it is **totally self-governed**. There is no independent oversight of the prison system. Therefore, there are **no checks and balances**, as there is no accountability for the operation of the prison system. By the same token, there is no independent oversight of the grievance process. Therefore, there is **no accountability** for the implementation of the grievance process. For this very reason a Step 1 Grievance is answered by the warden or assistance warden with exactly the same response literally 99% of the time: *"The officer denied all allegations; no further action is warranted."*

Because there is no accountability in place, a Step 2 Grievance essentially appealing the administration's response to the Step 1 Grievance and answered by the Regional Executive simply *echoes* the warden's or assistant warden's response to the Step 1 Grievance 99% of the time, regardless of the evidence presented supporting the claim by the inmate.

The only other recourse an inmate has in trying to resolve a complaint is to have their family contact the Ombudsman's Office or the Office of the Attorney General. There are two distinct problems with this. First, many prisoners have absolutely *no outside support.* Therefore, they have no one to pursue the matter outside the prison. For them, the grievance process is a dead end street. However, even for those who do have family or other outside support, taking the matter to either or both the Ombudsman and Office of the Attorney General is an exercise in futility because both agencies are *simply arms of the prison.* They will *echo* whatever response the warden or assistant warden have given in the

Step 1 Grievance process, which 99% of the time is, *"The officer denied all allegations; no further action is warranted."*

In addition to the rubber stamp responses at all levels of administration, as well as the self-governing of the prison system, those who administer over the prison system are just as corrupt as the people they administer over. Therefore, it is no surprise that the grievance process is ineffective.

Although I rarely submit grievances, last year an incident occurred that I believed was exceptionally serious and warranted a grievance. It occurred as I was getting ready to leave my assigned work area in the unit kitchen.

Prison protocol requires that all inmates be strip-searched before leaving their assigned work area. After I was stripped by one officer, the first article of clothing I put on was my boxer-shorts. Once my boxer-shorts were on, I bent over to pick up the rest of my clothing so that I could dress and move out of the way of the other inmates who were still waiting to be strip-searched. When I bent over to pick up the rest of my clothing, a sergeant walked up behind me and hunched me with his radio antenna, poking me on the behind in a most inappropriate way. The sergeant did this in front of other officers and staff, as well as several other inmates, and then he began to laugh.

As an instinctual reaction, I abruptly turned around and pushed him into the wall and told him, "I don't play that way."

Although the manner in which the radio antenna hit me was clearly deliberate, the sergeant apologized stating that what he had done was an "accident." Then, realizing I was not playing and would likely file a grievance against him for sexual misconduct, he repeatedly asked me if the incident was over.

I responded by saying "Yes," because at the time all I cared about was getting as far away from this particular guy as I possibly could.

After I returned to my housing area, I immediately called a family member and informed them of the incident. Because of the severity of this sergeant's behavior, following expected protocol my family contacted the Ombudsman's Office. The Ombudsman's office told them that due to the sexual nature of the allegation the matter would be turned over to the investigative division housed on the same prison unit where the incident occurred.

My family member, having previous experience with these matters, recognized that an internal investigation was an exercise in futility and would only result in defending the officer. Therefore, they brought the matter to the attention of their State Representative who just happened to be a member of the State Corrections Committee.

At the same time, following expected protocol, I wrote a Step 1 Grievance which was quickly returned to me with the expected routine response, **"The officer denied all allegations; no further action is warranted."**

Encouraged by my family member to follow expected protocol, I then filed a Step 2 Grievance. This too was returned to me with a rubber stamped response, echoing that of the unit warden, **"The officer denied all allegations; no further action is warranted."**

Because of legislation related to any sexual assault inside a prison, whether by inmate or staff, I also contacted the Safe Prison Department, which of course is housed on the same prison unit where the incident occurred. It is essentially an arm of the Office of the Attorney General which in and of itself is only an arm of the prison system.

All efforts that I made through the prison's identified grievance process were to no avail. Even though this particular incident was reported immediately, no medical evaluation was done, and no inmate that was present when the incident occurred was ever interviewed. Therefore, I was left to wonder if other officers and staff present were even interviewed. It is unlikely they ever were.

My family member continued to persistently pursue the matter through the State Representative's office.

In the meantime, because I grieved this particular incident and because questions were now coming from the State Representative's office, the sergeant and his co-workers responded (as is common practice when an inmate refuses to stop grieving) by retaliating against me. This retaliation was indicated by officers making degrading comments to me (typically racial and sexual in nature) and creating and writing me up for bogus cases. Their retaliation persisted as the matter continued to be investigated from the outside.

Believing the allegation to be true, the State Representative personally called the Director of the State Prison System and inquired about the case. In an apparent attempt to sound as though he had done his job, the Director responded by saying he had sent a letter on the matter to the Representative on the preceding day.

The Representative then indicated the allegations were very serious, and the prison Director responded by saying he did not recall the allegations. To this the Representative reportedly refreshed his memory, telling my family member that the Director clearly had no knowledge of the case, because his response was "frantically," "Oh! Disregard my letter. Please disregard the letter I sent yesterday and I'll get my best investigator on this immediately. Just disregard that letter."

The additional investigation that resulted from the prison director's involvement only intensified the retaliation against me by the prison staff. Even the warden called me in and told me to "tell my family member and 'her representative' to back off" and additionally presented me with a pre-typed statement, ordering me to sign it. The statement was written as if I were saying the incident was of no importance and the matter was resolved. When I refused to sign it, stating that I preferred to write my own statements, the retaliation of course continued against me.

Ultimately, because of the outside pressure initiated and pursued by my family member, who requested I be moved off the unit where the incident occurred, and because of the support we received from the State Representative, I was relocated to a new unit.

After this experience, I vowed to never write a grievance again, because they don't work and you will be retaliated against if you don't stop grieving.

Once on the new unit, I was assigned field duty, usually a work assignment given to new inmates or those being disciplined. While I made no complaints about the assignment, after working in the fields for several months I attempted to talk with the field lieutenant concerning a problem I was having with being denied the right to use the restroom while at work in the fields. The lieutenant cursed at me and told me to get back in the field line before he writes a case on me.

On this same day another inmate also had to use the restroom and was similarly denied the right to do so. As usual, the only thing the officers would say to him was, "Hold it," as they laughed at the inmate. The inmate again attempted to inform the officer that he was sick and urgently needed to use the restroom. Again, the officer's response was "Hold it!" Unfortunately the inmate could not "hold it" any more and defecated on himself in front of everyone there. The officers all laughed at him and would not even allow him to remove his socks to clean himself up.

Horribly appalled by the incident, but because of my vow to never write another grievance again, I contacted my family member immediately by phone once I returned from the fields and told them what had just happened. Also disgusted and appalled, my family member asked my suggestion of how to address the situation. I suggested they begin by calling the major on the unit and report the incident, as I had heard he was someone who would actually listen.

My family member called the major and although later reporting to me that the major immediately became defensive, telling her, "You can tell anyone about this you want; it is not true," within about ten minutes of her call, the inmate who had defecated on himself and I were called into the major's office. I was confronted with having reported the incident to someone outside of the prison. However, it is interesting to note that not only were port-a-potties installed in the fields two days later, but although I had never complained or grieved about working in the fields, which is considered among the lowest of menial jobs—even used as punishment, I was actually asked which job I would prefer. I gave my preference and have been working in that job ever since.

No. The grievance process does not work. It is totally useless and unless you have **outside support that is persistent in pursuing the matter**, you either live with the abuse and humiliation presented by the officers or as some prisoners do, you find other more devious ways to attack them.

The bottom line is that grievances are totally ineffective. From my experience, the only thing that works is going outside the prison to hold officers accountable for what they are supposed to do. Although we haven't done so yet, probably the best way to address a grievance is to shine the light of the media on the officers, the unit and the entire prison system when they are in the wrong. They don't like the public to know what really goes on behind these prison walls, but once exposed, they will respect it.

FEDERAL LAW: REQUIREMENT TO FILE A GRIEVANCE BEFORE SUING THE PRISON

The question of whether it is right that there is a law that a grievance must be filed before suing the prison system is actually a "Catch 22." I say this because despite believing the grievance system is a total sham, if the grievance system actually worked, there would be little reason for filing lawsuits against prison systems. Unfortunately, this is not the case.

Almost assuredly many frivolous lawsuits from inmates made this law a necessity. However, filing a lawsuit should legally be a right of any individual who believes their rights have been violated or a crime has been committed against them. Surely, serious cases of abuse of power by correctional staff should definitely by-pass the grievance system, because they are in fact *criminal* acts. If the officer was in the free world, the act would be punishable by law. For example, the sexual act that was committed against me would be considered at the very least sexual harassment, if not rape by a foreign object, if it occurred in the free world. As such, a lawsuit certainly should be allowable without going through an internal grievance process. However, less serious acts could probably be handled judiciously within the prison system and not need legal action, *if the grievance process were managed in a fair and just manner* as the system was intended.

I write this for family and friends of prisoners, because I know that if they are reading this they are genuinely concerned for the welfare of their loved one. Too often when prisoners attempt to explain circumstances such as I have described here, even the most well-intended family and friends cannot bring themselves to believe members of the administration of our prisons would act in these ways.

My loved ones know me. They know what I say to them and what I say here is true. I want families and friends of other inmates to believe their loved ones when they come to them for help with incidents like these.

Families and friends may not believe it, but they do have power when they stand up and advocate for their loved one in prison—especially when they remain persistent in their pursuit of justice. No person should be made to feel as though they are not supported. It is my hope that you will use this information to provide your loved one in prison the support they need to be safe and free from humiliation or abuse.

PRISONERS' RELATIONSHIPS

People are consistently looking for fulfillment in life, and prisoners are no exception. Many people think they will find fulfillment through material things such as money, houses and cars; others think that social status that comes from job positions and titles will bring fulfillment. True, all of the above might bring fulfillment to a certain degree, but in reality true fulfillment in life comes from establishing meaningful relationships.

It is quite a challenge trying to establish meaningful relationships while in prison, but although prisons are abnormal environments in many ways (especially with regard to relationships) relationships are maintained and developed while in prison. In fact, relationships are necessary components in the growth and development of each prisoner.

There are two classifications of relationships within the prison environment. The first classification is "Relationships Established *Before* Prison;" the second classification is "Relationships Established *In* Prison."

To be well equipped to become the most effective member of your incarcerated loved one's support team, and in all honesty to be well equipped to *avoid* becoming the next victim of the grave manipulation and deception embedded throughout the prison culture, it behooves families and friends of prisoners to acquire knowledge about the realities of relationships in the prison culture. Knowledge is power.

RELATIONSHIPS ESTABLISHED BEFORE PRISON

Relationships established before prison typically consist of family, friends and associates the prisoner knew before becoming incarcerated. This would of course include biological family, adoptive family, church family, co-workers and friends met through various community activities. Those who fall in this category of relationships actually have the greatest potential to influence the life of the prisoner in either a positive or a negative direction—that just depends on the character of those **who actually maintain contact** with the prisoner.

It is likely you fully intend to maintain contact with your loved one and are reading this book because you want to become knowledgeable about the prison environment in order to become the most **positive** support your incarcerated loved one has from the outside. The following list includes several ways that family and friends can provide meaningful support that will influence prisoners' lives in a positive direction. Several of the methods for providing meaningful support have been discussed in detail previously, including:

Written Correspondence - Mail or e-mail: We have previously talked of the importance of written communication between prisoners and their loved ones. Regardless of why prisoners are incarcerated, they are human beings and like all human being they have the same needs and desires as any other person to be loved and cared about. Simply put, receiving written communication offers tangible confirmation that they are cared about, but even more importantly your written correspondence is a valuable means of conveying positive values to encourage the prisoner in a positive direction.

Phone calls: Similarly, prisoners enjoy hearing the voices of those people they love: parents, siblings, children, spouses and genuine friends. Next to an actual visit, phone conversations are the most tangible means of conveying care and concern. Phone conversations also provide opportunities for those on the outside to discuss values and offer encouragement to the prisoner to maintain themselves in a positive manner. In fact, many prisoners actually stop themselves from engaging in negative behaviors out of fear that they will be caught by prison administrators and lose their phone privileges. So, having the opportunity to actually speak by phone with family and friends carries a lot of weight with prisoners.

Visits: Prisoners especially enjoy the opportunity to communicate in person with those they love and perhaps these face-to-face visits are the best times for family and friends to share values and encourage the prisoner. Visits offer loved ones the opportunity to actually see the prisoner's reactions and assess the veracity of their responses to information being offered. There is nothing like looking someone directly in the eye to best understand whether they are accepting the ideas being conveyed or whether they are heading in a positive or negative direction.

There are some other ways families and friends can show their support to their loved one in prison that we have not talked about yet.

Educational Materials: Although we did talk earlier about sending books and literature to the prisoner, we did not emphasize the potential educational value of these items. Educating oneself while in prison is well known to be a key to the prisoner's success when returning to the community. In fact, without the support of families and friends, it is highly unlikely the prisoner can or will receive any education at all while incarcerated.

Contrary to some widely held erroneous beliefs, while the prison system does offer a limited number of college and vocational course opportunities within prison facilities, other than GED classes the prison system neither provides nor pays for any higher education for prisoners, whether through classroom education or correspondence courses. In fact, the financial burden to enroll in education courses is that of the prisoner and if the prisoner has no personal resources to pay for these classes, the burden of course is passed on to family and friends who are willing to support the prisoner's pursuit of an education.

Some people may disagree, but education is one of the best investments with the greatest return, especially for those who are incarcerated. Statistics show that prisoners who have educated themselves before returning to society significantly decrease their chances of returning to prison. In other words, when prisoners educate themselves their recidivism rate is significantly lower than those who have received no education while in prison.

Undoubtedly families and friends of prisoners experience a wide range of financial difficulties, even difficulties that are directly the result of their loved one's incarceration. So it is understandable that some are unable to provide for the formal education of their incarcerated loved one. Higher education can be very costly. However, that is not an excuse to provide **no** educational support at all, as there are other ways to motivate the prisoner to educate them self that are not as costly as enrolling in college courses. In fact, some of the ways to motivate the prisoner's pursuit of education are almost free of any cost.

We are now in the technology-era with a vast amount of free or inexpensive educational resources available literally at our fingertips through the internet. Unfortunately, the prisoner usually has no access to the internet, however their loved ones do. Family and friends can easily ask the prisoner about their interests or the things they would like to learn more about. Once you know their areas of interest you can search for related items on the internet and copy and print articles on that topic and send them to the prisoner. If you don't have a computer or access to the internet, you can find free internet access at your local library.

While the self-education provided by free internet resources may not result in a diploma or degree, there are other free resources that do provide certificates of completion that can serve prisoners well in educating themselves. For example, the College Guild courses mentioned earlier in this book are one resource for learning various topics of interest such as history, philosophy; creative writing and even physics. Those courses are stimulating and enlightening and are completely free to the prisoner.

There are also a number of faith-based organizations that offer free Bible study classes via correspondence. In fact, we have just recently learned of a brand new resource that can result in an actual college degree in theology and it is completely free to prisoners. While this resource provides on-line studies, which are not accessible to most prisoners, family and friends can provide the contact information to the prisoner to enroll in the classes. This resource is called "Pilgrim Theological Seminary" and their information is at http://pilgrimseminary.webs.com/.

A little ingenuity and a bit of time invested in on-line searching will net a nice variety of available educational resources for prisoners. The most important role of family and friends is to *encourage* the prisoner to participate in these educational opportunities!

You can encourage the prisoner to pursue an education by providing informative books and even magazines that are available at a fairly reasonable cost. For example, the "Dummies" series of books are available on virtually every subject imaginable, as is the "Idiot's Guide" series. These and a great deal of other informative literature can be ordered on-line or from local book stores to be shipped directly to the prisoner.

Perhaps your loved one would like to learn more about technology that is so necessary for employment in today's society. Typically, prisoners do not have open access to the internet, but they may like to have *knowledge* of the many resources to be found there to prepare themselves for the technical skills they will need when they return to the community. A number of prisoners have read volumes of material from a wide variety of literature and as a result are quite knowledgeable about using the internet for various purposes, such as social media interaction and on-line investing. These educational and informative books can be found on-line for reasonable prices, and are even cheaper when purchased as used copies.

Even subscriptions to magazines on every imaginable topic can be ordered at reduced rates, especially for the first year of the subscription. Because these subscriptions arrive with the prisoner's mail on a monthly basis, they provide a steady stream of educational material. If the renewal rates seem too costly, it would just be important to be aware of when the subscription ends, as it will likely be automatically renewed at the higher rate, if the subscription isn't promptly cancelled.

You can really encourage and even help your loved one to educate them self by providing reading materials of an educational nature in any format. Remember, knowledge is power. *"When we know better, we do better."* (Maya Angelou)   Help your loved one "know better."

Financial Support: Although the prison system supposedly provides for the basic needs of each prisoner and while a person could survive with these provisions alone, what little the prison system does provide is often overrated. For example, the prison system in Texas does not provide for the most basic hygiene needs of prisoners, such as toothpaste or deodorant. It is my understanding that female prisoners are only provided five tampons and a couple pads for their monthly cycle. While the prisoner certainly won't die without these and other similar items, they certainly would be healthier and less troubled by having them. These and other items for basic hygiene needs are sold in the prison commissary. If families and friends are able to do so, a small monthly contribution to cover the cost of these types of items will at the very least provide adequate hygiene supplies for the prisoner.

Of course other items are available for prisoners to purchase through the commissary. Although some are certainly not a crucial necessity, such as snacks or greeting cards, some items can certainly help a prisoner be more comfortable. For example, in Texas where summer heat has consistently been in the triple digits for weeks on end (and contrary to popular belief, the prison cell areas are **not** air conditioned), the commissary does sell fans which are of some relief from the heat. For those prisoners who are working on legal matters, such as preparing their own writs for appeals, if they want the documents they submit to the courts to be legible and appear more professional, typewriters are even available for purchase in the commissary.

I am not fully familiar with how clothing is provided in other prison systems, although I do know that some states allow families and friends to actually send in certain articles of clothing to the prisoner. However, that is not allowable in many prison systems, including the Texas prisons. For example in Texas, inmates must purchase items such as thermal underwear, adequate work gloves or work boots to protect against the wet and cold when they are required to work in inclement weather conditions. These items are also available for purchase at the prison commissary.

In some prison systems it is even possible for family and friends to send in approved writing supplies and postage stamps. However, that is not allowed in other prison system. While the prison may provide an allotted amount of writing supplies to *indigent* prisoners, the allotment is not consistent or assured. Therefore, if prisoners even want to write home on a regular basis they must purchase writing materials through the commissary.

Those prisoners who need or even want such items as these, but have no outside financial support, will find "other ways" to acquire them. While these "other ways" are not always devious in the way of criminal behavior, they do require manipulation and "bending the rules" to achieve the desired outcome. For example, postage stamps are a common source of currency inside the prison. To simply have items they need or that make them more comfortable, indigent prisoners will steal items from their work assignments such as foods from the kitchen or laundry and cleaning supplies to exchange with other inmates for stamps.

They then accumulate their stamps and offer another prisoner a certain amount of stamps to order a needed item from the commissary. Once the needed item is obtained, it is then exchanged for the agreed upon number of stamps. Exchanging stamps for commissary goods, while certainly not considered a major crime to most free world people, is against the prison rules. So if family and friends are able to provide funds for truly needed purchases, it certainly can eliminate any wrong doing on the part of the prisoner, and the prisoner can avoid the risk of being written up if caught "bending the rules."

———

A Word of Caution about Providing Financial Support to Prisoners: Unfortunately, this is unvarnished truth you never hoped to hear, but prisoners routinely extort their own families and friends by inflating their stated need for money. While for some prisoners this type of behavior appears to be second nature, for others it is an act of desperation based on fear. Neither reason is justification for extorting those who are only trying to help. The latter reason is a *desperate cry* for help.

If you are providing financial support to a prisoner, it is perfectly appropriate to insist that they carefully budget what you send them; it is perfectly appropriate to inquire into their purchases; it is perfectly appropriate to research by computer or even by calling the unit commissary to verify prices of items. Because you are providing financial support, there are two very important reasons why it is necessary to make sure that those you are providing that support to use what you provide responsibly.

- **Some prisoners will use the money you provide irresponsibly and unwisely.** It is not fair to families and friends to provide money that is not used for the purpose they believed it would be used for, especially if the prisoner expects them to send even more money to replenish that which was used inappropriately.

- **Some prisoners will use the money you provide for unethical and even dangerous purposes.** Often prisoners will request money to cover gambling debts or bribes or to attempt to gain protection from threats by other prisoners. Loved ones should be aware of the prisoner's true financial necessities to be able to discern whether the prisoner is requesting extra money for legitimate needs or whether they are in trouble or even in danger.

If you truly want to help your loved one in prison become a better person, you will hold them accountable for inappropriate use of the money you send. Following is a list of activities and habits prisoners engage in that are extremely expensive and even dangerous.

- **Gambling** – Those prisoners who are not engaged in productive activities (such as educating themselves as was mentioned above) have too much empty time on their hands and often become involved in gambling. If they are using the funds their loved ones provide for gambling with other prisoners instead of for the purpose their loved one believed they needed the money, they are showing absolutely no appreciation or even respect for their loved one's support. Additionally, gambling is one of the primary causes of violence within the prison environment. Prisoners who gamble take their wagers very seriously. Not unlike gambling in the free world, when gambling debts (even for a bet on a football game) are not paid, violence erupts.

- **Drugs, Alcohol and Tobacco** – The absolute unvarnished truth is that the vast majority of the public erroneously thinks the prison environment is free from the chemical substances that brought so many individuals into prison because of their dependence on alcohol and/or drugs. With all of the "no smoking" laws, who would even think that prisoners would have access tobacco (or other) smoking products in prison? Well, the unvarnished truth is there is nothing you can get in the free world that you cannot get in prison, for a price.

  The fact is that there is a vast underground in prison that enables these substances to flow freely when purchased at a pretty high cost. For example, one self-rolled cigarette goes for around $1.50.

  In all honesty, this underground supplies more serious types of contraband, including hard street drugs. If a prisoner is making such underground purchases, they are obviously not committed to improving themselves while incarcerated, not to mention the fact that they are not showing respect for the hard earned monies their loved ones are depositing into their accounts for what was intended for legitimate purchases from the commissary.

- **Extortion** – Some prisoners extort each other and they also extort their family and friends. It is fairly self-explanatory as to how prisoners extort each other—bribes. Typically these bribes relate to promises for protection for the right amount of money. However, prisoners extort family and friends just as frequently by lying and deceiving family and friends about how they spend their money or by quoting higher prices for commissary items than are actually charged and by requesting more money than they actually need.

If you think your loved one won't lie to you concerning their "need" for money, simply insist that they provide you with their commissary receipts. If they have nothing to hide they will gladly send their receipts. However, if they do have something to hide, they will make all sorts of excuses as to why they cannot provide a receipt. It just seems logical that those who are providing financial support to prisoners should, at the very least have the right to know how their money is being used.

Mail; e-mail; phone calls, financial support; visits; educational materials are among the most important ways families and friends can indicate their support for a prisoner and each of these forms of support can be used as a means to influence a prisoner's life in a positive direction.

It is understandable that all of the aforementioned items can not be provided at one time by many families and friends because of financial limitations. However, it is unlikely that *none* of the above can be provided at one time or another during the prisoner's incarceration. At the very least, consistent expressions of love can be sent to those who are incarcerated by sending written correspondence at least periodically.

There are, however, some practices that undermine the good intentions of families and friends and send messages to the prisoner that can damage a relationship and send the prisoner in a negative direction if those practices persist.

There are a number of situations that can jeopardize relationships between prisoners and their families and friends. Following are the two most talked about complaints among prisoners when it comes to the relationships they had *before* entering prison.

- **Family and friends do not respond to the context of prisoners' letters.** Prisoners, like anyone else desire to be heard and expect answers to their questions, especially when they've asked the same question or made the same request multiple times.

While there is a typically held belief that prisoners have nothing but time on their hands, in fact the prisoner's time is extremely limited by rigid requirements and expectations that they be in certain areas of the prison at certain times or that they be immobile while being "counted," or that they respond to "lay-ins," (which are expectations that they keep appointments with prison personnel such as the infirmary, law library, education department, the chaplain or warden's office) or that they go to their work assignment at an appointed hour. So, when a prisoner does **find time** to write, they certainly appreciate it when there is some evidence that the person they wrote to actually **reads the context** of their letter.

I have been incarcerated almost thirteen years and although one of my brothers occasionally communicates with me via written correspondence he has never in all of those years ever responded to the context of my letters to him.

While I always make the effort to respond to his quick notes to me, for the entire time of my incarceration my brother has made the same request in each and every piece of his correspondence, asking that I add him to my visitation list. However, he has never responded to my consistently repeated requests that he send me his *home address* since I write to him at his post office box and an actual street address is required for the visitation list. How can I add him to my visitation list if I do not have the correct information to add him?

In fact, by not responding to my repeated requests he is actually sending me one of two messages—or both. First, he never really reads my letters and only sends off a quick e-mail when he feels guilty that he hasn't written me in quite some time. Or, second, he does not really want or plan to visit me anyhow, because if he genuinely wanted to visit me, would he not do everything possible to assure that I have the proper information to add him to my visitors' list?

I am not alone in making this complaint. Numerous prisoners can frequently be heard telling of family and friends who fail to respond to the *context* of their correspondence. They too are left to read between the lines in determining the reasons their family and friends fail to respond to the context of their letters. Most often, what they read between the lines is damaging to the relationship.

- The second most heard complaint among prisoners about relationships they had before coming to prison is that **family and friends do not keep commitments and break promises**. Often family or friends will agree to do something requested by the prisoner and even tell the prisoner they've done it, but the evidence that the task has actually been accomplished is never forthcoming.

When a prisoner is worried that they have not heard from their loved ones in quite some time or they have an urgent message they want to get to their loved ones quickly but are unable to call them for various reasons, they will ask another prisoner who is able to make phone calls to ask one of their outside contacts to try to reach their family to convey a message.

Recently another prisoner asked me if I would ask my family member to try to call his wife to see if she had put money on his account. He said that his wife had repeatedly told him she had already sent the money to the trust fund, but after several weeks had passed the money never appeared on his books. It had now been about two weeks since he had even heard from his wife, so out of concern that something was possibly wrong with her or that the money had been lost in the mail or even deposited to the wrong inmate's account, he asked for my help.

My family member agreed to try to contact the prisoner's wife and then reported back to me that the wife said she "had been busy and had not had time" to send the money yet, but would do so "by the end of the week."

Of course I conveyed that message to the other prisoner and needless to say he was very disturbed to hear that his wife had not done what she had repeatedly told him she had already done.

As clarification, because it was previously mentioned that prisoners will manipulate each other for devious purposes, I would like to interject that when inmates ask each other for the type of help I just described it is not considered "manipulative" or "devious" by other prisoners. Because the prison system is so volatile and even because meting out discipline is done in such an unjust manner at times, most prisoners try to arrange for an emergency back-up plan in the event they are in trouble and unable to directly contact their loved ones on the outside. Because all prisoners face this same dilemma, it is not considered a means of extortion to ask for help to contact loved ones. In fact, it is a relatively unselfish thing that prisoners do for one another. Virtually every prisoner knows they may need this type of help themselves at one time or another while they are incarcerated.

Many times prisoners ask for outside help from family and friends to acquire information related to appealing their convictions or for other legal matters. The person they contact on the outside assures them that they will go to the courthouse or call the District Clerk's Office to get the information or that they will copy legal information off the internet and send it to the prisoner. Then the prisoner patiently waits for weeks before sending letters or inquiring in phone calls about the information they are waiting to receive. Their outside contact will either make up excuses as to why they've been unable to fulfill the promise or they will blatantly lie and say the information is in the mail, when it actually isn't.

This kind of deception from family and friends only serves to destroy trust and damage the relationship. No one likes to be lied to. Family and friends should know that prisoners have a sufficient sense of reality to understand that their loved ones have busy schedules and many obligations and responsibilities other than fulfilling requests from the prisoner. Therefore, they are certainly willing to wait their turn if it will take some time for their request to be fulfilled.

What prisoners do not have is unlimited tolerance for being lied to, and when they are lied to those lies literally destroy relationships. Unfortunately, incarceration forces prisoners to be dependent on outside support to fulfill many of their absolute needs. This is a topic that requires many chapters to fully understand all of the relationship dynamics this type of dependency creates, so for simplicity's sake, let me just give you a brief example or two.

When I needed certain legal documents to work on a writ to appeal my case, I sent letters requesting this information to various courts. However, there is often a charge to obtain these records. I have no resources to include that money with my letter. Similarly, when I wanted transcripts of my academic records, I sent a letter to the college. However, the college responded by requesting a "transcript fee" before sending me the documents. As I have no access to money while in prison, the only possibility I had for obtaining the transcript I needed was to ask my family for help. I provided the letters to order the documents I needed and sent them to my family. After that, I was totally at the mercy of my family to actually write the checks or obtain the money orders required and to mail everything to the proper sources. Fortunately, my family did follow through and I eventually received the needed documents. Unfortunately, despite promises to do what was asked, that type of reliability and follow-through does not always happen for other prisoners.

There is no need to lie to a prisoner about having done something you have not done. It seems to me that there are two ways to avoid the destruction of relationships that results from lying. First, the family member or friends should simply tell the prisoner "No" if they cannot or do not want to do the favor being requested by the prisoner. Most anyone, including a prisoner can handle an honest "no" far better than an outright dishonest lie.

Second, the family member or friend should tell the prisoner the truth of the matter. If they have promised to do something for the prisoner and later realize they will be unable to do what was promised, they should simply explain that they will not be able to follow through on the promise, or tell the prisoner when they *will be able to do* what was promised, and then just do it.

NURTURING RELATIONSHIPS

We have discussed ways in which family and friends can support the prisoner (mail; e-mail; phone calls; visits; educational materials; financial support). We have provided information to assure financial contributions to the prisoner are used wisely. We have also detailed the two greatest complaints among prisoners (family and friends not responding to the context of prisoners' correspondence and not doing what was promised, with no explanation). Now let's discuss the most important element for nurturing relationships with a loved one in prison: *effective communication.*

Effective communication is not only key to avoiding, as well as resolving problems in relationships, but truly effective communication is the building block that can nurture relationships to unimaginable heights. Effective communication can also improve the quality of life for all of us. In fact, the primary reason we are writing this book is to *effectively communicate* information that will improve the prison family's quality of life as they travel the often rocky roads on the prison family journey—to make that journey easier and more productive for the entire prison family.

When people communicate even superficially, it is relatively easy for almost everyone to discuss things that they are happy about or that are fun and exciting. That is because happiness, fun and excitement are associated with pleasure. Everyone wants to feel good. However, many people, especially those in prison refuse to discuss anything associated with discomfort or fear and hurt. That is because discomfort, fear and hurt are associated with pain and no one wants to experience pain or feel uncomfortable, so they simply do all they can to avoid it.

However, pain can be a good thing to a certain extent. Pain lets us know something is wrong and needs our immediate attention. Whether physical or emotional, pain of any kind is a warning that lets us know we need to attend to the source of our pain before it is too late to do anything about it.

Prisoners know first hand that bad things happen in prison. Not only is communicating about these things uncomfortable and difficult for the vast majority of prisoners, but communicating about these bad things is also uncomfortable and difficult for the vast majority of prisoners' families and friends. Maybe family and friends are uncomfortable communicating with their incarcerated loved one concerning bad things that happen in prison because they do not know what to do to help. Hopefully what is shared here will help families and friends overcome their discomfort about discussing painful issues with their loved one in prison.

If there's any truth to the saying that "knowledge is power," the first course of action in resolving our problems is to admit there is a problem and then set out to learn as much as possible about the problem to ever be able to resolve it. If we never share our problem, others won't even know it exists and therefore they can do nothing to help us resolve it. When we communicate a problem, we are able to receive knowledge that gives us the power to do something to correct it.

Helping one another resolve problems actually nurtures relationships. To nurture your own relationship with your incarcerated loved one, you will need knowledge of the types of problems prisoners typically experience. Let's discuss the most common problems that occur in

267

prison that prisoners and their loved ones really need to discuss openly, but rarely do.

VIOLENCE IN PRISON: PHYSICAL ASSAULTS

Violence occurs frequently in prison, yet it is one of the most lied about acts that occurs in prison. Not only do prisoners lie to prison officials concerning physical assaults that have happened to them, but prisoners lie to their family and friends about those assaults, as well.

Prisoners often lie to *prison officials* about assaults because they are afraid of punishment for being involved in an altercation and also because they do not want to be labeled as a "snitch." Prisoners lie to their *family and friends* concerning assaults because they are embarrassed and ashamed and may feel they will be perceived as weak if they tell of these assaults.

Unfortunately, disclosing physical assaults to prison officials is not always in the best interest of the prisoner. Not only may the prisoner be disciplined for engaging in a violent act, but prisoners quickly come to realize that prison officials will not intervene to protect them in instances of violence. The unvarnished truth is that prison officials are downright lazy and hate doing paperwork, so they close their eyes to the violence that occurs right in front of them.

When an assault is reported, officers are required to complete incident reports. Many times, to avoid doing all the paperwork, if a prisoner continuously complains to an officer that something is wrong and repeatedly insists that the officer do something about it, the officer will actually **retaliate** by telling *other prisoners* that the inmate who has reported an assault or even the threat of an assault is "snitching" on them. This of course creates hostility between inmates that often results in violence. Presumably the officer believes they've successfully avoided filling out all the paperwork by letting the prisoners "handle the problem" for them.

VIOLENCE IN PRISON: SEXUAL ASSAULTS

Sexual assaults happen in prison far more than a person could possibly imagine. As with physical assaults, prisoners lie to prison officials and family and friends about being sexually assaulted or the prisoner just refuses to say anything at all and keeps the sexual assault a secret.

Because prisoners do not trust prison officials to do what is right, prisoners refuse to disclose such humiliating incidents. In addition to the humiliation of the sexual assault, if you factor in the fear and shame of being labeled as a "snitch" (if you tell), add the sense of feeling weak (because you weren't able to protect yourself from the assault), you have the **recipe for secrecy** among prisoners.

Prisoners do not disclose sexual assaults to family and friends because they are embarrassed and feel weak at not having been able to protect themselves. To encourage your loved one to talk with you about these types of violence so that you might be helpful in protecting them from it you must first have the knowledge necessary to know that a problem exists. Since the prisoner is highly unlikely to come right out and tell you there is a problem, you must know what to look for to determine whether there is a problem or not.

WARNING SIGNS OF VIOLENCE

Since most prisoners will never tell you of their fears about violence, to be able to help and even protect your loved one, you should be fully aware of the warning signs that a physical or sexual assault has occurred or is imminent. Here are the best clues to alert you to the fact that it is highly likely some form of violence or threat of violence has occurred.

- You actually see visible signs of violence such as scratches and bruises on the prisoner's face and various parts of the body. These visible signs very often indicate some form of violence has occurred.

- When you inquire about visible signs of injury, to avoid acknowledging violence has occurred the most common justification prisoners will provide to deflect you from the topic are such statements as: "I slipped and fell in the shower;" "I slipped and fell down the stairs;" "It happened while on the recreation yard playing basketball or handball."

- If a prisoner requests that family and friends deposit money in *another* inmate's account, you can almost be assured that they are being threatened with physical harm if they don't deposit a certain amount of money in another prisoner's account **or** they are paying another prisoner or group of prisoners (a prison gang) for protection against violence from other prisoners. The end result is extortion.

It will likely be very difficult for the prisoner to admit to you that anything is wrong. This is why building trust and effective communication between yourself and the prisoner is so important.

I am not saying that I have a "perfect" relationship with my family. However, I do have at least one person I believe I can trust implicitly to share uncomfortable information such as described here, if it does occur. That is why I was able to so quickly gain the support of my family member when the inappropriate sexual behavior of the officer occurred and even when the most distasteful incident of the inmate defecating on himself in the fields occurred. We had already built a relationship based on open effective communication that allowed me to know that it was safe to bring these incidents to their attention.

I did not fear their judgment of me, and because of the relationship that had already been nurtured between us, I knew they would believe what I had to say. I also knew that if I asked for their help they would assuredly do whatever was in their power to do to help me. I believe that if more prisoners had this type of effective communication with those on the outside that fewer prisoners would lie to their families and friends about what really goes on in prison.

Please note, while suggested safety measures have proven to be effective in many instances, those suggestions are **not absolute**. In instances where violence is involved or imminent, outside assistance may be required to maintain the prisoner's safety. If there are grave concerns that a prisoner may be in danger you are encouraged to contact PFFUnited for further evaluation of the situation and possible intervention assistance to resolve it. Our e-mail address is: info@pffunited.org.

RELATIONSHIPS ESTABLISHED IN PRISON

It would require volumes to explain in detail the pros and cons of relationships prisoners develop while in prison and we intend to elaborate on this topic in future editions of this book. However, to assure you have valuable information you may need now to determine whether your loved one is headed in a positive or negative direction, we will provide a synopsis of the most critical things families and friends need to know about prison relationships.

Everyone has the desire and even the *innate need* to be loved. It is actually a universal need of all human beings to belong to a group that embraces and unconditionally accepts us. We all consistently seek to belong to a group that provides us with support and encouragement regardless of who we are or what we have done. Of course, prisoners are no exception to this need to belong and feel accepted.

These innate needs for love and acceptance and belonging do not evaporate simply because a person is in prison. In fact, the need for love and belonging may be greater than ever when a person is isolated in the prison environment. Therefore, if a prisoner does not feel they have the love and support of their family or true friends on the outside, they will begin seeking other avenues to fill these needs. Not only might these other avenues be inappropriate or even unhealthy and dangerous, but it is anyone's guess how the other avenues a prisoner might seek to fulfill their need for belonging will influence them. It is also anyone's guess whether the influence they find through these other avenues will be temporary or will permanently direct the prisoner in a positive or negative direction.

Gang Members - We have discussed gangs fairly thoroughly. However, it is safe to say that since gangs are so pervasive in the prison system, it is virtually impossible for any prisoner to avoid having some interaction with gang members during their incarceration. The one thing that gangs do provide for those who join them is a sense of belonging. Those prisoners who are most vulnerable and most in need of the acceptance and sense of security that they believe a gang may provide will join a gang if those needs are not met by family and friends outside of the prison. Undoubtedly, prison gangs will lead those who join them in a negative direction.

Cellies & Other Prisoners - For the most part, prisoners do not make friends in the true sense of "friendship" with other prisoners. It is difficult to fully trust another person in an environment where you always must be looking out for yourself, because you never know when violence might erupt or when someone has reached their breaking point and simply goes berserk and might create a dangerous situation or even when another prisoner may become desperate and try to manipulate you into meeting their needs! In many ways, each prisoner must only look out for him or herself without concern for the others around them. This is a very selfish behavior of course, but it is a necessity for survival in prison.

Because of these survival factors, the prison environment is always tense and it takes a great deal of time to develop a sufficiently keen intuition to know who can be even moderately trusted and who cannot.

Prisoners usually refer to the person they share a cell with as their "cellie." Cellie assignments are pretty much the luck of the draw, because for the most part there seems to be no real formula for how the prison assigns those people who will live together and once assigned, cellmates can be and frequently are moved at the drop of a hat for no valid reason.

Prisoners' relationships with one another are generally aloof or superficial. Rarely will prisoners share deeply personal information about themselves with other prisoners. Some prisoners even maintain lies about who they are and where they're from and why they are in prison for the entire time they are incarcerated, always inflating their prowess of course, because they never develop any trust with other prisoners. While some moderately cordial relationships do occur, there will always be reservations about trust regardless of whether a cellie or another prisoner is leading or even willing to follow other prisoners in a positive or negative direction.

Ministries - Among the people you might meet while incarcerated are those from the free world who come into the prison chapel as volunteers, especially for faith-based ministry. In some cases these groups come in only once on their way through town. However, other ministries come on a regular basis. The group typically stays for a few hours and provides a spiritual program, and then leaves without having much direct interaction with the prisoners.

Occasionally there will be time for shaking hands and sharing a few words of pleasantry and encouragement. However, the interaction with ministry volunteers does not often lead to any sort of ongoing relationship. In fact, if the prison learns that one of the volunteers has become involved with a prisoner, or has even written an innocent friendly note to a prisoner, it is likely that volunteer will be banned from coming into the prison ever again. This stipulation usually keeps most relationships at a fairly superficial level.

However, on occasion a prisoner and a ministry volunteer (especially when of opposite genders) will connect on a deeper level and thereby risk it all to find ways to be together. We would hope that relationships formed with prison volunteers would serve to lead a prisoner in a positive direction. However, without intending to sound judgmental, the fact that both the prisoner and volunteer are violating some hard and fast man-made rules leads to speculation about the possibility that these relationships may not advance on solid footing.

Pen Pals - One of the most common sources for prisoners to attempt to fill voids in their innate need for a sense of belonging and to feel accepted and supported is through the numerous prison pen pal groups that are advertised in various magazines and newsletters that are mailed to prisoners. Because these groups range from the spiritual to the sexual, the type of relationship that might evolve from this type of connection most likely depends on the type of relationship the prisoner is seeking.

While we personally know those who met through these pen pal groups that have married and now live together in the free world and seem to have good relationships, there are some dangers to be considered in establishing a pen-pal relationship. It is sad to say, but the unvarnished truth is that **most of those dangers are for the free world correspondent** and not the prisoner.

While there are some very good people who are incarcerated, there are also some very dangerous and devious people in prison. These

274

prisoners, especially those without outside support will seek vulnerable pen pals from whom they can extort financial support by writing love letters like no movie scriptwriter has ever conceived. The end result of this type of relationship is always tragic for the well-intentioned free world pen pal who has given their heart and very often sent financial support down to their last penny to a prisoner who played the love game impeccably until they walked out of the prison gate.

Deception in pen pal relationships occurs far more frequently than we know, because the free world correspondent who engages in an ongoing "love affair" with a deceptive prisoner is typically too embarrassed at having been deceived to share their painful experience with others. On the other hand, the deceiving prisoners have absolutely no conscience at all about using pen pals for all they are worth for many years, and then totally abandoning the relationship at the end of their time in prison.

Engaging in a prison pen pal relationship is no different than engaging with an unknown person in a lonely hearts group on the internet. From falsifying personal information to sending photos of other (possibly more attractive) prisoners, to engaging in numerous pen pal relationships at one time, you have no idea who is really on the other side of the correspondence. Deception or not, there are certainly no guarantees about the direction in which either pen pal will lead the other.

Prison Personnel - We've alluded to it, but here we will say it directly: permitted or not; healthy or not; safe or not relationships often develop between prisoners and prison staff members.

All prisons hire employees of both genders. These individuals work in a wide variety of positions, including serving as officers, medical staff, office or kitchen employees and even educators. These employees have daily contact with prisoners and although it is expected that this contact will remain totally business-like and of course prison policy and training forbids staff members from engaging in any personal relationship with an inmate, intimate—very intimate relationships occur all of the time. These intimate relationships, whether solely for physical pleasure or whether genuinely emotionally intimate, are of both a heterosexual and a homosexual nature.

As with prison volunteers, of course prison staff are terminated if they are found to be intimately involved with a prisoner. Some staff members actually avoid being fired by quitting their jobs before being caught in an intimate relationship with a prisoner, for the sole purpose of continuing the relationship from the free world. Often these individuals marry and on occasion, these relationships do work out; however, most end in the same disaster described for pen pal relationships.

Very often "business relationships" develop between prisoners and staff who are motivated by promises of money to smuggle contraband into the prison for prisoners to sell. While explaining these underground business arrangements is a bit complicated, they apparently are fairly easy to arrange, because they happen all of the time. For example, you often hear of prisoners being found with large quantities of drugs or cell phones, which of course are considered contraband by the prison administration. Logic should clearly indicate that prisoners do not leave the prison to shop for these items; therefore they must be brought in from the outside.

While the prison would have you believe these items are **all** brought in by visitors, and administration even charges visitors and inmates with bogus cases for bringing such items into the prison, virtually all such contraband is brought in by prison personnel. Accomplishing such smuggling requires a good deal of collusion amongst the employees.

It is fairly well known that these underground arrangements are typically made when a member of the prison staff meets with a prisoner's outside contact who provides the requested items and pays the staff member an agreed upon amount to take the contraband to a specific prisoner. The staff member then pays off other staff to ignore the contraband when it is brought into the facility and handed to the designated prisoner. That prisoner then sells the contraband items to other prisoners for a high price. Both the prisoner and the staff members benefit financially from these arrangements.

Because there are so many unknowns with the potential to lead prisoners in unhealthy and unproductive directions, when it comes to relationships developed while in prison, it is very important that families and friends understand how critical their role is in the prisoner's life while they are incarcerated. If the prisoner has little or no outside support from those who have the potential to lead them in a positive direction, they will definitely turn to other resources to meet their needs.

IF NOT YOU, WHO?

While a loved one's time in prison can provide the ideal opportunity to strengthen relationships and improve the quality of life for the prisoner and their family, it can also become the ruin of the prisoner and their family. The outcome is largely determined by the type of support a prisoner receives from the outside—from family and friends, because the absolute unvarnished truth is that other than a few educational classes and possibly some chapel experiences, prison in and of itself provides absolutely nothing to improve the quality of anyone's life. In fact, prison barely provides for the most basic of human needs.

We know that many people who are unaware of the big picture of incarceration will state their belief that prisoners deserve nothing. Those people will say that prisoners have offended against society; they have harmed—even taken the life of other human beings, and they only deserve to face the consequences for their behavior. There are even those who will say that the harsher the punishment, the better. There are two facts such believers may have overlooked!

- Not everyone in prison is guilty, and

- Unless executed or otherwise dying in prison, all prisoners **will** return to society one day.

Tens of thousands of innocent people are trapped in our prisons. Every week we read of prisoners being exonerated or released from prison when found not to be culpable of the crime for which they have been incarcerated. Even other prisoners can think of nothing worse than being incarcerated for a crime that they did not commit. Yet, all the while they are in prison these innocent human beings are treated with the same degree of disrespect, humiliation and brutality with which all prisoners are treated. We believe that all human beings, regardless of their errors should and must be treated with dignity, and we especially believe this to be true for all of the **innocents** who are trapped behind bars.

With the exception of the death penalty and those who will otherwise die in prison, every single prisoner has a finite sentence and with or without being awarded "good time" will eventually return to their communities. When they do return to society, there are those in the community who will fear them, and with good cause.

We should all fear those who have spent years being humiliated and physically and sexually assaulted and endlessly witnesses to violence, experiencing daily injustices with absolutely no semblance of an effort at rehabilitation. Anyone enduring such circumstances is at high risk for perpetrating the same atrocities they have experienced on those they encounter in the free world, once released from prison. **The unvarnished truth is that prisons by their very nature are designed to de-humanize the prisoner, not humanize them.**

If the vast majority of prisoners will return to the community one day, isn't it just common sense to do everything possible to prepare them to return in better shape and not in worse shape than when they entered prison? Wouldn't making the effort to "rehabilitate" prisoners in a productive manner reduce the danger factors when prisoners are released into the community? If we truly wanted a safer society would we not speak out and demand that our prisons do all that can be done to improve the prisoner's chances for success upon community re-entry, rather than do all that we have already allowed prisons to do to assure the failure of sixty-five percent of prisoners upon their release?

Since the early 1940's it has been a widely understood and accepted "fact" that all human beings have certain basic innate needs that must be fulfilled to ensure they become healthy, productive and safe human beings within our society. This understanding is based on the widely accepted theory: *"Maslow's Hierarchy of Needs"* developed from the research and studies of the well respected psychologist, Abraham Maslow and typically explained with this diagram:

The Hierarchy of Needs tells us that unless a human being's most basic needs are satisfied, they will never achieve any degree of fulfillment, or as Maslow called it, "self-actualization." As a result of never becoming fulfilled, human beings will act out their frustrations and anger at not having achieved the satisfaction they are constantly seeking.

We might say that as adults, prisoners make their own choices, and some make very poor choices. That is true. However, let us look at how prison actually deters prisoners from making better choices by **thwarting** all efforts of prisoners to achieve their innate quest for fulfillment, thereby imperiling the quality of life in our communities as sixty-five percent of released prisoners return to prison time and again, largely because their most basic human needs remain unfulfilled.

Basic Human Need #1 – Physical Comfort. Our most basic human need, evidenced clearly from the moment of birth by the newborn's cries to be fed and cleaned, is our need for physical comfort. We must have our physical needs met before we can even think about achieving any goals or engaging in any relationships. For example, we will become totally distracted by hunger or an upset stomach, preventing our achievement of any other goal until the pain in our stomach is resolved. When we are freezing or burning up from extreme weather elements, all of our energy becomes devoted to reducing the discomfort rather than seeking lofty goals or expressing our love for one another. Thus, the *most basic human need* is to be physically comfortable—to be physically free from sickness, to have food in our belly, water to quench our thirst and sustain life and even to be sheltered in an environment that offers a comfortable temperature.

What Prison Provides to Meet Basic Human Need #1: While prisons by their very nature do provide a solid roof over a prisoner's head, they barely provide any of the other *most basic physical needs* of all human beings. We have already noted that prisons are attempting to feed prisoners on *less than* one dollar per meal. We challenge anyone to purchase adequate provisions for twenty-one meals per week for less than twenty-one dollars, especially in today's economy. Will those purchases stave off hunger? Will they provide adequate nutrition to maintain physical health or ample energy to carry you through a day's work—especially a day of physical labor?

Millions of children in the United States go to bed hungry and even suffer from malnutrition as occurs routinely in most third world countries. Sadly, while each one of those children internally aspires to escape poverty and starvation, how many actually do? How many actually perpetuate the cycle of starvation when giving birth to their own children? Whether deserved or not, like those starving children, malnourished and experiencing related medical problems, prisoners aspire to escape their "impoverished" conditions to have the energy to achieve their own dreams and goals, but most never do and in turn pass on their cycle of "starvation" to their own children.

While most prisoners rarely mention the temperature in the prison (because it is futile to do so), the cell areas of prisons are not air conditioned even in those states where temperatures soar into the triple digits for weeks on end. The result is much like the *illegal* act of leaving a child or animal locked in a closed car on a hot summer day for hours on end. Although for prisons it is apparently perfectly legal and goes mostly unnoticed when prisoners literally die from the heat from which they have no escape.

Prison uniforms provide no warmth from freezing winter weather and while jackets may be distributed in the winter, the flimsy and often threadbare uniforms do little to prevent unbearable chills and even frostbite if the prisoner is forced to work in unheated areas or even outside. In fact, although it has been many years ago, a good number of prisoners faced frostbite related *amputations* of digits and even limbs, when one prison unit in Texas refused to replace broken windows in the cell area during freezing winter weather. So, suffice it to say that prisons certainly do **not** provide for the most basic human need for physical comfort.

Basic Human Need #2 - Safety: The next most basic human need is to feel safe and secure from physical danger.

What Prison Provides to Meet Basic Human Need #2: What we have learned about prisons is that danger surrounds the prisoner twenty-four hours a day, seven days a week, year in and year out. There is never a moment the prisoner can totally relax and let down their guard with the assurance that at least for the next minute they will be safe from physical harm. To remain as safe as possible, prisoners must remain constantly vigilant as they know the next minute might bring the eruption of violence. And if violence erupts the prisoner knows that no one—not the prison guards or the prison administration—not even the prisoner's own "prison family" will intervene to protect them from harm or even death. With all of their attention and energy directed to maintaining their personal safety, prisoners have few if any internal resources remaining with which to aspire to meaningful relationships or higher achievement. Without persistent outside intervention from family or friends there is absolutely no sense of safety or security for the prisoner.

Basic Human Need #3 – A Sense of Belonging and Feeling Loved: Once a human being's innate need for physical comfort and safety is met, the next most important basic human need is to gain a sense of belonging and appreciation and love from those with whom one belongs.

What Prison Provides to Meet Basic Human Need #3: Since prisoners' most basic needs for comfort and safety are never met within the prison system, it is a rare prisoner who even strives to become a member of any substantial group outside of a prison gang, and they only join prison gangs to gain a sense of safety (basic human need #2). Prison offers no sense of belonging and certainly no sense of being loved. Therefore, if a prisoner is to attempt to fulfill this basic need for belonging, they must look somewhere outside of the prison environment.

Basic Human Need #4 – A Sense of Self Esteem and Respect: Having once fulfilled the first three basic human needs (comfort, safety and belonging), human beings instinctually strive for personal achievements and acquiring recognition for those achievements. These achievements give human beings a sense of positive self esteem which is reinforced by the praise they receive from others who admire their accomplishments.

What Prison Provides to Meet Basic Human Need #4: Prison provides absolutely nothing to build a prisoner's self esteem and in fact prison officials overtly and actively degrade and humiliate prisoners daily, offering absolutely no respect for prisoners—even those prisoners who are actively striving to achieve positive accomplishments. A prisoner's efforts to achieve meaningful goals, such as acquiring a GED or college degree go unnoticed, and rarely is respect let alone praise shown by prison personnel for any such accomplishment.

Basic Human Need #5 – A Sense of Self Actualization: When Maslow developed the theory of human needs he noted that all human beings are constantly and instinctually striving to achieve their highest potential. As we mature and gain knowledge, our potential to achieve constantly grows and changes. When human beings achieve one goal, they immediately set out to achieve their next goal. For example, once we accomplish graduation from high school, we may set our sights on graduating from college. When we graduate from college, we may immediately set our sights on acquiring a job and satisfying career. Once we achieve the career that we aspired to, we may set our sights on having our own business or starting a family—or both! So, while we constantly strive to achieve new goals, we never will fully realize our *total* potential, because there will always be *one more thing that we can achieve*!

What Prison Provides to Meet Basic Human Need #5: The unvarnished truth is that the prison provides absolutely nothing to meet a prisoner's need for self-actualization! The average prisoner has virtually nothing to accomplish while in prison other than to survive one more day. Because the prison environment barely provides for the most basic of innate human needs, an average of sixty-five percent of prisoners fail to succeed when they return to their communities.

The unvarnished truth is that if there is to be any hope for the prisoner to effectively mature and achieve positive growth while in prison, the stimulus necessarily must come from outside of the prison, from those who are willing to consistently invest their time and effort into providing the impetus, stimulation, encouragement and support required to fulfill the prisoners' basic human needs. If not you, who will the prisoner turn to?

HELPFUL FORMS FOR PRISON FAMILIES

DURABLE POWER OF ATTORNEY (POA) - Form

Without having a written, signed and notarized Power of Attorney to give to legal counsel, the prison or other entities on behalf of the prisoner, families and friends have absolutely no access to information regarding the prisoner.

This may not seem critical at the moment, but it is.

Tomorrow is not promised to any of us. Unfortunately, if an inmate becomes in any way incapacitated and is unable to speak for him or her self, he or she becomes the virtual property of the State/Prison and the State/Prison will be his or her *only* spokes person.

We have had numerous reports of an inmate being severely injured, even unconscious with life threatening head trauma, and because the prisoner's loved ones had no official documentation indicating their right to communication and decisions regarding that prisoner, they were unable to even receive medical updates on the inmate's condition, and were definitely denied visitation with that prisoner even while they were hospitalized.

Similarly, because prisoners do not have ready access to communicate with attorneys or other legal representation, often they ask their family or friends to make legal contacts and even legal decisions for them. Attorneys and other legal representatives will refuse to speak with the family member or friend without written authorization from the prisoner. A written POA will provide that authorization.

Of course, it is the prisoner's decision to appoint the person or persons of their own choosing to serve as their Agent or Attorney in Fact in the event they are unable to speak for them self.

It is not necessary to pay an attorney hundreds of dollars to run a POA form off of their computer. Instead, you may choose to use the form provided here which provides POA authority for both medical *and* legal issues. You can adapt it to address only one or the other, or any particular needs or preferences.

Once you and the prisoner are satisfied with the terminology of your POA, the prisoner must sign it before a Notary Public. There will be one at the jail or prison.

It is wise to have at least two ORIGINALS of the POA notarized. The prisoner may keep ONE ORIGINAL and provide the other ORIGINAL to their appointee.

NOTE: Always retain the ORIGINAL and only provide copies of the original to those individuals or entities, such as attorneys; the prison; physicians; hospitals, etc.

DURABLE POWER OF ATTORNEY

I _____, residing at _____ _____ hereby appoint _____ of _____ as my attorney-in-fact/Agent to exercise the powers and discretions described below.

This Power of Attorney shall not be affected by my subsequent incapacity.

I hereby revoke any and all general powers of attorney that previously have been signed by me.

My Agent shall have full power and authority to act on my behalf. This power and authority shall authorize my Agent to manage and conduct my affairs as described herein. My Agent's powers shall include, but not be limited to the power to:

1. Act on my behalf with regard to legal matters related to myself.
2. Sign documents, legal or otherwise necessary to pursue legal matters on my behalf
3. Employ professional and business assistance as may be appropriate.
4. Prepare, sign and file legal documents on my behalf.
5. Obtain information and documents from any source including any government or its agencies related to any legal or medical matters on my behalf.
6. Act on my behalf with regard to medical matters related to myself.
7. Act on my behalf in the event of my incapacity to do so.

This Power of Attorney shall remain in effect until rescinded by myself or until my death.

This Power of Attorney shall be construed broadly as a General Power of Attorney. The listing of specific powers is not intended to limit or restrict the general power granted in this Power of Attorney in any manner.

My Agent shall not be liable for any loss that results from a judgment error that was made in good faith. However, my Agent shall be liable for willful misconduct or the failure to act in good faith while acting under the authority of this Power of Attorney.

Date: _____ at _____

_____
Signature

State of _____

County of _____

This document was acknowledge before me the undersigned Notary on this the _____ day of _____, _____.

_____
Notary Public in and for

_____ County, _____

My commission expires: _____

RELEASE OF INFORMATION – Form

The prisoner may not agree to allow you to actually make decisions on their behalf or you may not agree to assume full responsibility such as that given in a POA. In that case, the prisoner may still give you the authority to obtain various types information on their behalf by requesting documents or discussing relevant issues with others. They can provide you the authority to obtain this type of information with a Release of Information form.

For example, perhaps they would like you to talk with their attorney about the progress in their case so that you can convey information to them while they are incarcerated. The Release of Information form will tell the attorney that it is alright to talk with you about the case.

The Release of Information is a very brief and simple form and is often used to obtain various types of information, such as legal or medical or education records or even counseling records. You can adapt this form for other purposes if needed by changing the words related to "legal" issues and inserting the correct terms for the information that is desired.

The form will need to be signed by the prisoner in front of a Notary Public and provided to you for the use specified.

It is wise to have at least two ORIGINALS of the Release notarized. The prisoner may keep ONE ORIGINAL and provide the other ORIGINAL to their appointee.

NOTE: Always retain the ORIGINAL and only provide COPIES of the original to those individuals or entities, such as attorneys; the prison; physicians; hospitals, etc.

RELEASE OF INFORMATION

By my signature, I, _____, residing at _____
_____ hereby authorize _____
_____, residing at _____ to obtain
written documentation and/or to discuss information about me and on
my behalf as pertains to the legal matters related to my current legal
case(s).

Date: _____

_____
Signature

State of _____

County of _____

This document was acknowledge before me the undersigned Notary on
this the _____ day of _____, _____.

_____
Notary Public in and for_____ County, _____

My commission expires: _____

LIMITED POWER OF ATTORNEY FOR THE CARE OF MINOR CHILDREN - Form

When a parent goes to prison and there is no other biological parent or legal guardian to care for the child(ren), the parent(s) must make arrangements for the children's care or they will be placed in the custody of Child Protective Services. The children will then be placed in foster care and it may take lengthy legal action to have them returned to a relative caregiver or any other person the parent would prefer to designate as caregiver. To avoid having the children placed in foster care it is very important that the parent sign over at least temporary guardianship of the children to a relative or friend.

Incarcerated parents may become fearful that by signing a legal document related to the care of their children they will permanently lose custody. If that is *not* the intent, take the time to carefully explain to the parent the difference between "temporary" and "permanent" custody and why making temporary arrangements is so vital. For example, without a legal document giving you temporary custody of the child(ren), you cannot enroll them in school or even get them medical care. Many relative caregivers have been unable to even get inoculations for the children to enroll them in school, because they do not have the *legal* authority to act on behalf of the child(ren.)

The following documents will provide for the *legal* temporary care and custody that all minor children need during their parent's incarceration. These documents should be signed as soon as possible after the parent's *arrest*. Even while the parent is in jail, the children need the security of knowing who will care for them in their parent's absence.

The parent (or both parents, if both are incarcerated) should sign the documents in front of a Notary Public.

It is wise to have at least two ORIGINALS of the Release notarized. The prisoner should keep ONE ORIGINAL and provide the other ORIGINAL to their appointee.

There is also a brief statement for the caregiver to indicate their willingness to accept the responsibility of caring for the child(ren) during their parent's absence. This statement is not mandatory and may or may not be notarized.

Also note that there is a document for the parent to provide relevant medical information. Unless you are absolutely certain you know the complete medical history of the child(ren) it is important that the parent provide this information to you. Provide sufficient copies for each child that will be in your care.

If the parent is unwilling to cooperate by signing the temporary custody agreement, it will unfortunately be necessary to pursue legal custody through the courts. While no one wants the child(ren) to go into foster care, it will probably be necessary for Child Protective Services to intervene until the legal issues are resolved.

NOTE: Always retain the ORIGINAL and only provide COPIES of the original to those individuals or entities, such as attorneys; the school; physicians; hospitals, etc.

LIMITED POWER OF ATTORNEY
FOR CARE OF MINOR CHILD(REN)

KNOW ALL MEN BY THESE PRESENTS:

That I, _____ (Name of
Legal Parent(s) residing at _____
(City), _____ County, State of _____, here-
inafter referred to as "Natural Guardian state the following:

1. I am the Natural Guardian of the following Minor Child(ren):

Name	Age	Date of Birth
_____	_____	_____
_____	_____	_____
_____	_____	_____

2. As Natural Guardian of the above named children, I have made, constituted and appointed, and by these presents do make, constitute and appoint,_____
(name), of _____
(address-city-state), as my true and lawful Attorney-in-Fact, hereinafter called "Attorney-In-Fact", to act with the limited powers, as specified herein, in regard the Minor Children named above.

3. The Attorney-in-Fact named herein shall have the following powers in regard to the health, education and general welfare of the Minor Child(ren) named in paragraph one (1), to wit:

(a) To act for and on behalf of the undersigned to consent to any x-ray examination, anesthetic, medical or surgical diagnosis or treatment and hospital care which is deemed advisable by, and is to be rendered under the general or specific supervision of any physician and surgeon licensed under the provision of the Medical Practice Act, whether such diagnosis or treatment is rendered at the office of said physician or at a hospital, during all times that the Minor Child(ren) is/are in the care and/or presence of said Attorney-in-Fact. It is understood that this power is given in advance of any specific diagnosis, treatment, or hospital care being required, but is given to provide authority and power on the part of our aforesaid Attorney-in-Fact to give specific consent to any and all such diagnosis, treatment, or hospital care which the aforementioned physician in the exercise of his or her best judgment may deem advisable; and

(b) To do and perform any and all acts necessary or required that a natural parent would perform in reference the education of said Minor Child(ren). It is expressly the intent of the Natural Guardian that the Attorney-in-Fact is hereby given wide discretion in education matters and that all educational institutions shall recognize and follow the instructions of the Attorney-in-Fact in regard to the education of such Child(ren); and

(c) To perform and provide discipline to said Child(ren) as if said Attorney-in-fact were the Natural Guardian of said Minor Child(ren); and

(d) To perform and act as Natural parent in reference to any and all legal matters necessary or desirable for the custody, care and education of said Minor Child(ren); and

(e) I do authorize my aforesaid Attorney-in-Fact to execute, acknowledge and deliver any instrument under seal or otherwise, and to do all things necessary to carry out the intent hereof, hereby granting unto said Attorney-in-Fact full power and authority to act in and concerning the premises as fully and effectually as the Natural Parent(s) may do if personally present, limited, however, to the purpose for which this limited power of attorney is executed. The Attorney-in-Fact may execute any and all such documents or other papers in the following form: "_____ - _____, Attorney-in-Fact for _____{name of applicable Child(ren}, a Minor Child".

4. The Natural Guardian hereby releases the Attorney-in-Fact from any and all liability and damages of any kind or character whatsoever for the performance of the duties herein provided in consideration for the Attorney-in-Fact's acceptance of the duties specified herein.

5. This Power of Attorney and the powers of the Attorney-in Fact shall begin on the date this document is signed and shall remain effective indefinitely, unless or until revoked in writing by the Natural Guardian.

6. This Power of Attorney may be terminated or revoked by the Natural Guardian, by delivery of a written Notice of Termination to the Attorney-in-Fact at any time.

7. Any person may rely upon the continued effectiveness of this Power of Attorney and the continued powers of the Attorney-in-Fact, unless or until such person has received actual written notice of the termination of same.

8. Natural Guardian further declares that any act or thing lawfully done hereunder and within the powers herein stated by said Attorney-in-Fact shall be binding on the Natural Guardian and their heirs, legal and personal representatives and assigns.

IN WITNESS WHEREOF, I have hereunto set my signature this the
_____ day of _____, 20___.

_____ (Signature: Natural Guardian)

_____ Printed Name

Witnesses: Signature   Address

_____

_____

_____

STATE OF _____

COUNTY OF _____

BEFOREMEonthisdate,personallycame_____
the undersigned who acknowledged to me that having signed, executed
and delivered the foregoing Power of Attorney for the purposes set for
therein.

GIVEN under my hand and seal of office, this the _____ day of
_____, 20____.

                         _____
                         NOTARY PUBLIC IN AND FOR
                         _____ **County,** _____**(State)**

My Commission Expires:
_____(date)

Acceptance by Attorney-in-Fact

I, _____ (name of Attorney-in-Fact), hereby accept the duties, powers and responsibilities contained in the above and foregoing Power of Attorney.

DATED this the _____ day of _____, 20____.

_____

Signature

CHILD'S MEDICAL INFORMATION SHEET
The following information is provided to the Caregiver of my Child

_____(Name of child)
Complete separate form for Each Child

Parent _____

Date Information Provided: _____

Contact Address for Emergencies ONLY:

Other Emergency Contact _____ _____Phone _____

Family Doctor _____ Phone _____

Insurance Co. _____

If None Please Check (__)

Insurance Policy Name and # _____

Medicaid: _____

Child's Social Security Number: _____

Known Medical Conditions

_____

_____

Medications? _____

Allergies? _____

Last Tetanus Immunization? _____

Other _____

_____

INDEX

ABOUT THE AUTHORS

CAROLYN ESPARZA, LPC

As a licensed professional counselor Carolyn's plans for a sedate comfortable career in family counseling went awry with one phone call that has now propelled her through over 30 years work with adult and juvenile offenders and their families.

As Founder and Executive Director of Community Solutions of El Paso, an organization dedicated to serving prison families, Carolyn's career in the area of criminal justice has been varied. She has provided court ordered psycho-social assessments for the courts in San Antonio; served as Family Involvement Coordinator and Social Service Administrator for a maximum security facility of the Texas Youth Commission and as the Treatment Director for a maximum security private youth detention facility in Colorado. She has been involved with prisoner ministries in both adult and juvenile facilities and was a member of a team of professionals engaged in a short lived effort of one concerned warden attempting to bring professional counseling inside one prison in Texas.

With a deep concern for children and families, Carolyn authored the book "The Parenting Business: Hindsight is 20/20" and has written several articles featured in magazines and newspapers. She has served as a university instructor for classes on The Study of the Family and Child Development and as a volunteer has provided parenting classes at a Federal prison. Currently she serves as the President for the El Paso Chapter of CURE, a prison reform advocacy organization and is a volunteer Reviewer for College Guild providing non-traditional courses in creative writing for prisoners across the country.

Carolyn speaks candidly of the phone call that changed the direction of her path in life and brought her into the field of criminal justice in many of the workshops and professional training sessions she facilitates. She believes it is the responsibility of those who have come to understand the destructive impact of incarceration on the prisoner's family to educate those who remain unaware. As such, she initiated the concept for the annual National Prisoner's Family Conference, which she currently chairs.

PHILLIP DON YOW, SR.

Best known for his extraordinary musical talents and song writing, Phillip has toured with a well known professional musical group and he has served as a music instructor on a variety of musical instruments. His exceptional leadership skills in coordinating musical groups consisting of both youth and adult musicians has earned him the recognition of many faith based and secular organizations.

Having a strong interest in the world of business, Phillip is currently pursuing his Bachelor's degree in business administration, with plans to continue his education to receive his Master's degree, also in business. He initiated the concept for P-khole Productions to utilize and promote the literary, artistic and musical talents of those affected by incarceration and he also serves as the Advocacy Director for Prisoner's Family & Friends United.

An avid reader with a penchant for writing, Phillip eagerly accepted the opportunity to collaborate on a book for prison families. He is currently outlining a book to encourage adolescents to pursue a higher education and positive career goals.

The co-authors of "The Unvarnished Truth about the Prison Family Journey" have had an association spanning over twenty-five years. They previously collaborated on the development of Prisoner's Family & Friends United (www.PFFUnited.org) an on-line resource for advocacy and support for prison families

With the clarity of 20/20 hindsight, the author provides vital and encouraging parenting tools straight from a well-worn counseling toolbox. Presented from poignant examples from the author's thirty years of counseling with some of this country's most troubled youth and many bungled parenting experiences with her own four children, she provides a valuable and helpful perspective on the challenges of raising children in today's turbulent society.

To Order "The Parenting Business"
Or
To Arrange Speaking Engagements with Carolyn Esparza, LPC

e-mail: carolynesparza@juno.com.